a

THE LIFE OF
SAINT THOMAS AQUINAS

St. Thomas Aquinas: from The Crucifixion *by*
Fra Angelico, in the Refectory, S. Marco, Florence

THE LIFE OF
SAINT THOMAS AQUINAS

BIOGRAPHICAL DOCUMENTS

Translated and Edited with an Introduction by

KENELM FOSTER, O.P.

LONDON
LONGMANS, GREEN AND CO

BALTIMORE
HELICON PRESS

HELICON PRESS
5305 EAST DRIVE, BALTIMORE 27, MD
LONGMANS, GREEN AND CO LTD
6 & 7 CLIFFORD STREET, LONDON WI
THIBAULT HOUSE, THIBAULT SQUARE, CAPE TOWN
605–611 LONSDALE STREET, MELBOURNE CI
443 LOCKHART ROAD, HONG KONG
ACCRA, AUCKLAND, IBADAN
KINGSTON (JAMAICA), KUALA LUMPUR
LAHORE, NAIROBI, SALISBURY (RHODESIA)
LONGMANS, GREEN AND CO
20 CRANFIELD ROAD, TORONTO 16
ORIENT LONGMANS PRIVATE LTD
CALCUTTA, BOMBAY, MADRAS
DELHI, HYDERABAD, DACCA

First Published 1959

Library of Congress Catalogue Card No. 59–6616

PRINTED IN GREAT BRITAIN BY JARROLD AND SONS LIMITED,
NORWICH. NIHIL OBSTAT: FR. DROSTANUS MACLAREN, O.P., M.A.,
S.T.L. IMPRIMI POTEST: FR. HILARIUS CARPENTER, O.P. PRIOR
PROVINCIALIS IN NATIVITATE DOMINI 1957. NIHIL OBSTAT:
JOANNES M. T. BARTON, S.T.D., L.S.S. CENSOR DEPUTATUS. IM-
PRIMATUR: E. MORROGH BERNARD VIC. GEN. WESTMONASTERII,
DIE IIA JULII, 1958

TO RUPERT GROVE

OF THE ORDER OF PREACHERS

spe sociae exultationis

Preface

It is easy to minimise the interest taken by other people in the things that one admires. So it is with my admiration for the writings of St. Thomas Aquinas: how little, I think, does the world appreciate them. But a fellow-admirer assures me that this is too sad a view. Is there not, he says, a steady, if limited, demand for translations of those writings, in selections and extracts at least, as well as for books and articles and lectures about them? And I have to agree that such signs of interest are not lacking, both in England and in America, not to speak of the rest of the world. As a Christian, moreover, I believe that Christian thinking will go on to the world's end; and this the more vigorously the more lucidly it possesses, spiritually, its past achievements. Such possession implies not only a re-thinking of principles already discerned but also a continual discovery of fresh applications and inter-connections. For what we are obliged to seek is wisdom, which is neither merely old nor merely new, but an understanding of how both age and youth are related to the eternal.

Here I am assuming that Aquinas was a wise man in the sense just indicated—a wise teacher, that is to say. It is not my business, here, to prove this assumption, but only to state it and so to conclude that if a wise teacher, then a man well worth knowing, so far as biography can make him known. Hence this attempt to gain, through the records of him left us by his contemporaries, some acquaintance with St. Thomas the man. My aim has been to show the man through the documents, letting these speak for themselves before adding comments of my own.

I like to think that many people who would not dream of calling themselves scholars may be interested by this subject and this way of presenting it. But there is a good deal of learning in the notes added to the documents, gathered from better scholars than myself. I put it there, first because the texts obviously needed a fair amount of historical commentary, and secondly because some readers may wish to follow up the subject for themselves a little, and it seemed only fair to provide them with aids to further study. Other readers, less curious or less leisured, can skip such details. And if the learned, for their part, find my notes at times too meagre, I can only plead that both the time and the space at my disposal are limited, and that this book is not primarily addressed to them.

The translation has been made with an eye to the style as well as the sense of the texts. Thus in Section II will be found much of the repetition inseparable from an official examination of a number of witnesses to the same matter. And if Section III reads, at times, like the random jottings of an octogenarian whose mind has begun to wander, that is what it is like, at times, in the Latin and what one might, in fact, have expected. Sections I and V, on the other hand, are fairly polished performances.

Some readers may find it helpful to read Appendix I, the 'Note on St. Thomas's Family', immediately after the Introduction and before beginning Section I.

My thanks are due to the fellow Dominicans who have helped me with this book in various ways; and in particular to Fathers Guy Braithwaite, Antoninus Finili, Walter Gumbley, Sebastian Bullough, Thomas Gilby, and Brian Monahan.

K.F.

Blackfriars
  Cambridge
CHRISTMAS 1957

Contents

Bibliography and Abbreviations

(Words in bold type are abbreviations used in the Notes)

I. TEXTS

1. **Fontes** *Vitae Sancti Thomae Aquinatis*, Toulouse (s.d.), containing:
   (*a*) the *Lives* by Peter Calo, William Tocco, Bernard Gui, ed. by D. Prümmer, O.P., pp. 1–261;
   (*b*) the 1st and 2nd Canonisation Enquiries, ed. by M. H. Laurent, O.P., pp. 265–510;
   (*c*) contemporary accounts of the canonisation, ed. by M. H. Laurent, O.P., pp. 511–32.

   All the above were published for the *Revue Thomiste*, Saint-Maximin (Var), between 1912 and 1934.
2. **Documenta,** ed. M. H. Laurent, O.P., being a supplement to the above *Fontes*, and consisting of documents relating to St. Thomas or his family between 1197 and 1325; published for *Revue Thomiste*, 1937.
3. *Acta SS.* (ed. Bollandists), *Martii*, I, pp. 655–747.
4. *Historia Ecclesiastica* (XXII, c. 17–XXIII, c. 16) by **Tolomeo** of Lucca, printed in L. A. Muratori's *Rerum Italicarum Scriptores*, XI, Milan, 1724.
5. *Vitae Fratrum* and *Cronica Ordinis* by Gerard de Frachet, O.P. Both of these texts are ed. by B. M. Reichert, O.P., in *Monumenta Ordinis Fratrum Praedicatorum Historica* (**MOPH**), I, 1897.
6. *Acta Capitulorum Generalium Ordinis Praedicatorum* (1220–1303), ed. by B. M. Reichert, O.P., in *Monumenta Ordinis Fratrum Praedicatorum Historica* (**MOPH**), III, 1898.
7. *Chartularium Universitatis Parisiensis*, ed. by H. Denifle, O.P., and E. Chatelain, I, Paris, 1889.
8. *Bonum Universale de Apibus*, by Thomas of Cantimpré, Douai, 1605.

II. STUDIES

(A selection from works used in preparing this book: an asterisk marks those that have proved especially useful)

*A. Walz, O.P.: *Saint Thomas Aquinas: a Biographical Study*, The Newman Press (Maryland, U.S.A.), 1951. This translation, by Fr. S. Bullough, O.P., from an Italian original (1945) is the most reliable *Life* of St. Thomas that I know. A comparatively short work, it is packed with information, supported by reference to sources. Most useful for students, it can be read with pleasure by the non-specialist too. I refer to it frequently in the Notes, under the heading **Walz**.

*A. Walz, O.P.: *Compendium Historiae Ordinis Praedicatorum*, 2nd edition, Rome, 1948.

A. Walz, O.P.: 3 cc. in *Xenia Thomistica*, ed. S. Szabo, O.P., III, Rome, 1925: 'De Aquinatis e vita discessu', pp. 41–55.

*'Historia canonisationis S. Thomae', pp. 105–72.

'Bulla canonisationis S. Thomae . . . illustrata', pp. 173–88.

San Tommaso D'Aquino, O.P.: Miscellanea Storico-Artistica, Rome, 1924. An extremely useful collection of studies by various scholars; referred to in my Notes as **Miscellanea**, with respect to the following chapters especially:

*'La Vita, la Famiglia e la Patria di S. Tommaso', by F. Scandone, pp. 1–110.

*'Discepoli e Biografi di S. Tommaso', by I. Taurisano, O.P., pp. 111–85.

'Fra i Monaci di Fossanova che videro morir S. Tommaso', by P. Fedele, pp. 187–94.

*'Le Carême de S. Thomas d'Aquin à Naples (1273)', by P. Mandonnet, pp. 195–211.

*P. Mandonnet, O.P.: 'S. Thomas d'Aquin, Novice-Prêcheur (1244–46)', *Revue Thomiste*, VII and VIII, 1924–5. This important series of articles is indispensable for the study of the entry of St. Thomas into the Order of Preachers, and indeed for the general history of the Order in the mid-thirteenth century.

*P. Mandonnet, O.P.: 'La Canonisation de S. Thomas d'Aquin, 1317–23', in *Mélanges Thomistes*, Le Saulchoir, Kain (Belgium), 1923, pp. 1–48. Another fundamental study by the chief Dominican historian of this century.

*P. Mandonnet, O.P.: *Thomas d'Aquin Lecteur à la Curie Romaine*, Rome, 1924. This is an offprint of an article which appeared in Latin in *Xenia Thomistica*, III, pp. 9–40, Rome, 1925.

*A Birkenmajer: 'Ad Litteras Universitatis Parisiensis de Obitu S. Thomae analecta nova', *Xenia Thomistica*, III, pp. 57–72, Rome, 1925.

M. Grabmann: *Thomas von Aquin. Personlichkeit u. Gedankenwelt*, Munich, 1946 (English translation by V. Michel, *Thomas Aquinas, his Personality and Thought*, London, 1928).

*M. Grabmann: *Die Werke des hl. Thomas von Aquin*, 3rd ed., Munster, 1949.

*M. Grabmann: *Mittelalterliches Geistesleben*, Munich, I, 1926, especially for the following:

'Mag. Petrus v. Hibernia der Jugendlehrer des hl. Thomas v. Aquin', pp. 249–65; 'Die italienische Thomistenschule des XIII u. beginnenden XIV Jahrhunderts', pp. 332–91; 'Die Aristoteleskommentare des hl. Thomas v. Aquin', pp. 266–313.

*F. Pelster, S.J.: 'Die älteren Biographen des hl. Thomas v. Aquin', in *Zeitschrift für Katholische Theologie*, XLIV, pp. 244–74, 366–97, 1920. These articles are indispensable for a comparative evaluation of the early 'lives' of St. Thomas.

F. Pelster, S.J.: 'La Giovinezza di S. Tommaso', in *Civiltà Cattolica*, LXXIV, pp. 385–400, 1923; and 'La Famiglia di S. Tommaso, *ibid.*, pp. 401–10.

H. Denifle, O.P.: 'Quellen zur Gelehrtengeschichte des Predigerordens im 13 und 14 Jh. (1) Magistri der Theologie . . .', in *Archiv für Literatur u. Kirchengeschichte des Mittelalters*, I, pp. 165–92 (**ALKM**).

Analecta Bollandiana, XXIX, pp. 5–116, 1910.

H. Rashdall: *The Universities of Europe in the Middle Ages*, ed. Powicke and Emden, I, pp. 269–584; II, pp. 21–6, 1936.

A. Mortier, O.P.: *Histoire des Maîtres Généraux de l'Ordre des Frères Prêcheurs*, I, Paris, 1903.

A. Dondaine, O.P.: *Secrétaires de S. Thomas*, 2 vols., Rome, 1956.

*M. D. Chenu, O.P.: *Introduction à l'étude de S. Thomas d'Aquin* (Univ. de Montréal, publications de l'Institut d'études médiévales, XI), Montreal and Paris, 1950.

M. D. Chenu, O.P.: *La théologie comme science au XIIIe siècle* (Bibliothèque Thomiste), Paris, 1943.

G. Verbeke: *Themistius. Commentaire sur le Traité de l'Ame d'Aristote; Traduction de Guillaume de Moerbeke*, Louvain, 1957. ('Corpus Latinum Commentariorum in Aristotelem Graecorum', I.) A critical edition of Moerbeke's translation of Themistius on the *De Anima*, with an important Introduction discussing St. Thomas's collaboration with Moerbeke and his utilisation of Themistius in the Commentary on the *De Anima* and the *De unitate intellectus*. The editor demonstrates the profound influence of Themistius on the later psychological work of Aquinas, especially with regard to the critique of Averroism.

M. B. Crowe, 'The Date of St Thomas's Commentary on the *Sentences*', in *Irish Theological Quarterly*, XXIV (1957), pp. 310–19.

*B. Schmeidler: 'Die Annalen des Tholomeus v. Lucca', in *Monumenta Germaniae Historica: scriptores rerum Germ.*, n.s., VIII, Berlin, 1930.

E. Gilson: *Le Thomisme*, 5th ed., Paris, 1948. The English translation (*The Christian Philosophy of St. Thomas Aquinas*, London, 1957) contains a valuable 'Catalogue of St. Thomas' Works' by I. T. Eschmann, O.P., pp. 381–439; referred to here as **Catalogue**.

W. Gumbley, O.P., and A. Walz, O.P.: 'S.R.E. Cardinales ex Ord. Praed. assumpti', in *Analecta Ordinis Fratrum Praedicatorum*, 1925, fasc. 4, pp. 187–207: a useful list of Dominican cardinals, with short biographies; referred to as **AOP**.

M. H. Vicaire, O.P.: *Saint Dominique de Calaruega, d'après les documents du XIIIe siècle*, Paris (Editions du Cerf), 1955. This is the best short work on the framework of Dominican life in the thirteenth century.

D. A. Callus, O.P.: *The Condemnation of St. Thomas at Oxford*, Aquinas Papers 5, London (Blackfriars Publications), 1946.

D. L. Douie: *The Conflict between the Seculars and the Mendicants at the University of Paris in the thirteenth century*, Aquinas Papers 23, London (Blackfriars Publications) 1954.

*D. L. Douie: *Archbishop Pecham*, pp. 280–301, Oxford, 1952.

Histoire littéraire de la France:
    XXXII, pp. 550–67, on Gerard de Frachet, Paris, 1898;
    *XXXV, pp. 139–232, on Bernard Gui, Paris, 1921.

We are indebted to the Mansell Collection for permission to reproduce the frontispiece.

Introduction

The aim of this book is to confront the reader as directly as possible with the personality of St. Thomas. It is not concerned with his doctrine except incidentally. We have many good studies of Thomism under this or that of its aspects; far less attention has been paid to the saint himself. And this is very natural, given his massive doctrinal achievement, but perhaps the man within the teacher has been unduly neglected. The writings themselves of St. Thomas, in their style and method, are partly the cause of this; so impersonal are they, so thoroughly didactic and abstract, that in their light the writer seems to vanish, like Dante's angel who 'col suo lume se medesmo cela'.[1] Second thoughts will suggest, of course, that, as a work gets its character from the workman, we may, with M. Gilson, take the *Summa theologiae* itself as evidence of its author's 'don total de soi', of 'la vie intérieure même de saint Thomas d'Aquin'.[2] And, speaking more generally, one knows that St. Thomas very powerfully impressed his personality on the technical procedures that he shared with his contemporaries; it has been a principal achievement of the modern historical study of medieval scholasticism to make this fact really evident. None the less, Thomism remains a system of doctrine thought out and expressed at a highly abstract level; and the very success with which it has imposed itself on Catholic Christianity, the prestige it enjoys, especially in our own time, has been won at the cost of much overshadowing of the man by the work. For modern Catholics, surely, St. Thomas Aquinas is, by and large, an authority rather than a saint, a sort of embodiment of theology or doctrinal orthodoxy rather than a lover of Christ. It is with an eye on this bias that I have written this book, intending it as a small counter-weight, as an attempt to draw more attention to St. Thomas the man and the Christian. Primarily, I have tried to see and exhibit him as (to quote Dante again) 'one of the Christians of the thirteenth century'[3]—giving 'Christian' its full weight of meaning.

[1] *Purgatorio*, XVII, 57: 'hides himself in his own light'.
[2] *Le Thomisme*, 5th edition (1948), p. 521.
[3] *Vita Nuova*, XXIX. The words refer, in the context, to Beatrice.

I

Not that I presume to try to show his sanctity directly—a thing in any case beyond the reach of biography, as of history in general, which 'cannot pierce the walls which enclose personal experience of God, His hidden action in souls'.[1] Nor is this even a straight biography, but a selective miscellany of records and facts. Yet out of the details I hope that the lineaments of a man may gradually become visible, emerging from the impressions which his contemporaries received from him and have transmitted to us. Thus their admiration may refresh and quicken ours. Its expression we may indeed, at times, find quaint and, where miracles are concerned, credulous; but it comes from the hero's own age and world, and there is a chance that he may appear more clearly to us for being seen through the eyes of men who knew him, or knew others who knew him, before a mounting and increasingly official glory had blurred his human countenance, his smile, and his tears.

All that we know of St. Thomas derives—apart from his own writings—chiefly from three sources: (a) the minutes of the first Canonisation Enquiry, held at Naples in 1319;[2] (b) three lives by members of the Order of Preachers, William Tocco, Bernard Gui, and Peter Calo—all written, probably, between 1318 and 1330;[3] (c) fifteen chapters from the *Historia Ecclesiastica* of Tolomeo of Lucca, also a Dominican, written by 1317.[4] Of this material I translate the bulk of (a), most of Gui's *Life*, and all that is relevant of Tolomeo. But before I explain my choice of Gui's *Life* (rather than Tocco's) and indicate the value of Tolomeo's witness, it will be useful to give the reader some idea of the developments that led to the canonisation of St. Thomas on 18 July 1323. This will serve also to introduce the important figure of William of Tocco.

Brother Thomas of Aquino (as he was called) died in the morning of 7 March 1274 at the Cistercian abbey of Fossanova, about 50 miles south of Rome, in the diocese of Terracina, while on his way to the Council of Lyons. His death and burial at the

[1] *Roman Catholicism in England from the Reformation to 1950*, by E. I. Watkin, Oxford University Press (1957), p. 234.

[2] Edited by M. H. Laurent, O.P., for the *Revue Thomiste* (1932–4) and reprinted in *Fontes Vitae S. Thomae*, pp. 264–407. This volume also contains the minutes of the 2nd Enquiry, at Fossanova in 1321, and other documents to which reference will be made later. As the 2nd Enquiry is only concerned with *post-mortem* miracles, it is omitted from this volume.

[3] Edited by D. Prümmer, *Fontes*, pp. 17–55, 57–160, 168–263.

[4] xxii, cc. 18–25, 39; xxiii, cc.1, 2, 8–16. The *Historia* is in L. A. Muratori's *Rerum italicarum scriptores*, xi (1724). This vast compilation is being re-edited, but Tolomeo's *Historia* has not yet, I think, appeared in the new edition (Carducci and Fiorini, Città di Castello, 1900 ss.).

abbey were accompanied by miracles which led to his being venerated as a saint in the monastery and its neighbourhood. The peasants began to bring their sick and infirm to his tomb, and many cures were reported.[1] Meanwhile his memory was alive and revered in the Order of which he had been so conspicuous a member and in which some of his former pupils were rising to eminent positions. At Naples—where Thomas had passed the last period of his life in the Order, and where, as a lad, he had first felt drawn to it—the priory of San Domenico became a centre of devotion to him.[2] It was to Naples that the Dominican who knew St. Thomas best, his *socius* Reginald of Priverno, returned from Fossanova after preaching at the funeral the panegyric on him. At Naples, Reginald remained for a while, and later we hear of him at Anagni. In the 1280s we lose sight of him, but he had done his work for his friend. The two chief witnesses at the Enquiry in 1319, William of Tocco (LVIII and LIX) and Bartholomew of Capua (LXXIX and LXXXI), largely depend on Reginald, directly or indirectly; he had become, in fact, the chief link connecting St. Thomas with the Dominicans of the early fourteenth century. Next to Reginald the most important link was William of Tocco, of whom more must be said presently. Outside the Order the south Italian cult of Aquinas at the end of the thirteenth century and in the early fourteenth had its chief representative in Bartholomew of Capua, a distinguished lawyer in the service of the Angevin kings of Naples, into whose lengthy deposition at the Enquiry flowed and mingled many memories and anecdotes —from the Roman Province of the Friar Preachers, from the Cistercians of Fossanova, from the laity and the secular clergy of Naples, and through the latter (as well as through the Dominicans) from the Schools of Paris.[3] With the Neapolitan tradition we may also associate that gifted and long-lived Tuscan, Tolomeo of Lucca, who accompanied St. Thomas to Naples in 1272, studied there under him, and was there at San Domenico, in March 1274, when news came of the master's death at Fossanova. And, as we shall see, Tolomeo lived long enough to supply Tocco with information at Avignon in 1318, after recording his own memories of the saint in his *Historia Ecclesiastica*.

From Paris, as early as May 1274, the Faculty of Arts had

[1] See *Fontes*, ed. Laurent, pp. 411–510.

[2] Canonisation Enquiry, e.g. VI, XL, XLII, XLV, LXIII–LXV, etc. On the rest of this paragraph, see Taurisano, *Miscellanea*, pp. 111–75.

[3] Canonisation Enquiry, LXXVI–LXXXVI.

begged the Dominican Chapter General, then sitting at Lyons, for the body of the dead master ('tanti clerici, tanti patris, tanti doctoris . . .') in a letter which bears striking witness to the admiration and veneration felt for St. Thomas in the University.[1] Yet Thomism was meeting with stiff resistance in the senior faculty of theology, both at Paris and at Oxford. Some points of St. Thomas's teaching on form and matter were included at least implicitly in Bishop Tempier's condemnation, in March 1277, of 219 'errors' current in the Faculty of Arts of the University of Paris;[2] and Tempier's example was followed, with an eye on Oxford and with a more explicit anti-Thomism, by two successive archbishops of Canterbury, Robert Kilwardby, himself a Dominican, and John Pecham (1277–92). Pecham was especially fierce against what he regarded as an impudently untraditional and unChristian view of human nature, while at the same time protesting his goodwill towards the Dominicans in general and alluding to Thomas himself as a man 'of holy memory'.[3] Meanwhile the Dominicans were closing their ranks around their greatest teacher.[4] It is doubtful to what extent this controversy affected the progress towards the canonisation of St. Thomas; but it did ensure that the doctrinal implications of that event would be quickly and sharply felt. Already in 1316, when the canonisation was 'in the air', the Dominican John of Naples (who was to bear witness at the Enquiry of 1319, being the only master in theology to do so) upheld, in a public disputation at Paris, the thesis that the doctrine of brother Thomas 'could be taught at Paris with respect to all its conclusions'.[5] And in 1325, after the canonisation, Stephen Bourret, bishop of Paris, formally revoked his predecessor's condemnation, so far as it 'touched or seemed to touch the teaching of blessed Thomas'.[6]

[1] See Section V below.

[2] Text in *Documenta*, ed. Laurent, pp. 596–614, and in *Chartularium Univ. Paris.*, ed. Denifle, I, pp. 543–55. But knowledge of the background is here quite essential: for a start, see Gilson, *Christian Philosophy in the Middle Ages*, pp. 402–10, 728.

[3] The text of Kilwardby's condemnation is in *Documenta*, ed. Laurent, pp. 615–17; and of Pecham's various utterances, *ibid.*, pp. 627–46.

[4] *Documenta*, ed. Laurent, pp. 621–2, 655–62; including texts from eight General Chapters between 1278 and 1300, aimed at promoting the authority of St. Thomas (still, of course, uncanonised) in the Order of Preachers; and a decree of the Chapter of the Roman province, at Arezzo in 1315, punishing a Florentine lector, Uberto Guidi, for having publicly spoken against his doctrine: see MOPH, xx, p. 197. Cf. Taurisano, *Miscellanea*, pp. 143–5. On this episode in general, see D. A. Callus, *The Condemnation of St. Thomas at Oxford*, Blackfriars publications, Aquinas Paper, No. 5, 1946.

[5] See *Xenia Thomistica*, II, pp. 23–104. Cf. Grabmann, *Mittelalterliches Geistesleben*, I, pp. 374ss.; Taurisano, *Miscellanea*, pp. 159–63.

[6] *Documenta*, ed. Laurent, p. 666.

It was Mandonnet's view that the initiative in the canonisation came from the pope, John XXII; and it is certain that John warmly favoured and furthered the project as soon as it was submitted to him.[1] But in fact the first move seems to have come from the south Italian Dominicans. In 1294 the Roman province of the Order (which was St. Thomas's) was divided by the creation of a new province for the Kingdom of Sicily, which included Naples.[2] The first Provincial was a Perugian, Nicholas Brunacci, who had been one of St. Thomas's companions on the return journey to Paris in the winter of 1268–9. Brunacci was in close touch with the man who, as it happened, was to undertake most of the preparatory work in view of the canonisation—William of Tocco; and at the turn of the century, no doubt, the influence and authority of Brunacci was an important factor.[3] Indeed, the chief living historian of the Dominican Order, Angelo Walz, sees in that division of the Roman province, with the consequent autonomy of the more actively 'Thomist' Sicilians—in the sense which included the Neapolitans—the real starting-point of the affair.[4] Yet no official step was taken until 1317.

The early Dominicans seem to have been somewhat unconcerned about canonising their holy men.[5] Whereas St. Francis was raised to the altars within two years of his death (1226–8), St. Dominic was left to wait thirteen years for this honour (1221–34); and even then it was the Holy See which took the initiative.[6] The next Friar Preacher to be canonised was St. Peter of Verona, in 1253, one year after his death at the hands of heretics in north Italy; but this again was due to the pope—to Innocent IV's desire to have a canonised Inquisitor.[7] Later the claims of the Catalan Raymund of Peñafort were urged upon the Holy See; three times indeed before the end of the century and

[1] P. Mandonnet in *Mélanges Thomistes*, pp. 3 ss. This important article is indispensable for an understanding of the canonisation, but it should be checked by reference to Walz, in *Xenia Thomistica*, III, pp. 105–72.

[2] A. Walz, *Compendium Historiae Ord. Praed.* (2nd edition, 1948), pp. 123, 142; *Acta Capit. Gen.*, MOPH, III, p. 279.

[3] On Brunacci, see Taurisano, *Miscellanea*, pp. 134–9; cf. Grabmann, *op. cit.*, pp. 332 ss.

[4] Walz, *Xenia Thomistica*, III, p. 121: 'Tota res canonisationis . . . ex statu velleitatum, quibus provincia Romana inhaesit, nunc per patres Neapolitanos educta est ad terminum gloriosum. . . .'

[5] Mandonnet, *op. cit.*, p. 1: '. . . l'Ordre des Prêcheurs n'a jamais témoigné d'une grande sollicitude pour le culte de ses propres gloires. Il a peu et mal écrit son histoire et n'a même tenu qu'assez mollement la main à la canonisation de ses saints.'

[6] Walz, *Compendium Historiae O.P.*, p. 204. St. Dominic's first grave, behind the high altar at Bologna, had been almost neglected before the translation of his body in 1233 was attended by miracles, which at last brought on the canonisation, by Gregory IX, in 1234.

[7] Walz, *Compendium Historiae O.P.*, p. 206.

2

again in 1318. But Raymund's cause was deferred, partly for political reasons; and in any case the Dominicans took only a minor part in proposing it.[1] As for St. Thomas, he had been from the start, as we have seen, the object of a local cult in South Italy; and scattered about the provinces of the Order were men devoted to his memory and sure of his holiness; there were records too of miracles and rumours of visions.[2] But all this remained merely dispositive until 1316, when John XXII became pope, and the autumn of 1317, when the chapter of the province of Sicily, sitting at Gaeta, commissioned William of Tocco and a younger friar, Robert of Benevento, to collect materials—reports of miracles, etc.—to be submitted to the Holy See in view of the canonisation of Thomas of Aquino.[3]

Brother William was already, for those days, an old man, probably about seventy.[4] Born at Tocco near Benevento, perhaps before 1250, he became a Dominican soon enough to be one of the community at San Domenico in Naples when St. Thomas lived there in 1272–3. His career was fairly distinguished—preacher general in 1288 (by an odd coincidence he received this honour along with Tolomeo of Lucca, at the provincial chapter held in that city), prior of Benevento in 1291, Inquisitor for the kingdom of Sicily from 1295 to 1301 (?), during which period he incurred the displeasure of the king, Charles II. A little later a common devotion to St. Thomas brought William into touch with Bartholomew of Capua.[5] The same interest took him, in November 1316, to Marsico in the Abruzzi to see the count of that place who was a nephew of the saint.[6] In the following September Tocco received the commission, mentioned above, from the provincial chapter at Gaeta; and in February 1318 he was again at Marsico, interrogating old Lady Catherine de Morra

---

[1] Walz, in *Xenia Thomistica*, III, p. 120. St. Raymund, who died in 1275, was at last canonised in 1601. Walz notes that when King James III of Aragon asked for Raymund's canonisation in 1318, it was the fourth time that this request had been made to the Curia; but during the first half of the fourteenth century the papacy was under French influence in this as in other matters; cf. Walz, *op. cit.*, p. 132, n. 3.

[2] See the first Canonisation Enquiry, *passim*.

[3] Mandonnet, *Mélanges Thomistes*, pp. 19–20; Walz, *Xenia Thomistica*, III, pp. 121 ss.

[4] On William of Tocco, see Walz, *Xenia Thomistica*, III, pp. 121 ss.; Mandonnet, *Mélanges Thomistes*, pp. 19 ss. Mandonnet, following Taurisano (*Miscellanea*, p. 148), doubts whether Tocco was a pupil of St. Thomas at Naples; they would have met there when Tocco was merely a 'passing guest' at S. Domenico. Possibly; but Tocco anyhow insisted that he had met St. Thomas quite often at this time—'pluribus vicis' (Canonisation Enquiry, LIX).

[5] Canonisation Enquiry, LXXIX.

[6] Walz, *Xenia Thomistica*, III, p. 122; Canonisation Enquiry, LX. Taurisano and Mandonnet placed this visit in 1317, wrongly, it appears.

whose memory went back to conversations, in her childhood, with St. Thomas's mother, Theodora of Naples.[1] Meanwhile Tocco had obtained letters, petitioning for the canonisation, from Queen Mary of Sicily (Charles II's widow) and various nobles and notables of the kingdom.[2] Armed with these documents and his list of miracles, the old friar, with his young companion Robert, then proceeded to Avignon, going part of the way by sea. They reached the papal city in August or late July 1318. In Avignon Tocco found two fellow-biographers of his saint: Tolomeo of Lucca, an old acquaintance, now over eighty and a bishop, and the distinguished French Dominican and indefatigable chronicler, Bernard Gui.[3] Gui was now about fifty-six years old and Procurator General of his Order. The three men no doubt compared notes, and it is possible that Gui now sketched the outlines of his own *Life* of St. Thomas, using the first draft of Tocco's as his source. But Tocco's immediate business was of course with the pope; and he could not have hoped for a better reception: John XXII declared himself certain that brother Thomas was 'in glory' and that by his teaching he had enlightened the Church 'more than all the other Doctors'.[4] He then appointed a committee (all non-Dominican) to examine Tocco's materials. This done, the pope, on 13 September, nominated, by letter, the three ecclesiastics who would preside at the official and final Enquiry.[5] With these letters the case was formally opened; the Enquiry itself being held at Naples a year later (see Section II). Tocco meanwhile returned to Italy: we find him at Anagni in December, and next year, 1319, at Fossanova from April to July, making his final preparations for the Enquiry which opened on 21 July.[6]

By mid-September the Neapolitan Enquiry was completed. The *acta* were sealed by the two presidents, the archbishop of

---

[1] Canonisation Enquiry, LXII.

[2] These letters have not apparently survived: they are referred to in John XXII's letter to the archbishop of Naples authorising the Enquiry of 1319 (*Fontes*, p. 270).

[3] Canonisation Enquiry, LX; mentioning the meeting with Tolomeo. Gui was in Avignon in August 1318 and, as Procurator General of the Dominicans, would have been concerned with so important a visit to the Curia as Tocco's, even had Gui not been interested, as a historian, in writing a biography of St. Thomas. For an outline of Gui's career, see p. 11, note 1 below.

[4] See the Supplement to Tocco's *Life*, no. 12, *Fontes*, ed. Prümmer, pp. 148–9. This was written after the official introduction of the cause (13 September 1318) but probably before the canonisation on 18 July 1323 (Mandonnet, *Mélanges Thomistes*, p. 24). Incidentally, it mentions (no. 11) a storm at sea which nearly drowned Tocco and his companions *en route* from Naples to Provence in July 1318.

[5] Text in *Fontes*, ed. Laurent, pp. 269–71.

[6] Canonisation Enquiry, LXI, LXIII–LXV; cf. *Fontes*, ed. Prümmer, p. 149.

Naples and the bishop of Viterbo (the third of the pope's nomi-
nees, his notary Pandulf Savelli, did not in fact attend the sessions)
and entrusted to two minor ecclesiastics, Mathew and Peter of
Viterbo, who were to take them by land to Avignon, whither
Tocco also now returned.[1] The delegates Mathew and Peter
crossed the Alps in mid-winter with their documents and reached
Avignon in February, after missing death by inches by the lake
of Geneva.[2] Tocco's journey, too, was eventful, and in a way
which helps us to date his biography of St. Thomas. He tells us
therein (c. 28) how, in a dream *en route*, St. Thomas appeared to
him and corrected a detail in the 'historia quam de eo scripserat'
—that it was not Peter of Sezze who praised the saint's chastity
in the sermon at his funeral, but Reginald of Priverno. Tocco, in
this passage, also makes it clear that this was but one out of
several possible corrections, the whole *Life*, 'tota historia', having
been already written. Now at the Enquiry (LVIII) he had named
Peter as the preacher in question, whilst in the *Life* as we have it
the name is altered to Reginald. Evidently, then, Tocco wrote
two drafts of the *Life*; one before the Enquiry—perhaps in those
summer months at Fossanova, April to July 1319—and a second
one, the *Life* as we have it, afterwards, and probably in 1320–1,
well before the actual canonisation.[3]

Back at Avignon for the second time, Tocco was kept waiting
more than a year, until, in June 1321, the pope ordered a further
Enquiry which would concern itself exclusively with miracles—as
it happened, with *post-mortem* miracles. This opened at Fossanova
on 10 November and was concluded on the 20th. Tocco was
present, but that is the last we hear of him.[4] He never returned
to Avignon, and may well have died before the canonisation for
which he had worked so hard. This took place at Avignon and
with exceptional solemnity on 18 July 1323.[5]

It was a great public occasion, as John XXII, supported by
King Robert of Sicily—who was present and made a speech—
clearly intended that it should be. The aged pope (he was nearly
eighty) associated himself in a particularly emphatic way with

---

[1] Mandonnet, *Mélanges Thomistes*, p. 31.

[2] *Fontes*, ed. Prümmer, pp. 158–9, 249.

[3] Mandonnet, *Mélanges Thomistes*, p. 24.

[4] The minutes of this second enquiry are in *Fontes*, ed. Laurent, pp. 409–510. Along with
parts of the first enquiry (e.g. XIX, XXII, XXVI, LXIII–LXV) it shows the popular cult of St. Thomas
which had sprung up around Fossanova after his death.

[5] Relevant texts in *Fontes*, ed. Laurent, pp. 511–30; cf. Mandonnet, *op. cit.*, pp. 35 ss.;
Walz, *Xenia Thomistica*, III, pp. 133–49.

the glorifying of Aquinas—as if doctrinal issues, as well as devotion, were involved. And so indeed they were, but that interesting topic is not to our purpose now: we must return, briefly, to Tocco's *Life* in order to introduce the contributions of Bernard Gui and Tolomeo of Lucca.

Tocco's *Life of St. Thomas* consists (after a prologue in praise of the Dominican Order) of seventy short chapters, the last dozen of which are concerned with *post-mortem* miracles and the fate of the saint's corpse. Then follows a supplementary list of miracles, perhaps by another hand.[1]

It is very far from being a masterpiece: Tocco is clearly no thinker, and as a writer he is tediously and conventionally rhetorical. Yet his *Life* remains—along with Tolomeo's more virile record and the first Canonisation Enquiry—our chief source of information about St. Thomas Aquinas. It is the first and fullest summary we possess of the Dominican tradition concerning him, as this took shape in the years that followed his death. Why then, it may be asked, have I passed over Tocco and chosen instead to translate the *Life* by Gui? Well, in the first place I have not ignored Tocco; he is referred to step by step in the Notes. Secondly, there are the claims of taste and convenience. To my taste Gui writes far better than Tocco, and he is certainly more concise. Whenever they describe the same event Gui uses fewer words than Tocco, and he usually conveys his meaning more clearly and forcibly because he allows less place to pious comment and rhetorical decoration. It is Tocco's rhetoric that makes him a bore. He is a slave to the tricks of the *cursus*—to the antithetical balancing of pairs of clauses, emphasised by assonance, and the persistent recurrence of certain set rhythms at the sentence endings.[2] These features were supposed to set off the nobility of noble themes, but they soon become wearisome in a mediocre writer like Tocco. Even in his own day this style was becoming old-fashioned. There is much less of it in Gui. Gui will sometimes

---

[1] *Fontes*, ed. Prümmer, pp. 57–160.

[2] 'Cursus' was the name given, in late antiquity and the Middle Ages, to the rhythmical (accentual) cadence of ornate prose. Cf. E. R. Curtius, *Europäisches Literatur und lateinisches Mittelalter*, especially pp. 156–9 (English translation, London, 1953, pp. 148–51). In case I seem too disparaging of Tocco's *Life*, let me cite the opinion of A. Walz: '. . . quae quidem magis ut expressio pietatis haberi potest et debet quam vitae tanti doctoris. . . . Ecclesiae condignum monumentum. Sancto Thomae, scholasticorum principi, non contingit habere authenticum vitae suae scriptorem sicut sancto Anselmo, scholasticae initiatori, in monacho Eadmero.' *Op. cit.*, p. 158.

reproduce a sentence or series of sentences from Tocco, rhythm and all; but more usually he shortens and clarifies, ignoring or moderating the standard jingles and omitting much of Tocco's pious commentary. The result has a certain crisp, sober elegance.[1]

It will be noticed that I imply that Gui wrote after Tocco. This was the view of the Bollandists, and is now so generally accepted that I do not feel obliged to repeat the arguments of Prümmer, Pelster, and Walz in its favour.[2] But the point has very little importance so far as Gui's reliability is concerned, since his work and Tocco's are virtually contemporary, and either one must depend on the other or most of both derive from a common earlier source. But the latter alternative cannot be proved and brings in a needless complication.[3] We have already taken note of evidence that Tocco wrote a first draft before the first Canonisation Enquiry (July to September 1319). Now in four places Gui seems to depend on this Enquiry and not on Tocco: in c. 5, for Thomas's age on entering the Order, in c. 27 for the name of his sister Theodora, in c. 43 for St. Albert's preternatural knowledge of St. Thomas's death, and in c. 51 for his account (fuller than Tocco's) of the vision of Albert of Brescia. On the other hand, there is evidence that Gui too had written a first draft of his *Life* before the Enquiry. Like Tocco, he has a supplementary list of *post-mortem* miracles—one hundred and two of them. This is preceded by three chapters (52–4), the second and third of which give a useful list of St. Thomas's works and the first of which alludes to the canonisation as already achieved. But in Gui's *Speculum Sanctorale*, completed in 1329, he says that after the first and second Enquiries (i.e. after November 1321) he drew up a list of St. Thomas's miracles as an appendix to 'the book I had *already* written about his birth, life and death'.[4] This phrase takes us back to the summer of 1319 at the latest. We know that Gui was in Avignon—returned from an unsuccessful papal diplomatic mission to Italy—in August 1318, when Tocco was also in that city with his dossier for the canonisation; and that in September 1318 Gui was sent by the pope on another mission to northern France. This journey lasted only a few months, and, if

---

[1] See the excellent study by F. Pelster, 'Die älteren Biographen'. etc.. *Zeitschrift für Katholische Theologie*, XLIV (1920), pp. 257–61.

[2] The *Acta SS.* (March, I, pp. 655ss.) print all of Tocco, but only excerpts from Gui. Cf. Prümmer in *Fontes*, pp. 9, 59-61; Walz, *Xenia Thomistica*, III, pp. 154–65; Pelster, *op. cit.*, pp. 254–68.

[3] Pelster, *op. cit.*, pp. 263–8.

[4] Cited by Prümmer, *Fontes*, p. 9, n. 2; cf. *Histoire littéraire de la France*, XXXV, pp. 162–5.

Gui was working on Tocco's material, he may well have found time to write his own first draft between August 1318 and July 1319. In any case, his *Life*, as we have it, was no doubt revised and published shortly after the canonisation (1323–5).[1]

In the main Gui's work reproduces Tocco, abbreviating but adding a few details from the first Enquiry and two at least from some other source (the name of the prior who received St. Thomas into the Order at Naples, Thomas Agni of Lentini, and the mention of a legal instrument which Reginald of Priverno had caused to be drafted for the recovery, by the Dominicans, of the saint's body from the Cistercians of Fossanova).[2] What Gui omits of Tocco does not, however, consist merely of rhetorical flourishes and pious observations; he also leaves out a few details and episodes. Two of these (given in Tocco, cc. 28 and 49) were of rather private interest to Tocco, and the same may be said of the names of people interrogated by him—or referred to by those whom he interrogated—in the course of his enquiries preparatory to writing his book, e.g. Count Thomas of Marsico (c. 37),

[1] From one MS. of Gui's *Legenda S. Thomae* (Vat. lat. 3847) we know that he dedicated this work to 'Master' Peter Roger, later Pope Clement VI. Since this dedication names Gui as bishop of Lodève, which he became in July 1324, and does not name Roger as abbot of Fécamp, which he became in June 1326, it very probably falls between these two dates. On Gui in general there is an excellent chapter by A. Thomas in the *Histoire littéraire de la France*, xxxv, pp. 139–232; which may remind us that this distinguished churchman is also, through his historical works chiefly, a considerable figure in medieval literature. Born *c.* 1261, into the 'petite noblesse' at Royère in the diocese of Limoges, Bernard Gui entered the Order of Preachers in 1279 and studied at Limoges and Montpellier. Between 1294 and 1307 he was prior at Albi, Carcassone, Castres, and Limoges. Appointed Inquisitor for southern France, with his headquarters at Toulouse in 1307, Gui held this office, nominally at least, until 1323. From 1317 to 1320 he was Procurator General of his Order, which office would have kept him with the Curia at Avignon, but for the fact that John XXII sent him on diplomatic missions (unsuccessful as it turned out) to northern Italy in 1317–18 and to northern France in 1318–19. In 1323 John made him bishop of Tuy in western Spain, but next year transferred him to the more congenial see of Lodève in Languedoc. Gui seems to have done much better as bishop than as diplomatist: he died at Lodève on 30 December 1330, with the reputation of a good shepherd of his flock.

All of Gui's many writings are in Latin. The bulk is historical and hagiographical. The following are the most notable: (*a*) the *Speculum sanctorale*, a hagiographical compilation finished by 1329; (*b*) *Flores chronicorum*, a history of the Roman pontiffs, dedicated to the Dominican Master General, Bérenger of Landorre, in 1316, but continued down to Gui's death; (*c*) *Practica officii inquisitionis*, a first-hand and very informative source for our knowledge of heretical movements in southern France (edited and translated by G. Mollat, *Le Manuel de l'Inquisiteur*, 2 vols., 1926); (*d*) various historical works on the Empire, the French monarchy, and the Order of Preachers; (*e*) the *Legenda S. Thomae*. This is our *Life* of the saint, consisting of (i) a biography in fifty-one chapters, written probably before the canonisation, at least in a first draft; (ii) three chapters on the canonisation and the works of St. Thomas; (iii) a supplementary list of 102 miracles. Gui is considered to have been, for his time, a careful and critical historian: A. Thomas notes his 'précision et exactitude', while finding his style 'sec et terne'; but the latter judgment should be compared with that of F. Pelster which I cite below, p. 12.

[2] Gui, cc. 5 and 45.

Raymund Severi (c. 27), Eufranone of Salerno (c. 36), Giles of Rome (c. 40). These names Gui omits. But he also overlooks some details of the saint's life itself, as Tocco presents this. Such are: the death of St. Thomas's baby sister in a thunderstorm (Tocco, c. 2); Roccasecca, as one of the castles where Thomas was held captive (c. 8); the books he read in captivity (c. 9); that Thomas studied Aristotle's *Ethics* under St. Albert (c. 12); the Master General's doubts, at first, as to Thomas's fitness for the baccalaureate in theology, and St. Albert's insistence in this matter, and the intervention of Hugh of St. Cher (c. 14); an appearance of our Lady to Thomas (c. 32); the use that St. Louis IX made of Thomas as a counsellor (c. 35); St. Thomas's insight into a certain brother's temptation (c. 46); the devil seen by John Blasio, who came to tempt St. Thomas (c. 55; cf. the Canonisation Enquiry, LXX); a conversation between St. Thomas and Reginald on the way to the Council of Lyons (c. 63; cf. Canonisation Enquiry, LXXVIII). For most of these details we depend on Tocco and on him alone. It should be remembered that Gui, a Frenchman who, so far as we know, only saw Italy once, and then for only about a year (1317–18), when he probably went no farther south than Bologna, had none of William of Tocco's familiarity with the rich south Italian tradition concerning St. Thomas. He did not know the saint's family, nor Naples with the memories that hung around San Domenico, nor Fossanova. In this respect Gui writes at a remove, at second-hand, and needs to be supplemented by Tocco and the Canonisation Enquiry and Tolomeo.

The editor of Gui's *Life* adds to it the same author's *Cronica brevis de progressu temporis sancti Thomae de Aquino*; but F. Pelster has shown that this little work adds nothing to our knowledge. And with Pelster's balanced judgment on Bernard Gui's biography of Aquinas we may conclude our own remarks on him. 'So far as its content goes', says this scholar, 'this *Life* has little value for historical research (apart from the valuable catalogue of St. Thomas's works that it contains) for it hardly adds anything that cannot be found in other sources. But from the point of view of form it is *ein höchst interessantes Zeugnis für den aufkeimenden Humanismus*.[1]

If Tocco gives us, in the main, the south Italian tradition, with anecdotes and memories from Paris and Cologne worked into it;

---

[1] Pelster, *op. cit.*, p. 272.

and if this material was then, by the Frenchman Gui, pruned of its verbosity, polished in style, and slightly reduced in content; with Tolomeo, the Tuscan from Lucca, we encounter memories from central Italy that reach back, farther even than Tocco, to the sixties of the thirteenth century. Tocco in 1272-3, when he stayed in the same priory with St. Thomas at Naples, was a very young man, probably still in his twenties; his relation to the saint, we may presume, was that of a young admirer to a venerated and rather overwhelmingly famous master. Somewhat different was Tolomeo's situation. Disciple and admirer he certainly was; but, as we read his chapters on St. Thomas, we may catch, unmistakably, the tone of a certain familiarity; not perhaps the tone of close friendship, but certainly that of a comrade in life and work; of, in some sense at least, an equal.[1]

By good luck Tolomeo lived to a great old age: born in the 1230s, he was a mere dozen years younger than Aquinas; and when the latter returned for the first time from Paris to Italy in 1260, Tolomeo had probably already entered the Order of Preachers at San Romano in his native Lucca. He may well have met Thomas at Viterbo or Orvieto between 1261 and 1265, or at any rate have attended his classes in Rome, at Santa Sabina, from 1265 to 1267. These contacts cannot, I believe, be strictly proved, since the exact chronology of Tolomeo's movements at this time is uncertain; but the contact at Rome, at least, is highly probable. He himself tells us that he knew Thomas personally for a long time ('cum ipso multo tempore conversatus sum familiari ministerio').[2] They were both of the Roman province of the Order, and Thomas, between 1261 and 1268, was frequently on the move in central Italy from one Dominican centre to another, attending provincial chapters and teaching. Tolomeo, a brilliant and quick-witted student, must have been eager to hear and meet the famous master, then at the height of his powers. We know, however, that he did not follow St. Thomas back to Paris in 1268. Nor could he have seen Thomas again until the spring of 1272, when the saint returned to Italy, with, now, less than two years' life before him. From the General Chapter at Florence,

---

[1] For the biography of Bartolomeo, or Tolomeo, of Lucca (sometimes called Ptolemy) my chief authority has been B. Schmeidler, the editor of his *Annales* in *Monumenta Germaniae Historica: scriptores rerum Germ.*, new series, VII (Berlin, 1930); cf. also Schmeidler, in *Neues Archiv*, XXXIII (1908), pp. 285–343; Grabmann, *Mittelalterliches Geistesleben*, I, pp. 354–60; C. H. McIlwain, *The Growth of Political Thought in the West*, pp. 234 ss.

[2] *Historia Eccles.*, XXIII, c. 8.

held in June that year, St. Thomas moved down to Rome, and thence, in the late summer, to Naples, being certainly accompanied, on this last stage of the journey, by Tolomeo, as well as by the inseparable companion Reginald. Since the saint left Naples again on his final journey in February 1274, Tolomeo was his pupil and companion there for little more than a year; during which time he would have met William of Tocco, a man about as junior to him as he was to St. Thomas.

One aspect of the difference between Tolomeo and Tocco, in their witness to St. Thomas, is that Tolomeo's interest is clearly more intellectual. He was not a notable theologian, his bent being rather political and historical—as indeed was Bernard Gui's also, but Tolomeo was more of a philosopher than Gui. He completed the *De regimine principum*, left unfinished by Aquinas: he wrote a notable work on the jurisdiction of the Emperor. Citizen of a Guelf commune, a papalist but a republican, Tolomeo carries with him something of the air of upper Italy, echoes of the old communal and middle-class resistance to the Empire and of the Guelf-Ghibelline polemic; echoes that recall the world in which Dante grew to manhood, though Dante ended on the side opposite to Tolomeo's. All this, it is true, remains in the background of Tolomeo's chapters on Aquinas; but we can clearly discern in them the watchful observer of public affairs, and likewise the student, appreciative of the Aristotelian scholarship of Thomas and of his master Albert, and always ready with allusions to texts and books.

Tolomeo left Naples for Tuscany before 1276. About 1281 he wrote (anonymously) his *Determinatio compendiosa*, a small 'Guelf' work on the limits of the imperial jurisdiction in Italy; and shortly afterwards left Italy for Provence. He returned, however, in the 1290s, saw Celestine V crowned at Aquila in August 1294, and was among those who begged this pope not to make his 'gran rifiuto' of the tiara a few months later. In 1295 he was prior of his convent at Lucca, and in 1301 of S. Maria Novella at Florence just before the crisis that issued in the exile of Dante. In 1302 we find him at the General Chapter of Bologna. He worked at his *Annales* through this decade. In 1309 he was at Avignon (whither Clement V had now transferred the Curia), and, after a brief return to Italy, settled at Avignon more or less continuously between 1311 and 1319, working at his *Historia Ecclesiastica* in the house of the Dominican cardinal William Godin, to whom that work was dedicated on 12 September 1317.[1] In March 1318 John XXII made Tolomeo bishop of Torcello near Venice—the title he bears in Tocco's deposition at the Canonisation Enquiry (August 1319). As we have seen, he and Tocco met in Avignon in August 1318. The responsibility for Torcello cannot have given Tolomeo much to do now; even his prodigious vitality was almost spent. Yet he lived to see St. Thomas canonised, dying in 1326 or 1327.

The third of our early biographers need not detain us long: Peter Calo, also a Dominican and perhaps from Chioggia near Venice; but exceedingly little is known about him.[2] The view entertained by his editor, Prümmer, in 1911, that Calo's *Life* is particularly primitive—preceding Gui and perhaps Tocco—has not found favour with later scholars. It contains (c. 26) an allusion to the Enquiry of 1319, and what seems to be a word-for-word quotation of the Bull of Canonisation of 1323 (cf. *Fontes*, p. 520, line 14, and Calo, c. 4). Yet it probably dates from before the death of John XXII (cf. c. 12). Shorter even than Gui and half the length of Tocco, this *Life* forms part of an ample *legendarium* or collection of lives of the saints, which the chief modern authority on Calo, the Bollandist Poncelet, dated between 1330 and 1342. It is a lively little work and gives three or four details not found elsewhere; the most interesting of which is that the child Thomas, at Monte Cassino, used to ask his master *anxie et frequenter*, 'What is God?' In the Notes to Gui's *Life*, below, cross-references will be found throughout to Calo.

Of far more value to historians are the writings of Gerard de Frachet: the compilation called *Vitae Fratrum* and a brief Chronicle of the first half-century of Dominican history. These works contain very few allusions to St. Thomas, which is not surprising, for the *Vitae* was finished by 1260 and both redactions of the Chronicle not much later. Whatever their obvious shortcomings these writings form a most precious record of early Dominican life. In Section IV of this book I give the chapters of the *Vitae Fratrum* that refer to St. Thomas, and some passages from the Chronicle

---

[1] Godin (died 1336) was one of the three Dominican cardinals at Avignon when Tocco arrived there with his dossier on St. Thomas in July–August 1318; the others being the Tuscan, Nicholas of Prato, bishop of Ostia (died 1321), and the Norman, Nicholas de Fréauville (died 1323). See Gumbley and Walz, in AOP (1925), pp. 189 ss.

[2] Calo's *Vita S. Thomae* is in *Fontes*, ed. Prümmer, pp. 17–55. For Calo in general, see Poncelet, in *Analecta Bollandiana*, 29 (1910), pp. 5–116; cf. Pelster, *op. cit.*, pp. 366–97.

which throw light on the background. On de Frachet himself a few words are called for here.[1]

He was from Chalus near Limoges, a gentleman by birth, and he entered the Order in November 1225, at St. Jacques in Paris, and made his religious profession to Bd. Jordan of Saxony a few months later. In 1233 he was prior of Limoges, and in 1251 became provincial for Provence; holding this office until 1259, when the General Chapter of Valenciennes (which St. Thomas attended) relieved him of it; whereupon de Frachet was at once elected prior of Montpellier (1259–63). He died in 1271. Bernard Gui calls him a fine preacher, a man 'gratiosus et dilectus Deo et hominibus, persona cunctis spectabilis'.[2]

Initially the *Vitae Fratrum* was a product of de Frachet's own province of Provence; the provincial chapter at Montpellier in 1252 having ordered a collection of edifying accounts of deaths of the brethren to be made and sent to the provincial (de Frachet himself). This initiative was taken up by the General Chapter at Paris in 1256, sitting under the fifth Master General Humbert of Romans, who extended the range of investigation to the whole Order and made it include any exemplary doing or saying of the brethren, whether alive or dead. The material that came in was then passed on to de Frachet, who shaped it into his book. This was approved in 1260 and published, within the Order only, with a preface by Humbert. Of its five parts, the first two concern the beginnings of the Order and St. Dominic in particular; the third is about Dominic's immediate successor as Master General, Bd. Jordan; the fourth and fifth are concerned with the 'progress' of the Order and with deaths of the brethren respectively. Neither the whole nor any part forms a continuous narrative, but rather a series of incidents and anecdotes, including many miracles and visions which one does well, of course, to take *cum grano salis*; while at the same time heartily thanking the 'nimis credulus'[3] de Frachet for so much richly informative material.

The Chronicle—*Cronica Ordinis*—begins at 1203, with St. Dominic's first journey into southern France, and ends with the General Chapter at Budapest in 1254, which elected Humbert of Romans as the fifth Master General. It exists in two redactions, of which the second is rather the longer. I give two sections from

[1] See MOPH, 1 (1897), containing the *Vitae Fratrum* and both redactions of the *Cronica Ordinis*, ed. B. M. Reichert.

[2] Quoted by Reichert, *op. cit.*, p. xii.

[3] Reichert, *op. cit.*, p. xvii.

each. It was Denifle who showed that this work was by de Frachet and drew attention to its value as a source for our early history;[1] and readers of Mandonnet will recall how that great, if sometimes intemperate, scholar liked to insist, in general, on de Frachet's importance in this respect.[2]

The letter of the Faculty of Arts of the University of Paris lamenting the death of St. Thomas (Section V below) will be found, I hope, sufficiently elucidated in the Notes attached to it to excuse me from discussing it here.

Of the texts which I present, only Gui's *Life* is anything like a biography in the modern sense of the term; it does at least survey the life of St. Thomas from birth to death. But Gui, like Tocco, is not in the least concerned with the details and dates of the story, except in view of edification: his chronological indications—such as they are—relate only to the first thirty years and the last year of the saint's life. We are given successive glimpses of Thomas's childhood and youth, of his entering the Order of Preachers and the curious ordeal that followed, of his studies under St. Albert and his own brilliant début at Paris. This takes us as far as c. 12 and the year 1256 (though Gui gives no precise dates except those of the death and canonisation). This first part of the book is then rounded off by cc. 13 and 14; the former a general eulogy of Thomas as a light of the Church, with a special word of praise for the *Contra Gentiles* and an eloquent, if conventional, comparison of the saint with three figures from Holy Scripture, Moses, Solomon, and Thomas the Apostle; while the latter completes the praise of Thomas's writings by praise of his speech *viva voce*, with a well-known example of its persuasiveness.

So far Gui, *more suo*, is following Tocco (cc. 1–22), apart from two notable differences: first, Tocco's list of St. Thomas's writings appears already in his c. 17, whereas Gui, who is better at arranging things, puts his catalogue right at the end (cc. 53–4); and secondly—a more interesting difference—Gui omits altogether the content of Tocco's cc. 18–21. In these chapters Tocco stated the four chief errors 'destroyed' by St. Thomas—namely Averroism, the anti-Mendicantism (so to call it) of William of St. Amour and the secular Masters at Paris, the heretical, pseudo-mystical Utopianism of the Fraticelli, and finally the schismatical

[1] *Archiv für Litteratur u. Kirchengeschichte des Mittelalters* (Berlin, 1885ss.), ii, pp. 170ss.

[2] Notably in the important series of articles, 'Saint Thomas, Novice Prêcheur', in *Revue Thomiste* for 1924 and 1925.

theology of the Greeks. This may seem a curious list; we are so accustomed to thinking of Thomism in terms of the Aristotelian movement of the thirteenth century, with the special threat of rationalism which this entailed, that we find it hard to conceive how William of St. Amour and the Fraticelli could be considered major preoccupations of St. Thomas's mind, on a level with Averroes. How much space do Master William or the Fraticelli occupy in the two great *Summae*, compared with Averroes and his followers—in other words, with the rational defence of the very foundations of Catholic dogma? How much space, for that matter, do the *errores Graecorum* occupy? But I only note this apparent anomaly to draw attention to the danger of reading the past with the eye of the present. Tocco's chapter on the 'error' of William of St. Amour is more than twice as long as his chapter on the 'error' of Averroes. But that was how Tocco, a fervent Dominican but no philosopher, regarded these two issues; to his not especially gifted mind the lesser victories of his hero could seem more important than what were to prove his more enduring achievements. And though Gui strikes one as more intelligent than Tocco, yet even he hardly saw things differently; he leaves out all four of these chapters and adds nothing of his own that might interest the historian of philosophy or theology.

At c. 15 Gui suddenly abandons even the vaguest chronological indications, and when twenty chapters later (c. 36) he resumes them, the end of the story, the death of St. Thomas, is already in sight.[1] Chapters 15 to 35 present a character, not a consecutive story; a character in abstraction from the time-series in which it grew and realised itself. Today we can reconstruct that time-series and date the course of St. Thomas's activities between 1256 and 1272; we may even be able to discern, in part, the growth of his mind through these years; though it is notorious that his thought shows a strange and striking self-consistency from the earliest works to the latest—a fact of which his contemporaries were aware and which they were inclined to regard as a considerable merit. But the spiritual character, the holiness of St. Thomas is still, to us, as it is presented by Tocco and Gui, a thing not measured by growth in time; I mean that we have no means of measuring this growth. We cannot see St. Thomas developing in holiness—as, in some degree, we may see the holiness of St. Augustine or St. Teresa of Avila or St. Thérèse of Lisieux or of

[1] This is, in outline, Tocco's arrangement also.

Charles de Foucauld develop and grow through time. For, unlike those more introspective people, St. Thomas tells us nothing about his own growth in grace. So here, perforce, we are left with the method of Bernard Gui. Gui's facts we can supplement with details from Tocco and the Canonisation Enquiry; but the perspective in which we see all this is still the timeless and abstract one exemplified by those central chapters of Gui's *Life*. We have no means of altering it essentially. We may no doubt relate St. Thomas's holiness to some historical 'type' of sanctity, according to our view of what was characteristic of medieval Christianity, as distinct from Patristic, Counter-Reformation, or modern. But that, for what it was worth, would still only relate St. Thomas, with his age, to other ages; it would not relate one phase of his life to another. And we should, of course, come no nearer achieving this perspective by considering St. Thomas's as a typically Dominican, as distinct from Franciscan or any other, holiness.

But this is not to deny that, through our texts, we may partly discern his holiness; and it is worth while to insist that it is precisely with holiness, not with theological or philosophical eminence, that Gui and Tocco and, of course, the Canonisation Enquiry are above all concerned. Of the twenty-one central chapters of Gui (cc. 15–35), only one comes anywhere near to a consideration of St. Thomas's intellectual greatness in and by itself; and a glance at this one chapter (32) suffices to show how little the author was disposed, even at his most 'secular' moments, to consider the saint's intelligence apart from its loving absorption in God. All the rest, in any case, is nothing but a point-by-point consideration of a spiritual quality, or rather cluster of qualities; each linked with one or more appropriate anecdotes, which serve also to introduce a few visions, raptures, and miracles. It will be convenient now to set out this material, briefly, following Gui's own order.

The whole of this central portion, cc. 15 to 35, may be subdivided into two sections: cc. 15 to 28, and cc. 29 to 35. The former, comprising fourteen chapters, is dominated by one theme, St. Thomas's habit of prayer. And c. 15 states as a presupposition the aspect particularly characteristic of this prayer—its relation to understanding or wisdom. Essentially it was the prayer of a Christian student, consumed by a hunger for the 'length and breadth and height and depth' contained in 'the unsearchable riches of Christ'.[1] All the intellectual activity of Thomas is shown as continuous with his prayer, as both the expression of and the means of fulfilling his desire for union with God; and, in a special way, with the God who confronted him, even now on earth—at once challenging faith and stirring intelligence—in the Sacrament of the Altar, to which, we are here told, 'he had a particular devotion'. In c. 16 follows a pre-eminent example of God's answering that desire for understanding, in the colloquy with SS. Peter and Paul on the text of Isaiah. These two chapters derived, we can be sure, from the first-hand witness of Reginald of Priverno.

Chapters 17 to 21 give us five more examples of answers to prayer—two miracles and three visions—but these, except perhaps that given in c. 19, are less emphatically related to the desire for wisdom. Chapter 22 rounds off this series. But with cc. 23 and 24 the theme of the quest for wisdom that is 'in Christ' returns with very great power, and with special relation, again, to the Eucharist. These are the great levitation scenes, with those famous words spoken (we are told) to the saint by Christ: 'you have written well of me, Thomas' (c. 23) and 'Thomas, you have written well of this sacrament of my body' (c. 24). From this height the following chapters descend. The theme is still, in general, the absorption of Thomas's mind by divine things, his habitual disposition to 'abstractio mentis', to a sort of intellectual ecstasy, whether in sheer thought, as a theologian (cc. 25, 28), or in direct prayer (cc. 26, 27); but the raptures are not accompanied now by visible miracles.

With c. 29 begins a new section which continues to c. 35. Less unified than the preceding one, this section is concerned not with St. Thomas's direct dealings with God but mostly with his relations with his fellow-men. We are shown him as a preacher (c. 29); we are shown his humility (cc. 30, 31); his intellectual power, with a moment's return to the theme of rapture (c. 32); his fraternal charity (c. 33); his unworldliness (c. 34); and finally his appearance and physique (c. 35). Gui has now completed his account of Thomas's character and person. Chapter 36 begins a brief narrative of his last days on earth, moving from Naples to Fossanova. Miracles accompany his sickness at Naples (c. 36) and the journey north towards Lyons (c. 37). Then the virtues already noted shine out at Fossanova (c. 38), with a glimpse of the

[1] Ephesians, 3: 8–19.

visionary gift, now in the form of prophecy. In c. 39, the climax of the story, there is a sudden, dramatic return, at the moment of death, to the dominant theme of cc. 15, 23, and 24, the devotion to Christ in the Blessed Sacrament. Death is encountered with a full, conscious and explicit faith, expressed in terms of belief in the Real Presence and of obedience to the teaching authority of the Church. And then this soul, faithful to the last to the mediation of the God-Man through outward signs and doctrinal formulae, goes on to the unveiled vision, to the fulfilment of that longing expressed in the eucharistic hymn:

> Jesu, quem velatum nunc aspicio,
> oro fiat illud quod tam sitio,
> ut te revelata cernens facie,
> visu sim beatus tuae gloriae.[1]

Of the remaining fifteen chapters of Gui's *Life* (omitting the supplementary list of *post-mortem* miracles) eleven concern the funeral at Fossanova and the subsequent fortunes of the saint's body.[2] A chapter follows on the vision seen by brother Albert of Brescia. This is of interest for the history of the cult of St. Thomas in the Dominican Order prior to his canonisation; but since the Canonisation Enquiry records it in more detail, I have not translated Gui's account. The last three chapters (52–4) are likewise omitted: c. 52, we have already noted, records the canonisation, while 53 and 54 contain a catalogue of St. Thomas's works.

As I end this Introduction the image of St. Thomas that I recall most vividly is the figure—often reproduced—in Fra Angelico's Crucifixion group in the chapter-room of S. Marco at Florence. Unfortunately the head of this figure has been much

---

[1] From the noble rhymed prayer *Adoro te devote*, ascribed to St. Thomas since the fourteenth century; but its authenticity, though probable, is not beyond dispute. Dom A. Wilmart made an important study of the MSS. and restored the text, but he was inclined to reject its ascription to St. Thomas; see *Recherches de théologie anciennes et médiévales*, I (1929), pp. 21–40, 149–76. Grabmann favoured authenticity, but with hesitation (*Die Werke*, pp. 367–70); cf. Eschmann, *Catalogue*, pp. 424–5. Dr. F. J. E. Raby, writing in *Speculum*, xx (1945), pp. 236–8, pointed out what he considered 'an unmistakable reference to the *Adoro te*' in one of the *Laudi* of Jacopone da Todi (no. xlvi. on p. 178 of F. Ageno's edition, Florence, 1953). This 'reference' does not mention St. Thomas, but if Dr. Raby is right it would almost certainly place the *Adoro te* within the thirteenth century, since the Laude in question was most probably written before 1300; perhaps within ten years of the death of St. Thomas in 1274.

[2] I give only some of these; for commentary, see notes *in loco*.

'restored', so that now its facial expression can be only approximately what the artist intended.[1] Even so, it seems to me singularly convincing; certainly more so than the calm, not to say cold, countenance that looks out of most other portraits of the saint. Tranquillity is doubtless appropriate enough; what the conventional portraits lack, but this one does suggest, is the burning intensity that glows through the early biographical records and the eucharistic hymns and even, for him who reads it aright, through the severe pages of the *Summa*. Even to turn from that conventionally impassive countenance to the handwriting of Aquinas—surviving in such abundance—may surprise one by the contrast: 'tranquil' is hardly the word for this furiously rapid script.[2] Nor is tranquillity the thing most evident in that Crucifixion portrait at S. Marco. The broad face is almost fiercely thoughtful; the eyes express an intense attention and deep longing. It is not hard to imagine that St. Thomas really looked like this, in prayer before the crucifix. Let us not think of him as placidly sagacious; nor, even, as some oracular master of all the answers. If he is a prodigious master, it is because he himself was mastered—held by a vision of God's presence in the world's being (*esse*) and fascinated by the mystery of God incarnate and crucified. It is hardly possible, surely, to exaggerate either the clarity of this man's awareness of the divine presence in all existence—*esse . . . proprius effectus Dei*[3]—or, on the other hand, his sense of the complete 'otherness', the utter transcendance of the divine nature with respect to things created: to name only one, from a thousand instances, we could consider how St. Thomas lingers and ponders, in the *Contra Gentiles*, over those words from *Job*: 'Lo, these things are said in part of His ways; and seeing we have heard scarce a little drop of His word, who shall be able to behold the thunder of His greatness?'[4]

But all this natural religious sense is, in St. Thomas, turned Christwards; as much as his master St. Paul, this religious metaphysician is a captive and slave of Christ, in whose body 'dwells all the fulness of the godhead'.[5] Thomas was a slave of love, and what he loved he in part saw, but that vision drew him on to the

---

[1] See J. W. Pope-Hennessy, *Fra Angelico* (London, 1952), pp. 179–83.

[2] See A. Dondaine, *Secrétaires de S. Thomas* (Rome, 1956), 2 vols.; and *infra*, note 77 to the *Life* by B. Gui.

[3] 'existence, the effect proper to God', or 'the effect that God and God alone produces', *Summa theologiae*, 1a, xlv, 5.

[4] Job, 26: 14 (Douai version). I refer to *Contra gentiles*, IV, 1.

[5] Colossians, 2: 9.

limits of his strength and even beyond. And so he wrote the *Summa*, but could not, to his eternal honour, complete it; and perhaps the best comment on the great silence that envelopes the last months of St. Thomas's life will again be found in words of St. Paul: 'Not that I have already attained to it, that already I am perfect; but I press on to make it my own, as Christ Jesus has made me his own.'[1]

Is there a single word or phrase that might indicate the kind of person Aquinas was, as our sources reveal him? I suggest 'a Christian seer' as perhaps the least inadequate, provided the adjective be given enough force to include sanctity. 'Saint' alone is too general a term, 'sage' is too secular, 'prophet' too ambiguous, 'theologian' too narrow. 'Contemplative' might do, except that this term hardly conveys the immense *effort* towards vision that marked the vocation of St. Thomas, and except that this was an effort also to render *intelligible*, in terms of human rational discourse, all such vision as could be gained; and so to communicate it to others, according to the ideal of the Order of Preachers, *contemplata aliis tradere*.[2] In him contemplation stupendously fertilised reason; that we know from his books. What a reading of these other records of his life may help us also to see is something of the love that made this possible, and of the effort this love entailed. We learn, here, of his raptures, but also of his tears. We learn of the life which his writings so magnificently, yet only partially, express.

---

[1] Philippians, 3: 12–13. Here I venture to make my own version.

[2] 'To communicate things contemplated.' Cf. *Summa theologiae*, 3a, xl, 1 *ad* 2: '. . . absolutely speaking the contemplative life is better than the active life . . . but if the latter consists of preaching and teaching, by which things contemplated are communicated to others, then it is a more perfect (*perfectior*) life than mere contemplation, since it already presupposes a wealth (*abundantia*) of contemplation'. Writing this, Aquinas must have had his own vocation in mind; and he himself was genuinely *good*, i.e. holy, precisely through fidelity to it. Therefore the *way* of his holiness is specifically Dominican. The point is well stated by Fr. Chenu: 'dès le début de son enseignement, Thomas d'Aquin est porté par la grâce de l'Ordre, qui se reconnait en lui'. *Introduction à l'étude de S. Thomas d'Aquin* (Paris and Montreal, 1950), p. 38. To complete this note, one should stress—it is hardly possible to overstress—the word *teaching* in that passage from the *Summa*. Thomas's Christian 'seeing' envisaged, essentially, not only the mystery of Christ to be seen but also the minds of men that were to be brought to see it. In this sense his seeing was intensely practical. On this point, on St. Thomas as *teacher*—and this is to say, concretely, as *saint*, the two aspects being inseparable in his achievement—Josef Pieper says some really excellent things in *The Silence of St. Thomas* (London, 1957), pp. 27–32.

AN OUTLINE CHRONOLOGY
(only the principal writings are mentioned)

1224 or 1225	Birth of Thomas at Roccasecca, near Aquino, south Italy.
1230 (?)	To the abbey school, Monte Cassino.
1239 (?)	To the University of Naples.
1243 or 1244	Enters the Order of Preachers at Naples.
1244 (May?)	Captured by his brothers and interned at Montesangiovanni and Roccasecca.
1245 (summer)	Released: goes to Paris with the Master General, John the German.
1245(?)–8	Studies at Paris under St. Albert the Great.
1248–52	Studies at Cologne under St. Albert the Great.
1252–5	Lectures as Bachelor at Paris. Writes *De ente et essentia* and Commentary on the *Sentences*, etc.
1256	Made a Master in Theology.
1256–9	Lectures as Master at Paris. Writes Commentaries on Isaiah and Boethius's *De Trinitate*; the Questions *De veritate*; and much of *Summa contra Gentiles*.
1259	General Chapter of Valenciennes: reorganisation of studies in Order of Preachers. Then Thomas goes to Italy.
1260	Named a 'Preacher-General' for the Roman province.
1261–4	With the Curia of Urban IV at Orvieto. Finishes *Summa contra Gentiles*. Writes Commentary on *Romans* and *I Corinthians*, cc. 1–10; the *Contra errores Graecorum*; the Office of Corpus Christi.
1265–7	Regent of the provincial *studium* at Rome (S. Sabina). Begins the series of Commentaries on Aristotle and the *Summa theologiae*; writes Questions *De potentia* and perhaps *De malo* and *De spiritualibus creaturis* (but all three groups of Questions may overlap the later years in Italy).
1267–8	With the Curia of Clement IV at Viterbo. Thomas refuses the archbishopric of Naples. Continues the Aristotelian Commentaries; the *Summa theologiae*; the series of Disputed Questions.
1268–9	Returns to Paris.
1269–72	Teaching in Paris. Writes 2a *pars* of the *Summa theologiae*; the *De eternitate mundi* and *De unitate intellectus*; probably the Questions *De anima* and *De virtutibus*; the Commentaries on Aristotle's *Metaphysics, Posterior Analytics, Politics*; finishes that on the *Ethics*.
1272	Returns to Italy; perhaps attends General Chapter at Florence in June.
1272–4	Regent of the *studium* at Naples. Writes 3a *pars* of *Summa theologiae*; the Commentaries on *De coelo et mundo* and *De generatione et corruptione*.
1273 6 December	Ecstasy at Mass; he stops work on the *Summa theologiae*.
1274 Jan.–Feb.	Leaves Naples on the way to the Council of Lyons; he falls sick at Maenza.
7 March	Dies at the abbey of Fossanova.

I

The 'Life of St. Thomas Aquinas' by Bernard Gui

I

That great and holy teacher, Thomas of Aquino, of the Order of Preachers, came of the noble and famous family of the counts of Aquino, lords of the border country between Campania and the kingdom of Sicily. The name of his father was Landulf, and of his mother, Theodora. She was a Neapolitan lady, and distinguished by her own virtues as well as by her children's.[1]

The birth and the future career of Thomas were divinely foretold through the mouth of a holy man of that neighbourhood (named appropriately 'Bonus'), one of a number of hermits living in the hills around Roccasecca, and a famous man in those parts. One day God inspired this hermit to come to the castle of Roccasecca and speak to the countess, who was then bearing the child in her womb. 'Rejoice, my lady,' he said, 'for the son you are bearing shall be called Thomas, and he shall be famous throughout the world for learning and sanctity, and a member of the Order of Preachers.' And the countess replied, 'May the will of God be done!' This prophecy was all fulfilled in due time. Meanwhile the noble babe was born, and christened Thomas, and entrusted to the care of a good nurse.[2]

2

One day, while Thomas was still a babe unweaned, his nurse was about to give him a bath, and as she was taking off his clothes he put out his hand and seized and held on to a piece of paper that was lying unnoticed on the ground. And when the nurse tried to open his hand and remove the paper, so that she might finish washing him, the child began to cry loudly; but when she let him keep it he was quiet again. And while she

25

washed, dried and clothed him, he still clutched the paper. But his mother, in spite of his protests, at last extracted it from his grasp; and she found written on it nothing but the angel's greeting, *Ave Maria, gratia plena.* . . . And surely it was appropriate, that in this way Providence should indicate in the boy what was to be so conspicuous in the man, a love of the doctrine of salvation which it would be his vocation to teach. It was the divine Spirit that led him to find that paper.[3]

3

After his fifth birthday the child's parents, having decided to offer him to God, sent him, duly attended, to the Benedictine abbey of Monte Cassino (as Samuel was sent to Heli[4]) in order to be trained in good morals and taught his letters.[5] And this also was providential—that he who was so clearly to illuminate the Church should not be reared in a dark place, and that so bright a mirror of virtue should never be tarnished by contact with the ways of the world. And once at the monastery, it was astonishing —and significant—how quickly divine grace led the boy to seek for knowledge of God, though he was still so young and inexperienced that he knew not his own self. The future was to show that he who sought God sooner than others would write of Him with greater clarity than others, receiving from God to the measure of his desire. And already the holy Spirit claimed him, drawing him away from the childish occupations of the other noble lads, his companions in that school. As far as possible he shunned all frivolous conversation. He began to love solitude, and was continually to be seen pondering over the books which contained the little exercises and lessons suited to his age. He was a quiet boy with an unusually mature bearing; saying little, but already thinking much; rather silent and serious and, seemingly, much given to prayer.

4

And since, as Scripture says, we judge that a boy is worth something if we see him interested in the right things,[6] we need not wonder that the abbot of Monte Cassino (prophetically, as it turned out) began to think that the future held much in store for Thomas. And in this opinion he persuaded the boy's parents to send him to the University of Naples, to study the liberal Arts.[7] And once at Naples, Thomas was soon distinguished among the students of his own age by his lively intelligence. In all the usual scholastic exercises—the repetition of lectures and compositions and so forth—he showed a depth and subtlety of mind that won general admiration. All, in fact, 'were astonished at his understanding and his answers'.[8] But even as he made such swift progress through grammar, logic and natural science,[9] God had begun to inspire him with the idea of wholly renouncing the world by entering the Order of the Preaching Friars; and in this way of restoring with interest that talent of intelligence which he had received. A Dominican who knew him at this time and admired him has spoken of a visible radiance that seemed to shine from the face of young Thomas.[10]

5

While then the youth's fame and promise were on everyone's lips and he, for his part, was inwardly pondering his vocation to the Order of St. Dominic, a celebrated friar of the Order, John of San Giuliano, had occasion to speak with him and encourage him along the way. So the holy Spirit made use of brother John to decide the matter; and Thomas was able to be received into the Order (as the Bull of Canonisation states) while still below the age of puberty.[11] And so on the lampstand of the Church a light was placed that was to guide the feet of many who were walking in darkness.

He received the Dominican habit from brother Thomas Agni of Lentini, at that time prior of Naples and afterwards bishop of Cosenza, before being transferred to the patriarchate of the holy city of Jerusalem.[12] The event gave joy to the brethren and caused wonder in the city—the people marvelling over the entry into the Order of a youth of such high birth and promise. Meanwhile his mother—a lady whose memory should be held dear by all good men[13]—when she heard what had happened found consolation in recalling the prophecy concerning her son which the man of God had made and which now seemed in course of fulfilment. So the good woman hastened with her retinue to Naples, rejoicing in the Lord and hoping to see Thomas there and encourage him in his purpose; for she wished to be his mother in the spirit as well as in the flesh. However, the brethren, hearing that she was on the way, took fright, for they thought her moved by carnal affection only and that she cherished some feminine design for unsettling her son. So, to forestall her, they had Thomas taken to Rome, and thence put on the road north to Tuscany, with Paris as his destination. She then, missing her son at Naples pursued him to Rome, where again he was not to be found. This was a real grief for her mother's heart; yet she still protested that the only motive she had for wishing to see Thomas was a desire to confirm him in his resolution to enter the Dominican Order.[14]

6

In the end, however, the friars' refusal to believe in her good intentions so angered the countess that she completely changed her plans. She sent a message to her other sons to inform them of what had occurred and to order them, on pain of forfeiting her maternal blessing, to stop their brother on his way north and bring him to her by force. Those other sons were attached to the court of the Emperor Frederick, who happened just then to be encamped at Acquapendente in Tuscany. They repeated their mother's command to the Emperor and obtained his leave to put it into effect; and then (thus unjustly justified) swooped like bandits on their prey. They found Thomas, with four friars of the Order, resting from the fatigues of the journey by a wayside spring; and immediately—behaving like enemies rather than brothers—seized him and carried him off by force. But first they tried to make him take off his religious habit—ordering him to do so at first, and then, since he would not obey, attempting to tear it from him violently; but he put up such a resistance that, for fear of wounding him, they had to let him continue to wear it. And so, closely guarded, they sent him off to his mother.[15] The countess was delighted to see her son again, but, woman-like, she made a show of the grief she had suffered in the hope of inducing him to doff the habit. However, his mind was a match for any woman's; not even a mother's coaxing could make it

waver; its foundations were solid rock. So he was shut up—innocent as he was—in the castle of San Giovanni, pending the arrival
of his brothers who were expected to come soon. Meanwhile the
friars, who had been his companions on the journey and seen him
snatched away, took the matter to Pope Innocent IV, himself in
Tuscany at the time, protesting against the outrage; whereupon
Innocent wrote to the Emperor demanding an enquiry into the
crime and due punishment of those responsible. But since the
Emperor's response to this move was a favourable one, the friars,
for their part, thought it best to let the matter drop, for fear of
causing still greater scandal and disturbance of consciences.[16]

7

Now God's child was in prison; but light shone into his mind
through the outer darkness: in this period he studied and learned
much and committed much to his memory. He taught his sisters
too; indeed, one of them, who had done her utmost to turn him
from his holy purpose, he so persuaded (with God's help) of the
love of God and the worthlessness of the world that she proceeded
to take a vow of chastity and become a nun; and in the course of
time was elected abbess of the Benedictine convent at Capua,
where she died still faithful to her calling.[17]

Meanwhile the holy youth, though, like another Joseph, bodily
in prison, roamed mentally through the free spaces of heaven.
God spoke to him in his studies and with him, most sweetly, in
his prayers. Yet he had also many troubles to bear at this time,
and even, if we may believe reports, some particularly odious
temptations. This was when his brothers (in the flesh, not the
spirit) returned to the castle. They tried the expedient of tearing
his habit, in the hope that, by the shame of being seen in rags,
their brother might be induced to put on the clothes they wished
him to wear. But he took this nuisance very calmly, clinging to
his rags; the more they outraged him, the greater was his patience.
He was unconquerable.[18]

In the end—that no temptation might be left untried—these
brothers in the flesh but enemies of his soul had recourse to the
arms of the devil himself: the beauty of woman, they decided,
must be brought into play to destroy the lad's innocence. For
how (they reasoned) could this boy show more prudence than

father Adam, more strength than Samson, more justice than Lot, more piety than David, more wisdom than Solomon? Let a lusty girl, shameless in look and deed, be brought to him; surely she would bring down that tower which had repulsed every other threat and blandishment! Let us then, they said, kill the lad's soul, that we may have his body, and drive the divine Spirit out of him, that we may possess his own! Such were the thoughts and designs of his own flesh and blood, of those bound to him by ties of natural affection. . . . So a lovely but shameless girl, a very viper in human form, was admitted to the room where Thomas was sitting alone, to corrupt his innocence with wanton words and touches. But if she expected a man, she found an angel. And yet—that 'power be shown more perfectly through weakness'[19] —the young body of Thomas did feel a stimulus; but quickly controlled by the wise and virile soul; for only in the flesh was he adolescent. Chastity and indignation leapt up together. Springing towards the fire that burned in his room, Thomas seized a burning log from it and drove out the temptress, the bearer of lust's fire. Then, his spirit still aflame, he drew on the wall of the room, with the charred tip of the log, the sign of the holy cross; and fell to the ground weeping and begging God to grant him the gift of a constant virginity. He prayed that what he had done he would have the strength to do always. And so praying, he fell asleep. And then, while he slept, two angels came to tell him that God had heard his prayer. Then they bound his loins so tightly that he felt the pain of it, saying to him: 'In God's name we bind you, as you have asked to be bound, with a bond of chastity that never shall be loosened.' That sacred touch of angels woke him, crying aloud with pain; but to those who, hearing him cry, came running to ask what ailed him he said nothing of the vision. And to the end of his life he kept it secret, except to brother Reginald his *socius* and intimate, to whom he spoke of it humbly. But from that time onwards it was his custom always to avoid the sight and company of women—except in case of necessity or utility—as a man avoids snakes.[20]

8

For about two years[21] he remained virtually a prisoner, though the above-mentioned brother John of San Giuliano, who loved him dearly, was able to visit him frequently and bring him changes of clothing by the expedient of coming dressed in two habits, one of which, as soon as they were alone, he would take off and give to Thomas.[22] Thus he whose mind was thriving so vigorously did not lack what the body required. O happy prison alight with the splendours of intelligence! O goodly shackles which gave such liberty to the mind! O happy temptation, the proud Enemy's confusion and the glory of him whose strength was in God! O ripe fruit of inward merit and virtue, that this attack from both sides of our nature, this assault of pleasure and of fear, should so triumphantly be repulsed! O manly stripling, victorious over so old and seasoned an Enemy! O happy way-farer through this world, who won on earth the citizenship of heaven, and through chastity the company of angels! Who fighting for chastity on earth achieved a heavenly purity!

Finally, however, his mother, realising that the hermit's prophecy must perforce be fulfilled, and that to resist her son any longer would be to resist Providence, gave orders, cunningly, to relax the guard and so make it possible for him to escape; which he did, by a rope let down from his window. Certain brethren of the Order, being advised of this, were there waiting, and, receiving him with joy, conducted him to Naples. And they found him so advanced in his studies since the imprisonment began that it was as if he had passed through a long period of study in the Schools.[23]

9

Restored then to the Order (which in spirit he had never left) Thomas was sent from Naples to Rome, whence the venerable father John the German took him to Paris.[24] From Paris he was sent to Cologne, where that great teacher the lord brother Albert the German directed a flourishing school of philosophy and theology. And Thomas was delighted to find himself at Cologne, sitting at the feet of such a Master: it seemed to him that he had found what he was seeking and was drinking of the water for which he thirsted.[25] Ardently he began to study. As a bee gathers honey he busily stored his mind with the sweet treasure of doctrine that in due time would enrich many others. And as it befits a learner to be silent, gentle, and docile, Thomas so studied

to be quiet that his fellow students began to call him 'the dumb
ox'. An ox indeed he was, browsing in God's pastures and
building up the spiritual strength that would later be revealed.
And who doubts that the way to learn is to listen, and let oneself
be taught before presuming to proclaim one's own opinions? But
the moment came at last when Thomas showed what was in him.
It was when Albert was lecturing on the *Divine Names* of Denys.
To Thomas, who was following the course attentively, one of the
other students, not aware of his intelligence, offered to explain
a particular lecture. Thomas accepted the offer with cheerful
humility; but when the explanation itself began to falter, suddenly he broke silence and started himself to expound the lecture,
very lucidly and with additions of his own. Much surprised,
the other student went to the Student Master and said, 'That
Neapolitan, Thomas, knows a great deal; he has explained the
Master's lecture to me today, and so well that he has made it
seem clearer than the Master himself did.' The Student Master,
wishing to test the matter, placed himself next day where, without being seen, he could overhear Thomas's explanations; and
what he heard impressed him even more than the student's
report. So he lost no time in informing Master Albert.[26]

10

It happened about this time that Master Albert conducted a
formal disputation for the students. The subject was a difficult
one. Thomas took careful notes, in writing, on the argument; but
these he later dropped near the door of his cell when he was
leaving it in a hurry, and they were picked up by another student
and shown to Albert, who realised at once, on reading the notes,
that under the deep reserve of the exemplary student who had
written them some extraordinary grace was at work. He asked
the Student Master to tell Thomas that at the next disputation
it would fall to him to defend a certain extremely difficult thesis.
Though humility prompted Thomas to decline the honour he was
also bound in humility to obey; so, after recourse to prayer, he
got ready for this his first public defence of a thesis. The disputation took place the next day. After setting out the arguments for
and against the thesis, Thomas then proposed a certain distinction

as sufficient to solve the problem and answer the objections: whereupon Master Albert said: 'Thomas, you seem to be not only discussing the question—which is your task—but deciding it too!' Then he began to press Thomas with many strong and, one might have thought, decisive objections; but to each one Thomas had a sufficient answer. And the story goes that at last Albert exclaimed: 'We call this lad a dumb ox, but I tell you that the whole world is going to hear his bellowing!' Such praise would breed conceit in most young men, but on Thomas it had no such effect, for his heart was grounded in humility. Nor was the simplicity of his ways in the least affected, although after that day Albert always chose him for the chief part in the more difficult disputations. He was, clearly, the outstanding student, and in all the scholastic exercises he continued to conduct himself admirably. Clearly the holy Spirit was in him. But while he outshone the rest in knowledge and understanding, he was never found guilty of despising his companions or of using any arrogant language or of giving himself airs.[27]

I I

When this course of study under the Master was completed, Albert, now fully aware of Thomas's quality, both moral and intellectual, advised the Master General of the Order to send him to Paris to take the degree of Bachelor of Theology.[28] So Thomas was told to betake himself to Paris and prepare to lecture on the *Sentences*. This honour too he would have declined, but that obedience imposed it. Once, however, possessed of the degree and started on his course of lecturing, God graced his teaching so abundantly that it began to make a wonderful impression on the students. For it all seemed so novel—new arrangements of the subject-matter, new methods of proof, new arguments adduced for the conclusions; in short, no one who heard him could doubt that his mind was full of a new light from God. The divine splendour hitherto hidden in his soul was now shining out, and all were amazed at the glory and lucidity of his utterance.[29]

12

Then, with the completion of this period of lecturing as a Bachelor, on the *Sentences*, the time came for him to proceed, in name as well as in fact, to the degree of Master in Theology; and the Chancellor of the University wrote in this sense to the prior of the Friars Preachers in Paris. Thomas tried to excuse himself on the ground of insufficient age and learning; he was now, in fact, about thirty years old.[30] But since obedience left him no escape, he had recourse as usual to prayer. In the spirit of truth he prayed to the supreme Teacher, using those words of the Psalmist, *Salvum me fac Deus, quoniam diminutae sunt veritates a filiis hominum.*[31] With tears he begged for that understanding of divine things which had become so rare among men, and also for inspiration as to the theme he should choose for his inaugural lecture. Then he fell asleep and dreamed. He seemed to see an old man, white haired and clothed in the Dominican habit, who came and said to him: 'Brother Thomas, why are you praying and weeping?' 'Because,' answered Thomas, 'they are making me take the degree of Master, and I do not think I am fully competent. Moreover, I cannot think what theme to take for my inaugural lecture.' To this the old man replied: 'Do not fear; God will help you to bear the burden of being a Master. And as for the lecture, take this text, "Rigans montes de superioribus suis, de fructu operum tuorum satiabitur terra."'[32] Then he vanished, and Thomas awoke and thanked God for having so quickly come to his aid. And the text given him he not only used for the inaugural lecture but later fulfilled in every particular; for he watered the mountains, that is the minds of teachers to come, with the divine floods which poured into his own, and filled the whole earth with the fruits of his husbandry. For never has anyone studied, in the right spirit, the writings of Thomas without receiving abundance of knowledge and wisdom and wisdom's fruits. The spiritual flood of his teachings has both increased the wisdom of the wise and nourished the minds of little ones.[33]

13

For as the sun's splendour increases from east to west, from morning to high noon, so the teaching of Thomas has become an object of admiration for almost the entire world. It instructs the studious, corrects the wayward, guides the wanderer. For he teaches divine matters in the way which most aptly and discreetly employs all those human means which can serve in the work of man's salvation. This is not the place to describe at length the errors which the razor edge of Thomas's mind has cut off at their root; enough to say that the errors and follies of unbelievers have never, to this day, met with so terrible an adversary as the author of the *Summa contra Gentiles*. His penetration, too, of the deep things contained in Scripture and in the mysteries of our Faith was such that in all truth it may be said of Thomas that he 'searched the depths of the rivers and brought hidden things to light'.[34] Through the fields of secular knowledge he passed, gathering all its flowers. He filled his arms with the fragments of the teaching of the Apostles, those fragments which God Himself has commanded be gathered into baskets, lest they be lost to future generations. From the rich barns of the Fathers, stored with the harvest of both Testaments, Thomas gathered into his books (the number and names of which it will be found convenient to give in a later chapter) all that may serve the needs of our time.

Another Moses, we may fitly call him; rescued from the waters of worldly vanity—which are the high estate of the lords of Aquino—and restored as by Pharaoh's daughter to mother Church, to be filled at her rich breasts with the milky wisdom of God. Another Moses, for God first spoke to him in the spirit, and then sent him out to be the leader of his brethren, not without signs and great wonders. Another Moses, to lead the faithful out of Egypt's darkness behind the twin columns of cloud and of fire, which are the twofold doctrine; for the cloudy column, rising from the ground, is human science drawn up from the world of sense, whilst the fiery column is that flame which falls from the right hand of Him who sits on high, when He inspires the receptive spirit. Another Moses, whose humble prayers made waters of divine wisdom flow from the rocky obscurities of Scripture. Another Moses, aloft on the mountain of contemplation and writing down in his memory, as on the two tables of stone (if it was not, rather, Another's finger which wrote in him), the science of the old and new Testaments. Or again we might call him a Solomon for the range of his consideration which swept down from the cedar of Lebanon to the hyssop that grows out of the wall, from the Son of God as the splendour and brilliance born of the Father down to the same Son as born of a virgin with a body like ours. So from truth to truth went the movement of his mind and the course of his life and writings, each to its happy end. Or again, lastly, is he not another Thomas? Not indeed like Didymus in doubting, for our Thomas's hold on divine things was firm and sure; but resembling that Apostle in entering the abyss of the side of Christ (does not Thomas mean 'abyss'?)[35]— entering as one invited, and therein searching out and expressing the mysteries contained there, with such assurance that it is as if his hands had handled what the finger of his intellect points to.[36]

14

Nor was it only in his writings that greatness appeared, but also in his living speech, to which truth itself gave a force that none could resist, except only those whom an untamed pride or blindness made impervious to it. Consider, for example, the effect his words had on the two Jews, rich men and learned in their Law, whom he met at the castle of Molara near Rome, a property of the lord Cardinal Richard. It was the season of Christmas and Thomas was a guest of the Cardinal, along with these Jews, who were accustomed to stay at the castle every year for the festival. At the Cardinal's suggestion Thomas entered into conversation with them, and the ensuing discussion continued for a long time, Thomas using the Scriptures in various ways to demonstrate the coming into the world of its Lord and Saviour. Then he made an appointment with them for the following day, on the understanding that either they would refute his arguments or profess themselves believers; and in the meantime he gave himself to prayer on their behalf, begging Him who was born for sinners to come to these on His birthday. And next morning the day-star had risen in the hearts[37] of these two Jews: they came to the place appointed, shed their outworn Jewish errors, and were clothed with the lord Christ in baptism.[38]

15

In Thomas the habit of prayer was extraordinarily developed; he seemed to be able to raise his mind to God as if the body's

burden did not exist for him.[39] He had a particular devotion to
the Sacrament of the Altar;[40] and no doubt the special profun-
dity of his writings on this subject was due to the same grace
which enabled him to say Mass so devoutly. This he did every
day, unless prevented by sickness; after which he would hear, and
usually also serve, another Mass said by his *socius* or some other
priest.[41] We are told that at the elevation of Christ's body it was
his custom to exclaim devoutly: *Tu rex gloriae, Christe, tu Patris
sempiternus es filius*, etc.[42] While saying Mass he was utterly
absorbed by the mystery, and his face ran with tears. At night,
when our nature demands repose, he would rise, after a short
sleep, and pray, lying prostrate on the ground; it was in those
nights of prayer that he learned what he would write or dictate
in the day-time. Such was the normal tenor of his life—a minimum of time allowed to sleeping and eating, and all the rest given
to prayer or reading or thinking or writing or dictating. Never
an idle moment, always a holy activity. When compelled by
charity or courtesy to interrupt his studies and go to the parlour
to talk with one of the brethren or with some important visitor,
even then no time was wasted: having dealt with whatever
required his attention, he would briefly recall some good example
or let fall some observation with a moral point to it. Then if he
still had time on his hands before he need return to his cell, he
would get up abstractedly—it did not matter who had been
speaking with him—and wander off absorbed in meditation. It
was as though the prayer of his mind never ceased, and in fact
no external business could ever distract it from the thoughts in
which he delighted and the revelations for which he prayed.[43]
He never set himself to study or argue a point, or lecture or write
or dictate without first having recourse inwardly—but with tears
—to prayer for the understanding and the words required by the
subject. When perplexed by a difficulty he would kneel and pray
and then, on returning to his writing or dictation, he was accustomed to find that his thought had become so clear that it seemed
to show him inwardly, as in a book, the words he needed. All
this is confirmed by his own statement to brother Reginald that
prayer and the help of God had been of greater service to him in
the search for truth than his natural intelligence and habit of
study. This he told Reginald as a secret; but after his master's
death Reginald often mentioned it in his lectures or on other
occasions.[44]

4

Here too we may touch on Thomas's habit of reading from time to time in one of those collections of *Homilies of the Fathers*, which he did in order to offset the aridity which is so often the result of abstract and subtle speculative thinking. He himself used to say that after a spell of this sort of reading he found it easier to rise into speculation, so that it did both his heart good by increasing devotion and his intellect by deepening its considerations. And in this Thomas was but following the example of St. Dominic, of whom we are told that he often had the same collection of homilies in his hands, and that he learned much from it of spiritual perfection.[45]

16

Moreover, there was such a power of grace in his prayer that whatever he asked for God was sure to grant. Sometimes this came in the form of fresh light on some difficulty,[46] sometimes as new knowledge suddenly presented to him. Once at Paris, when writing on Paul's epistles, he came to a passage which quite baffled him until, dismissing his secretaries, he fell to the ground and prayed with tears; then what he desired was given him and it all became clear.[47] On another occasion it was an obscure text of Isaiah that puzzled him, and so much that for many days he could get no farther with it, though he prayed and fasted assiduously, begging for light to see into the prophet's mind. At last, one night when he had stayed up to pray, his *socius* overheard him speaking, as it seemed, with other persons in the room; though what was being said the *socius* could not make out, nor did he recognise the other voices. Then these fell silent and he heard Thomas's voice calling: 'Reginald, my son, get up and bring a light and the commentary on Isaiah; I want you to write for me.' So Reginald rose and began to take down the dictation, which ran so clearly that it was as if the master were reading aloud from a book under his eyes. This continued for an hour, and then Thomas said: 'Now go back to bed, son; there is little time left for sleep.' But Reginald fell at his feet and said: 'I will not leave this room until you tell me who was speaking with you.' And this demand he made calling on the name of God. Yet did Thomas refuse it; to grant it, he said, would serve no purpose. But Reginald continued urging and begging him, until at last

Thomas—not wishing even to seem indifferent to the Name by which Reginald was adjuring him—said, while tears ran down his cheeks:

> My son, you have seen the distress I have suffered lately because of that text which I have only now finished explaining. I could not understand it, and I begged our Lord to help me, and tonight He sent His blessed Apostles to me, Peter and Paul, whose intercession I had also begged for; and they have spoken with me and told me all I desired to know. But now, in God's name, never tell anyone else of this as long as I live. I have told you only because you adjured me so strongly.[48]

O wondrous mystery of Providence, that at first God conceals the meaning of His Scripture and then at last reveals it, in order to show how far short of His mysteries comes human understanding and that whoever desires the least insight into them must have recourse to Him who chose to reveal His secrets to the Prophets and the Apostles! O happy soul whose prayer was heard by God in His mercy, who thus teaches us, by this example, to possess our questioning souls in patience, so that in the study of divine things we rely chiefly on the power of prayer! O happy master, to whom heaven's Key-bearer opened the gate of the Scriptures, to whom the heaven-climbing master of marvels, Paul, showed secrets of heavenly truth! Happy teacher, already a citizen of heaven while still a wayfarer on earth, conversing with your fellow-citizens while still a pilgrim in the body! And O most true and trusty teaching, that such a master received from such teachers!

17

Then there was the occasion at Paris when during the night, as Thomas was praying, he found that one of his teeth had grown in such a way as seriously to impede his speech; while the next day he was expected to sum up and conclude a public disputation. In his perplexity he turned to Reginald, who advised him to let it be known in the Schools that he was unavoidably prevented from performing the task; for in Reginald's view an operation was required to get rid of the bad tooth. But Thomas, considering that his absence might be misinterpreted in the University and the danger of the proposed operation, replied that he preferred to put himself in God's hands. So he went to the church and prayed long and earnestly, and behold the tooth suddenly came away in his hand easily and painlessly; and he could speak as well as ever. This tooth he kept for a long time as a souvenir.[49]

18

Nor was it only for himself that his prayers had such power. Reginald being down once with a recurrent fever, Thomas visited him to show his sympathy and gently to recommend patience. Then, blessed Agnes having been mentioned as one whose prayers might help Reginald to recover, Thomas, who had a special devotion to that virgin, took a relic of her which he (no less a virgin) used to carry about on his person, and laid it on the sick man's chest and prayed; whereupon Reginald rose at once from his bed perfectly cured.[50]

19

One day, as the holy teacher was at prayer in the church of our Order at Naples, a certain brother Romanus appeared to him. This Romanus had been a Master in Theology and succeeded Thomas in his chair at Paris, and he had recently died, though Thomas did not know this. On seeing him there in the church Thomas said to him: 'Welcome brother; when did you arrive?' To which Romanus answered: 'I am, in fact, dead; but I have permission to visit you because of your merits.' This astonished Thomas at first, but, recovering, he replied: 'Since God allows you to visit me, I will ask you a question. How do I stand with God? Are my works pleasing to Him?' Romanus answered: 'Go on as you are; God is pleased with you.' Then Thomas again: 'And what about you?' 'I', replied the other, 'am now in the eternal life, though I was kept fifteen days in Purgatory for neglecting to attend promptly to a will for which the bishop of Paris had made me responsible.' Then Thomas asked him: 'What is the right solution of that problem we used often to discuss together, whether knowledge gained in this life remains in the soul after death?' But Romanus replied: 'I see God. Ask me no more!' And when Thomas pressed him, saying: 'Have you an immediate sight of God, or only by means of some image?', the other merely replied: 'As we have heard so we see, in the city of the Lord of hosts. . . .' Then he vanished, leaving Thomas in wonder at so strange a vision, but also greatly comforted.[51]

20

On another occasion, at Paris this time, his deceased sister appeared to him as he was praying, and said that she was in Purgatory and needed Masses and prayers; which he was quick to arrange that she should have. Some time later, Thomas being now at Rome, she appeared again to say that she was now in glory, as a result of this help. He took the opportunity to ask her about the state of his two deceased brothers, the lords Landulf and Reginald. Landulf, she replied, was in Purgatory, but Reginald already in the glory of God. Then Thomas asked about himself and got this answer: 'You are in a good state, brother, and you will soon be joining us; but to receive a greater reward than ours because of your labours for the Church of God.'[52]

21

Another time, while praying and desiring to know what had become of his brother the lord Reginald, a figure appeared to him and showed him an open book in which names were written in gold and blue, those in gold being the names of martyrs; and these, Thomas saw, included the name of his brother; for Reginald's death by order of the tyrant Frederick was counted to him as martyrdom, because he suffered in defence of the Church and bore his torments patiently.[53]

22

And since in his prayers Thomas sought only what he believed to be according to God's will, he never failed to obtain what he prayed for. Hence at the end of his life he could say to Reginald his constant companion (who was in tears, for he saw that Thomas's death was imminent):

> My son, do not be sad: God has given me everything I asked him. I have prayed for three things: first, that my mind should never be perverted or softened by the world or the flesh; secondly that I should never be lifted out of the ranks of the Order to any high dignity in the Church; and thirdly, that I should know what had become of the soul of my brother Reginald who suffered so cruel a death in defence of the Church. And all three prayers my God has answered; I know this by revelation.

O truly happy soul, never coarsened by the world or made slack by sensuality or inflated by ambition; and to whom a brother's eternal bliss was divinely revealed![54]

23

One effect of Thomas's amazing concentration in prayer was that several times, as he prayed, his body was seen lifted off the ground, as if it followed the movement of his mind, as with him who said 'The Spirit raised me up between earth and heaven.'[55] This happened once in our priory at Salerno. He was praying one night after Matins at the high altar, when two of the brethren (one was his *socius* Reginald, the other a certain brother James, a particular admirer of his and for this reason accustomed to observe him closely) saw him lifted about three feet off the ground. The body was following the mind; that wonderful obedience, in him, of flesh to spirit was revealed visibly by the power of God, the outward miracle showing the inward grace.[56]

A similar thing took place in the priory at Naples and was seen by an old lay-brother, a man of holy life and scrupulous conscience, Dominic of Caserta. This brother, who was the sacristan, had noticed that Thomas would often leave his cell quietly before Matins and go down to the church to pray alone; and one night, happening to observe more attentively than usual, the brother saw Thomas, praying in the chapel of Saint Nicholas, raised off the ground about two feet. For a long while brother Dominic remained watching in wonder; then suddenly, from the crucifix at which Thomas was gazing, he heard a clear voice say these words: 'You have written well of me, Thomas; what do you desire as a reward for your labours?' And Thomas replied: 'Lord, only yourself.' It should be noted that this occurred at the time when the last part of the *Summa theologiae* was being composed, which treats of the Incarnation, birth, suffering, and resurrection of Christ; and with that mention of 'reward' Thomas was no doubt given to understand that the end of his labours was near at hand; and indeed he wrote little after this. And how appropriate was that answer to the question our Lord put to him, that his only reward should be to be filled with the sweetness of Him whom he had so vividly foretasted on his way through this life![57]

24

Consider the power of the prayers of this holy teacher: they taught him understanding of mysteries; they brought him all he desired. As an example, take that profound problem of the way in which our Lord's body is present in the marvellous Sacrament of the Altar—how dimensions and accidents can exist in this sacrament without their substance. There were many discussions at Paris among the learned on this matter; and many differences of opinion. But finally all the Masters agreed to abide by whatever conclusion brother Thomas should reach; they knew his persistent subtlety in searching out the true answer to any question and his clarity in expressing any truth that he had found. So the question was written out with each man's reasons and objections, and then submitted to Thomas's judgment; but he, like another Moses, considered that recourse should be had to God. So he prayed first and then wrote down what the Spirit moved him to write, and finally took the sheets of paper to the altar and laid them before the Master of masters, Christ. Then lifting his hands towards the Crucified, he prayed thus: 'Lord Jesus Christ, who are really and truly in this sacrament and wonderfully work therein as the divine Wisdom by which all things are, grant me, I humbly beg you, if what I have written of you be true, the power to teach and expound it clearly; but if what I have written should in the least degree be out of harmony with the Faith, then do not allow me to utter it.' O wonder! Suddenly the *socius* of Thomas and other brethren there present saw Christ Himself appear! He stood on the altar, above the sheets of paper, and spoke to His servant in these words: 'You have written well, Thomas, of the sacrament of my Body; you have answered the question put to you as well as it can be answered, in human language, by man still living this mortal life.' And after this Thomas continued long in prayer; and as he prayed the onlookers saw him raised nearly two feet from the ground. This was seen with their own eyes by the prior and several other brethren who had hastened to the place, and was reported to those who were absent, for the glory of God and as a testimony to the truth of the saint's teaching. And he, reassured now concerning the truth of his doctrine, expounded it before the University with a clarity which matched his interior illumination.[58]

25

When praying or thinking he often seemed to be rapt out of himself; but what he saw on these occasions he generally preferred not to speak of, even when asked to do so; though sometimes he did say a little, to the joy of his hearers. To those who lived with him it was wonderful to see him—a man using his senses on sensible objects like anyone else—grow suddenly abstracted and rapt out of himself and human company into the divine world, as though his mind was no longer where his body happened to be. There is a story to illustrate this of a dinner to which he was invited at Paris by the illustrious king of France, Saint Louis. Thomas wished to decline the invitation on the plea that he was busy with study and writing; but his prior, on behalf of the king, made him accept. So he went to the dinner and was given a seat next to the king; but his mind was still full of the heresy of the Manichees, which at that time he was engaged in refuting. And sitting there at table, suddenly the truth about this heresy flashed into his mind, and he struck the table, exclaiming: 'That settles the Manichees!' Then, calling his *socius* by name, as though he were still at study in his cell, he cried, 'Reginald, get up and write!' But the prior touched his hand, saying, 'Master, master, you are at dinner with the king of France, not in your cell!' Then Thomas, coming to himself, blushed and, bowing to the king, said: 'Pray excuse me, your majesty; I thought I was at my desk. . . . I have begun a work against the Manichees.' But the holy king, marvelling at such detachment from the senses and much edified, had the presence of mind to call at once for a secretary to write down there and then the thoughts with which the master had been inspired.[59]

A similar thing is said to have happened once at Naples. A certain cardinal legate, recently arrived in the kingdom of Sicily, had heard great things about brother Thomas from lord Peter, at that time archbishop of Capua and formerly one of Thomas's pupils. The legate asked the archbishop to arrange a friendly meeting with the saint; who was therefore called away from his studies one day to talk with the two prelates. They made him sit down between them; but his mind was miles away and he said scarcely a word to them. And after a long silence, while they waited for him to say something, suddenly his face brightened and he exclaimed, 'Ah, now I have it!' The legate meanwhile had been wondering why this friar gave him and the archbishop no sign of reverence; and in his heart he was beginning to despise him. But the archbishop said to him: 'My lord, don't be surprised, he is often like this; with a mind so abstracted that he cannot be got to talk, whatever the company he is in.' Then he took hold of Thomas's cloak and tugged it sharply, saying, 'Wake up, master! Here is the cardinal legate, come on purpose to see you!' Thomas came to himself then, as though waking from sleep (the sleep indeed of contemplation) and, seeing the prelates on either side of him, bowed reverently to the cardinal and begged his pardon, saying, 'My lord, please excuse me: I thought I was still in my cell. A beautiful idea has just occurred to me for the work on which I am engaged at present—a really wonderful idea it was and it gave me such pleasure!' The cardinal was surprised at this reply, but very pleased all the same by the encounter. And the archbishop used to enjoy telling the story afterwards, and often did so. The work mentioned by Thomas as engaging him just then was the *Summa contra Gentiles*.[60]

26

On another occasion, at Naples, while he was saying Mass on Passion Sunday, he was observed by many people present to become so deeply absorbed in the mystery that it was as if he had been admitted to a share in the sufferings of Christ. For a long while he remained as in a trance, his face bathed in tears. At last some of the brethren came up and touched him and brought him back to himself, and he went on with the Mass. But afterwards, when asked by the brethren and by some knights who were friends of his what had happened to him during that trance, he refused to tell them.[61]

During Lent, at the singing of the versicle *Ne projicias nos in tempore senectutis*, the brethren used to see him absorbed in thought while the tears ran down his cheeks.[62]

27

In the last year of his life, happening to be at his sister's castle of San Severino with Reginald, his companion, and several other of the brethren, he was rapt in ecstasy almost continuously for three days. His sister, the lady Theodora, became very anxious and asked Reginald what was the matter with her brother; to which Reginald replied that Thomas was often affected in this way, but that this trance had lasted longer than any previous one in his experience. It was finally ended by Reginald's tugging violently at his master's cloak; who, coming to himself from the sleep of contemplation, said with a sigh: 'Reginald, my son, I will tell you a secret which you must not repeat to anyone while I remain alive. All my writing is now at an end; for such things have been revealed to me that all I have taught and written seems quite trivial to me now. The only thing I want now is that as God has put an end to my writing, He may quickly end my life also.'[63]

Thus it was with him as with Moses and Paul, to whom God revealed things that surpass human understanding, to the one as the mediator of the Law to the Jews, to the other as the preacher of Grace to the Gentiles.[64] For it was fitting that to this holy teacher Thomas, who from the Throne on high received the book of both Laws and expounded it in the presence of the whole Church, should be shown things beyond the reach of natural reason, as pledges of a still greater vision to come. O happy teacher, enlightened in the present and seeing far into the future! Who from those things you were found worthy to write of rose to a vision of yet greater things!

28

During these trances of which I am speaking Thomas became sometimes completely insensible to wounds inflicted on his body. Once, for example, when the doctor had ordered that his leg should be cauterised, he asked his *socius* to let him know beforehand when the hot iron was to be brought to him. Then, at the time appointed, he went to the infirmary, and, uncovering his leg, fell into such an abstraction that he felt nothing of the heat at all; as was clear from the fact that his leg did not move during the operation.[65] At another time, while dictating in his cell the Commentary on the *De Trinitate* of Boethius, a candle that he was holding burned right down to his fingers and was finally consumed, while his fingers remained motionless. His secretary meanwhile did not dare to interrupt, since Thomas had previously ordered him to keep a strict silence, whatever he might happen to see.[66] Similar occurrences were often noticed at Paris. For example, when it was his turn to be bled, he would put himself into a state of contemplation and so be quite insensible to the cutting of the vein. Yet we are told that his natural constitution made him extremely sensitive to pain.[67]

29

His preaching must not be passed over in silence. To the ordinary faithful he spoke the word of God with singular grace and power, without indulging in far-fetched reasoning or the vanities of worldly wisdom or in the sort of language that serves rather to tickle the curiosity of a congregation than do it any real good. In his sermons Thomas always used his own mother tongue. Subtleties he kept for the Schools; to the people he gave solid moral instruction suited to their capacity; he knew that a teacher must always suit his style to his audience. The people, on their side, heard him with great respect as a real man of God.[68] He was a teacher who taught others to do what he himself was already doing, or rather God in him, according to that saying of the Apostle, 'I dare speak of nothing except of what Christ has done in me.'[69] Hence his words had a warmth in them that kindled the love of God and sorrow for sin in men's hearts. Moreover, God Himself confirmed these effects by miracles. In Rome once, in Holy Week, Thomas preached on the Passion of our Lord, moving his hearers to tears; and the next day, preaching on the Resurrection, he roused them wonderfully to joy in the Lord. And when he got down from the pulpit a woman who had long been afflicted by a flow of blood and found no remedy in medicines, came forward and touched the hem of his cloak, believing that through his merits she would be cured. And at once she felt that she was cured; and followed him back to Santa Sabina, where she convinced brother Reginald, the *socius*, of the fact; as he afterwards declared to many people on different occasions. O happy teacher, privileged to work a miracle similar to Christ's—a mere touch on the hem of his garment revealing the holiness that dwelt in his soul![70]

30

Thomas's fidelity to the example and teaching of his master, the lord of all things, Jesus Christ, was shown also in his gentleness and sincere humility. It is said that he himself declared—the purity of his conscience bearing him witness—that he thanked God that neither his learning nor his rank as a Master in Theology nor his successes in the Schools had ever made him really conceited.[71] Slight feelings of vanity had come from time to time, but never so that reason could not control them. And how indeed could his mind have soared so high to things divine without starting from that ground of humility which excludes all human conceit? Conscious as he was of receiving his knowledge from God, aware from day to day of the inflow into his soul of divine truth, what use could Thomas have found for vainglory? Knowing that wisdom dwells only with humility, he could always find the way back to lowly things from the summits of speculation. So he was ever courteous in speech, gentle, and approachable; clearly showing, in this, that his heart was formed on the example of Him whose life he was found worthy to contemplate with his understanding and to comment on in his writings. The outward bearing of Thomas came from an inward humility, it expressed what he really was.

31

We are told (for example) that once when staying at our house in Bologna he happened to be in the cloister, walking meditatively around as he was wont to do, when a brother from another priory who did not know him approached and said: 'Good brother, the prior says that you are to come with me.' The prior had in fact given that brother permission to take the first man he should happen to meet as his companion on some business that he had to see to in the city. Thomas bowed his head at once and followed. Now the other was a fast walker, too fast for Thomas, who could not keep up with him and got many hard words in consequence, but each time begged the other's pardon. And this was noticed and wondered at by people in the city: for they recognised the great teacher who was hurrying after that undistinguished friar; and, thinking there must be some mistake, they at last told the latter who his companion was. And he, turning round, then apologised to Thomas, begging him to excuse his ignorance. But Thomas, seeing the people salute him respectfully and hearing them ask why he had let himself be treated in this way, gently pointed out that the way to perfection lies only through obedience; and if God, he said, had humbled Himself for our sake, should not we submit to one another for God's sake? O happily humble soul, you did not stand on your dignity, you did not plead your position as a Master in Theology as an excuse for not obeying the prior through his spokesman! Though the habit of meditation made you a slow mover in the market-place, you were speedy enough in obedience—obedience the teacher of all virtues when joined to humility![72]

Another instance of the same thing happened at Paris once when brother Thomas, as representing the Chancellor of the University, had to examine a certain religious for the Licentiate. The examination took place, as usual, in the afternoon. To the questions proposed to him the candidate answered in a manner contrary both to the truth and to conclusions which Thomas himself had publicly maintained; but in his gentle way Thomas made no objection to this, ignoring the contradiction and judging it of no importance that a newly fledged master should thus oppose him. In his magnanimity he could overlook any slight to himself; and so went home quite tranquilly. But the brethren accompanying him were not disposed to take the matter so lightly. 'Master,' they said, 'this is a serious offence. That tyro was setting his view against yours. It was an affront to the truth, which you should not have tolerated, with all the masters of the University present!' To which he gently and quietly replied: 'It seemed to me kinder to say nothing; I don't like to put a new master to shame on his first public appearance. As for my teaching, I am, thank God, sufficiently sure about that; it is based on authority and reason. But, since you insist, I agree to say something on the subject tomorrow.' So the next day when the masters and bachelors were assembled again, as the custom is, in the bishop's hall, and when the new master had repeated without any alteration his views of the previous day, our holy teacher said gently: 'Master, this opinion of yours cannot be maintained without prejudice to the truth; for it is clearly contrary to such and such a Council. Hence you must either contradict a Council of the Church or think again.' Then the other began to express himself differently but without any real change of his meaning. So rather more forcibly Thomas repeated his objection, explicitly citing the definition of the Council. Then the other at last was put to shame and admitted his error and humbly asked Thomas to instruct him. And all the masters and others present were amazed at the calmness of mind and speech which Thomas displayed; at his manner of addressing an opponent as though he were teaching a pupil; at his ready command of the appropriate authority; at his ability to meet, simultaneously, the claims, on the one hand, of virtue and, on the other, of truth.[73]

32

The extraordinary fineness of his intelligence was due no doubt to the most subtle Spirit of divine Wisdom who dwelt in him. It is reported that he once said, in conversation with his pupils (and not to give himself airs, but rather as giving the glory to God), that he had never read any book without (with God's help) thoroughly understanding it.[74] Entirely devoted as he was to the study of divine things, who can wonder that the Spirit filled with clear thought this 'man of desires'[75] up to the measure of his need? Of the subtlety and brilliance of his intellect and the soundness of his judgment, sufficient proof is his vast literary output, his many original discoveries, his deep understanding of the Scriptures. His memory was extremely rich and retentive: whatever he had once read and grasped he never forgot; it was as if knowledge were ever increasing in his soul as page is added to page in the writing of a book. Consider, for example, that admirable compilation of Patristic texts on the four Gospels which he made for the lord Pope Urban and which, for the most part, he seems to have put together from texts that he had read and committed to memory from time to time while staying in various religious houses.[76] Still stronger is the testimony of Reginald his *socius* and of his pupils and of those who wrote to his dictation, who all declare that he used to dictate in his cell to three secretaries, and even occasionally to four, on different subjects at the same time. It was as if a great torrent of truth were pouring into him from God. No one could dictate simultaneously so much various material without a special grace. Nor did he seem to be searching for things as yet unknown to him; he seemed simply to let his memory pour out its treasures. His knowledge was like an overflowing river of Scriptural doctrine, sprung from the fount of Wisdom on high and then branching out through all the variety of his writings. One of his secretaries, a Breton called Evan from the diocese of Tréguier, relates that Thomas, after dictating to him and two other secretaries, would sometimes sit down to rest from the work and, falling asleep, would go on dictating in his sleep; Evan meanwhile continuing to write just the same.[77]

33

This holy man was full too of charity and kindness; indeed his goodness to others had a sort of quick spontaneous alacrity which, in a way, paralleled the divine outshining of his doctrine. He was a wonderfully kind-hearted man, gentle in speech, generous in deed; so that it was evident who dwelt habitually in his mind from the sweet graciousness of the words of his mouth. They understood this best who were his daily companions. He was indeed—he so innocent himself—severe on sin, and even on sinners in the sense that his zeal for justice and the salvation of souls made him strict in requiring from those in authority—when they asked for his advice—the exact correction of abuses; since he held that a good superior is always the active enemy of wrong-doing and that only thus would the true interests of the subject be served. Yet Thomas always found it hard to believe in the sins of his fellow-men; seeing them like himself in nature, he thought them like him in innocence; and when it was brought home to him that anyone had fallen into sin through human frailty, he would grieve as if the sin were his own—like the Apostle whose charity caused him to feel the failings of others like a scorching fire.[78] So much charity and kindliness had a wonderful effect even on his outward appearance; as we know from the constant and loving testimony of those who knew him; they say that it was a refreshment to the spirit merely to live with him and to be able from time to time to speak with him.[79] All this is clear evidence that the Holy Spirit was in him; such fruits have no other root than the divine Love. Let us recall too his wonderful compassion towards the poor and needy; he readily gave them all he could, whether clothes or other things, keeping nothing for himself but what was strictly necessary.[80]

34

Dwelling with the wisdom that excels all the wealth of this world, the wisdom he had chosen as his bride in youth, how could worldly desire find a place in his heart? He was, we know, of noble birth; had he wished to take advantage of his position he could have enjoyed wealth and worldly honours; but all the riches and glory he desired was to follow Christ in poverty and humility. There are stories told that illustrate this also. Thus, one day, while returning with some students to Paris from a visit to the relics at Saint Denis, as they drew near the city the students said to him, 'Look, Master, what a fine city Paris is! Wouldn't you like to be the lord of it?' To tell the truth they expected an edifying answer, and they got one. 'I would rather,' replied Thomas, 'have Chrysostom on Matthew. If I had to concern myself with Paris, I should lack time for contemplation; it would interfere with the study of Scripture, which gives me such joy. Besides, it would be dangerous; the more desire for this sort of thing, the less for heaven.'[81] The same indifference to wealth and honours which led him to renounce all that he might have inherited by right of birth appears also in his attitude to such honours as were in fact offered to him—particularly Pope Clement IV's offer of the archbishopric of Naples together with the revenues of the monastery of St. Peter *ad Aram*. Clement (who was very fond of Thomas) actually sent him the Bull appointing him to this office, but Thomas utterly refused to accept either it or those revenues, and begged the pope never to press such things on him again. O happy teacher, who lived according to the doctrine you taught, reckoning earthly things as nothing compared with the foretasted joy of heaven![82]

35

Concerning his appearance and physique some details have been preserved. He was tall and stout. He held himself erect, as men of an upright character do. His complexion was healthy, as of one who shunned excess of any kind; and in colour like ripe wheat. He had a large head, with a full development of the organs that minister to reason. He was somewhat bald. His body had the delicately balanced texture that goes with a fine intelligence; yet virile also, robust and prompt to serve the will, and trained never to shrink from any pain or peril by a soul that drew its confidence from God. It was, in short, a noble instrument for noble deeds, showing that God Himself had designed it for this purpose. But in thunderstorms and tempests Thomas would fortify himself with the sign of the cross and say: 'God came to us in the flesh, He died for us and rose again.'[83]

36

In the same year in which he died the following sign of his sanctity occurred. He was at Naples, and being ill and in bed, he was visited one day by a certain John Coppa, a Neapolitan, and by John's brother who was a Friar Preacher. These men both saw a bright star come in at the window and remain for a while over Thomas's head. The star was about as large as the window through which it came. Then both witnesses saw it pass slowly out of the window again.[84]

37

After the event just narrated the order came that Thomas was to go to Lyons for the General Council called by Pope Gregory X. It was to begin in May 1274. Gregory, of course, required Thomas to attend the Council as an outstanding theologian, but in particular he needed his help with regard to the Greeks; against whose errors Thomas had written a book (at the behest of Urban IV) which he was now told to bring with him. So, leaving Naples, he took the road for Rome. His way across the Campagna took him to the castle of Maenza, the property of his niece, lady Frances. And here he fell sick, almost entirely losing his appetite. . . .[85]

[Here follows an account of the miracle of the herrings; see the Canonisation Enquiry (Section II), IX and L. Gui (c. 37) says that Thomas would not himself taste the herrings miraculously provided, 'after the example of David who refused the water for which he had thirsted and which the three warriors obtained for him'.[86] And Gui adds that the miracle was witnessed by many people, some of whom ate of the herrings, and that 'it is still spoken of in that neighbourhood'.]

38

Some days later the holy man had recovered his strength enough to continue the journey to Rome; but, passing near the Cistercian monastery of Fossanova and receiving a warm invitation from the abbot and community to stay there a while until his health should be perfectly restored, Thomas accepted the invitation and turned aside to the abbey. And after saying a prayer before the high altar of the abbey church, as he entered the cloister the hand of the Lord came upon him, and he knew in his spirit that he had now reached the end of his life; and turning to Reginald of Priverno, in a clear voice which was heard by many of those present, Thomas said, 'Son Reginald, "haec requies mea in saeculum saeculi, hic habitabo quoniam elegi eam"'—as though to say, 'Here is my journey's end, here I shall finally rest from my labours.' O happy soul, to whom it was given to know at once the end of your life in time and its beginning in eternity—your labour's end, your entry into peace!

The abbot kindly gave him a room in his own apartments,

with all the comforts that could be provided, as was fitting for such a guest; and being now utterly exhausted, he was put to bed and waited on by the monks with all reverence and humility. It was winter and they kept a fire burning in his room, carrying the logs in from the wood on their shoulders. And seeing this, Thomas said, 'Who am I that the servants of God should wait on me like this?' And now with every day that passed his body grew weaker; yet still from his spirit flowed the stream of doctrine. For, being asked by some of the monks to leave them some memorial of his stay with them, he gave a brief exposition of the Canticle of Solomon. And it was indeed appropriate that the great worker in the school of the Church should terminate his teaching on that song of eternal glory; that such a master in that school, when about to pass from the prison of the body to heavenly wedding-feast, should discourse on the bridal union of the Church with Christ her Spouse.[87]

39

Feeling his strength ebbing away, he devoutly asked for the most holy body of Christ: and when the abbot, accompanied by the monks, brought it to him, he did reverence to it, prostrate on the ground; weak in body, but with his mind, as it were, running strongly to meet his Lord. And being asked, as the Church's discipline requires, whether he believed that this was indeed the body of the Son of God which was born of the Virgin and hung on the cross for our sake and on the third day rose again, Thomas answered with a strong voice and alert devotion and shedding tears:

> Even were it possible for us wayfarers through life to have some greater knowledge of this truth than sincere faith gives us—faith inexpressibly true—yet now in that faith alone I declare that I truly believe and most certainly know that this is indeed true God and Man, Son of the eternal Father, born of the Virgin mother, the lord Jesus Christ. This I sincerely believe and profess.

Then with tears and devotion he received the life-giving sacrament. But first (according to report) he said also these words:

> O price of my redemption and food for my pilgrimage, I receive You. For Your sake I have studied and toiled and kept vigil. I have preached You and taught You. Never consciously have I said a word against

You. But if I should have said or written anything amiss on this sacrament or any of the others, I leave it all to the judgment of the holy Roman Church, in obedience to whom I desire to end my life.

On the following day he asked for and received the Last Anointing. His mind remained clear through the ceremony and he answered the prayers himself. Then, joining his hands, he peacefully gave back his spirit to its Maker. It was the morning of 9 March in the year of our Lord 1274. He was beginning the fiftieth year of his age.[88]

40

At this happy death many Friar Preachers were present, from various priories, especially from Gaeta and Anagni whence a number of the brethren had already been to visit Thomas during his sickness. And since there were not lacking indications that he had died as a saint, the abbot and the community, with the other religious present and some of the nobility of the district, celebrated the funeral with a certain solemnity. The bishop of Terracina, lord Francis, a Friar Minor was there, and also a number of noblemen of the Campagna, some drawn by the tie of blood, since Thomas had many relatives in those parts, others merely by the deceased's reputation for learning and holiness. So the funeral rites were solemnly performed. And Thomas's niece, the lady Frances, also came; since the rule would allow no woman beyond the monastery gates, she had to wait outside; but at her request, and as a particular favour, her uncle's body was brought to her at the gates for her to see it.[89]

The crying and wailing and lamentation that went on—after the fashion of the south Italians—almost passes belief. It affected even the mule on which the saint had been carried; snapping the rope that tethered it in the stable, the animal came bounding out and—with nobody to show it the way—ran straight towards the bier, where, on seeing the corpse, it immediately collapsed and died, although in other respects it was in perfectly good health. Doubtless God wished that even the animals should play their part in showing what a light of the Church had been extinguished.

When all was done the holy remains were carried to the church and interred before the high altar, like a vessel of white alabaster concealed in clods of clay.[90]

41

Then Reginald of Priverno, of the Order of Preachers, stood up to preach. Everyone was eager to hear his testimony to the merits of his master. Here is the gist of what he said.

> I am able to bear true witness to the life of this holy man in its entirety; to his outward behaviour and also to the secrets of his conscience, for I was many times his confessor, and even now, as he lay dying, it fell to me to receive his general confession. And before God I declare that I have always found him like a little child for purity, as if no corruption of the flesh had ever touched him. And I am sure that he never gave willing consent to a mortal sin.[91]

Such was the testimony of brother Reginald, the particular and constant companion of St. Thomas, his ever-faithful helper and servant. Reginald indeed served Thomas with the devotion of a pupil for his master, of a son for his father, of a devout soul for a saint. Let us remember too that he had to be as a nurse to his master, supplying his needs as one supplies the needs of a child, because of that frequent, nay almost continuous, absence of mind and absorption in heavenly things which rendered Thomas unable to look after his own body and needing to be protected from accidents and have his food put on the plate before him, so that he should take only what he required and avoid eating absent-mindedly what might have done him harm.[92]

42

[Signs accompanying the death of St. Thomas. Gui reports two such occurrences at Fossanova. A star was seen (by one of the monks in a dream) to fall towards the monastery and then rise into heaven; and another star 'like a comet' was seen for three days before the saint's death.[93] Then Gui recounts the 'vision' of brother Paul of Aquila, then at S. Domenico in Naples, who in a dream saw St. Paul enter the hall where St. Thomas was lecturing on his Epistles.[94]]

43

We must not overlook a rather similar experience which the reverend master and bishop, brother Albert the German, had on the day that St. Thomas died. While sitting at table in the refectory Albert suddenly began to weep. The prior and several of the brethren were present. And when the prior asked him the reason for his tears, Albert replied: 'Thomas of Aquino, my son in Christ and a light of the Church, has died.' The prior took note of the date, which was later seen to coincide with that of Thomas's death.[95]

44 *and* 45

[Various miracles at Fossanova.[96]]

46

It seems to have been in the design of Providence that the holy teacher should have died at Fossanova, in the monastery of an Order—and a great one—other than his own; and that he should have been buried there where the trusty testimony of so many religious, who saw the miracles that took place around his corpse, could keep his memory green. These miracles were indeed so manifest that the monks were, in a sense, compelled to bear their witness to his sanctity; which is a point to be noted, for in fact they seem to have wished to conceal what they must have suspected to be the truth, fearing that if miracles were reported the Dominicans would be so much the more eager to gain possession of the body. That powerful, sweet fragrance, for example, which was experienced at each opening of the tomb—how would all suspicion of some ingenious contrivance have been excluded if the scent had not arisen and become apparent to everyone from under the very hands of precisely those who did not wish it to be noticed?[97]

There is also this to be considered, that both the journey itself, which was interrupted by the death of Thomas, and the manner of his death bore the clearest witness to his perfect obedience to the Roman Church. He died, as he had lived, obedient.

NOTES TO BERNARD GUI'S *LIFE*

1. See Appendix I for a note on St. Thomas's family.

2. Tocco, c. 1. Calo, c. 1. Canonisation Enquiry, LXII.

3. Tocco, c. 3. Calo, c. 2. Canonisation Enquiry, XC. Tocco adds that the incident happened at Naples.

4. I Kings (I Samuel), 2: 11–20.

5. Tocco, c. 4. Calo, c. 3. Tolomeo, XXII, c. 20. Canonisation Enquiry, LXXVI. This is part of the important deposition of Bartholomew of Capua, who states, on the authority of two Dominicans whom he had known at Naples in his youth—John of Caiazzo and John of S. Giuliano—that the intention of Thomas's father was that his son should eventually become abbot of Monte Cassino (cf. Tocco, c. 1). Walz gives reasons for thinking that Thomas was a Benedictine 'oblate' (pp. 9–13). Tocco, c. 4, adds that the boy's mother was delighted by the reports of her son's swift progress in the monastery school. But it is Calo who adds the extremely interesting detail that Thomas used 'often and earnestly' ask his masters, 'What is God?' (c. 3). Incidentally, where did Calo get this? No one else tells us of it: writing after Tocco and probably after Gui, Calo seems occasionally to tap a source unknown to them.

The two friars mentioned above with Bartholomew of Capua were of the older generation of the Roman province contemporary with St. Thomas; indeed, John of S. Giuliano, as we shall see, played an important part in his vocation (see Note 11). On John of Caiazzo (not to be confused with James of Caiazzo, Canonisation Enquiry, XLII), see Taurisano, *Miscellanea*, pp. 124–6; Canonisation Enquiry, LXXV and LXXVI, where we are told that John was 'very familiar with brother Thomas and had been his pupil both at Paris and in the *Regno* (i.e. at Naples)'. He was provincial from 1285 to 1288.

6. Proverbs, 20: 11.

7. Tocco, c. 5. The abbot is Landulf Sinibaldo (1227–36), who is said to have been related to the d'Aquino (Walz, p. 11). Thomas seems to have gone to the University of Naples in 1239, aged about fourteen (Walz, pp. 17–18, with references). The move may have been occasioned by an occupation of the monastery by the troops of Frederick II in April 1239.

8. Luke, 2: 47.

9. On the University of Naples in the thirteenth century (it was founded by Frederick II in 1224, perhaps as a rival to Bologna—but it never rose nearly so high), see Rashdall's *Universities of Europe in the Middle Ages*, ed. Powicke and Emden, II (1936), pp. 21–6. Tocco, c. 5, names Thomas's teachers at Naples: Master Martin in grammar and logic, and Master Peter of Ireland in natural science. Calo, c. 4, refers to Martin only as teacher of grammar (the 'first art', as Dante calls it, *Paradiso*, XII, 138), saying that Thomas passed on quickly from Martin's tuition to study logic and natural science under Master Peter. On Peter, see Grabmann, *Mittelalterliches Geistesleben*, I, pp. 249–65; M. B. Crowe in *Studies* (Dublin), XLV (1956), pp. 443–56.

10. Tocco, c. 5. Who this Dominican was is not known.

11. St. Thomas's age when he entered the Order is uncertain, but it is most improbable that he was as young as Gui's words imply: 'infra annos pubertatis'. The 'years of puberty' would usually coincide with coming to a

sufficient use of reason to dedicate oneself to God in the religious life, according to St. Thomas himself in *Summa theologiae*, 2a, 2ae, clxxxix, 5. But in this article the saint expressly states: (*a*) that the Church does not recognise as solemnly binding (i.e. as constituting one a member of a religious Order) any vow taken when 'below the age of puberty'—for boys, 'about fourteen', for girls, 'about twelve'—and (*b*) that in any case a boy below the age of puberty is 'naturally in the power of his father', who still has therefore a full right to decide whether his son's vow is to take effect or not. If, then, Thomas did enter the Order before puberty, he broke the rule that he states in this article, for he certainly entered against the wish of his parents. It is true that both Bartholomew of Capua (Canonisation Enquiry, LXXVI) and the Bull of Canonisation (*Fontes*, ed. Laurent, p. 520) agree with Gui's statement; and that Calo, c. 4, says that Thomas entered at thirteen. Tocco, however, seems to distinguish, in respect of Thomas's having reached puberty, between the boy (*puer*), who joined the University at Naples, and the youth (*juvenis*), who joined the Dominican Order there (cc. 5 and 6). And in any case to suppose that Thomas was still, say, only thirteen when he joined the Order would imply, either that he was born as late as 1230–1, or else that he became a Dominican before 1240; both extremely improbable suppositions. Mandonnet discussed the matter pretty thoroughly in *Rev. Thomiste*, VII, pp. 243–67, concluding that Thomas received the habit in the spring of 1344, and so at the probable age of nineteen. This may be a trifle too definite, but Pelster, Grabmann, and Walz tend to agree with Mandonnet. It is safer to follow these scholars and suppose that Thomas became a friar in his later 'teens; even Tolomeo's 'sixteen' (XXII, c. 20) is probably too early.

The place was certainly Naples, and Thomas became and remained a member of the Roman province. Naples had a Dominican priory since 1231, dedicated to St. Dominic in 1234 when the latter was canonised. On the Dominican novitiate in the thirteenth century, Walz is informative, pp. 32–3. For the little to be learned about John of S. Giuliano, the spiritual director of young Thomas, see Taurisano in *Miscellanea*, pp. 120–2. This friar as an old man was acquainted with Bartholomew of Capua, who refers to him as a source in the Canonisation Enquiry (LXXVI). John will reappear in connection with the imprisonment of St. Thomas at Roccasecca (Gui, c. 8). Bartholomew says that John 'received' Thomas into the Order, but this is expressly given as hearsay (Canonisation Enquiry, LXXVI) and is probably untrue; see next note.

12. A detail not given by Tocco, but there seems no reason to doubt it. Thomas Agni of Lentini (Sicily) was in fact the first prior of S. Domenico at Naples; and, later, provincial of the Roman province before filling the other posts mentioned by Gui; he died *c.* 1278: see Taurisano, *Miscellanea*, p. 120, n. 3; Mandonnet, *Rev. Thomiste*, VII, p. 372, n. 1.

13. A rather curious 'aside', but Tocco also approves of Theodora, and even presents her as rejoicing when she first heard that her son had become a friar (c. 7); a point that Mandonnet begs leave to doubt, *op. cit.*, VII, p. 534.

14. Tocco, c. 8, and Calo, c. 4, agree in focusing attention on Theodora's annoyance with the friars for keeping Thomas out of range of her caresses, and they make this annoyance the chief cause of the violent action described

in the next chapter. See also Tocco's deposition in the Canonisation Enquiry, LXII. Bartholomew of Capua, on the other hand, throws the blame on Thomas's father, Landulf (*ibid.*, LXXVI); and the same is hinted by the Bull of Canonisation (*Fontes*, ed. Laurent, p. 520). But Landulf may well have been dead by the end of 1243 (Walz, pp. 39, 200), and Mandonnet takes his death at this time as support for thinking that John of S. Giuliano had restrained Thomas for a time from joining the Order: the great knight's death, on this view, would have seemed to brother John to leave the way open at last (*op. cit.*, VII, pp. 385 ss.). As for the journey of Thomas and his Dominican companions from Naples to Rome, Tocco says they went by Terracina and Anagni, which implies that they took the Via Appia along the coast and then turned inland, perhaps through Priverno and Frosinone. They went, of course, on foot (see below, Note 83); Mandonnet calculates, at the rate of 40 km. a day. At Rome they lodged at Santa Sabina, which Honorius III had given to St. Dominic in 1220, according to one account, or to his brethren soon after his death in 1221.

15. Tocco, c. 8. Calo, c. 4. Tolomeo, XXII, c. 20. Canonisation Enquiry, LXI, LXII, LXXVI. *Vitae Fratrum*, Part 4, c. 17 (MOPH, I, p. 201). In outline the incident is clear. Theodora appeals to her other sons (but which of them, apart from Reginald?) to recover Thomas by force from the Order. These young men are serving under the emperor, who is encamped at Acquapendente, a little north of the lake of Bolsena, well placed for a swoop on the road (the Via Cassia) that the friars were taking from Rome to the north. The brothers (or at least Reginald), mounted and with men-at-arms, find Thomas and four other friars resting by a roadside spring. Thomas is seized and, after a struggle, got securely on to a horse, and then carried off beyond Rome to the south—first, probably, to Montesangiovanni near Frosinone, and thence to the chief castle of the d'Aquino, Roccasecca. 'All this', says Walz, p. 35, 'happened probably during the first half of May 1244.' We know that Frederick II was warring in the neighbourhood of Acquapendente at that time. And on 22 May 1244 the General Chapter of the Dominicans opened at Bologna, a fact which lends support to the assertion of Tolomeo and de Frachet that the Master General himself, John of Wildeshausen ('Teutonicus', the German), was with the little band of Dominicans; and if so, the friars were presumably bound for Bologna, whence Thomas would have continued his journey to Paris, his intended destination (Gui, c. 5, Tocco, c. 7).

Tolomeo makes the saint's brother Reginald the chief abductor; the other sources are vague. Tocco, Gui, and Tolomeo all make the Emperor Frederick responsible, at least as permitting the action. Tolomeo adds that the great Peter de Vineis—Dante's Pier delle Vigne, *Inferno*, XIII—was Reginald's companion in violence; but this is implausible. Tocco, in his deposition at the Canonisation Enquiry (LXII), names the lady Catherine de Morra as his informant on the incident. Lady Catherine was a niece of St. Thomas—a daughter of his sister Mary and William San Severino—whom Tocco met and conversed with about her uncle, in February 1318. On the incident as a whole, see Mandonnet, *op. cit.*, VII, no. 30, pp. 529–47; and Walz, pp. 34–5.

16. Tocco, c. 8. Calo, c. 5. At Montesangiovanni, Thomas may have been kept for only a short time, *en route* for Roccasecca. Montesangiovanni was in

papal territory, while Roccasecca was in the 'Regno' directly governed by Frederick. Tocco, c. 8, names both as places to which Thomas was taken, but is otherwise vague; in his deposition at the Canonisation Enquiry (LXI and LXII) he seems to distinguish the two places by this, that Thomas's brothers were with him at Montesangiovanni, but not (until some time later) at Roccasecca. This may have a bearing on the famous 'seduction' scene to which Gui comes in c. 8 (see Note 20). Any reconstruction of the sequence of events must be partly conjectural; Mandonnet proposes the following: Thomas's brother, or brothers, attempted to seduce him with a girl soon after their arrival at Montesangiovanni; having failed in this they hastened back to the emperor's camp and Thomas was taken on to Roccasecca (*op. cit.*, VIII, pp. 222ss.). This theory is based on Tocco's deposition at the Enquiry, but Mandonnet has to press this text rather hard, and he gets no support from Tocco's *Life*, in which the seduction appears (as it does in Gui also) as the *last* act of the imprisonment, a sort of climax. But obviously this may be an 'edifying' rearrangement. . . . It is clear, anyhow, that those who attempted the seduction were Thomas's brothers (see Note 20), and that they must have attempted it, either at once, before their return to Frederick, or later, when they were once again free to deal with their difficult junior. The place may have been Montesangiovanni *both* times, but this is unlikely if, as seems probable, Thomas spent the greater part of his captivity at Roccasecca. As well as Mandonnet, *op. cit.*, see Scandone in *Miscellanea*, p. 107. Walz, p. 35, leaves the question open; I have not been able to consult his article, 'Il detenuto di Montesangiovanni', *Memorie domenicane* Florence, S. M. Novella, vol. xxxii (1956) pp. 162–72.

As for the Dominicans' complaint to the pope, Tocco and Calo agree with Gui that the pope was Innocent IV; which helps to date the episode, since he was elected in July 1243. And all three sources say that Innocent was in the neighbourhood, and so not far from his imperial rival. Moreover, Frederick was still excommunicated (since 1239) and at war with the pope's allies in Central Italy. Given this delicate situation, it is understandable that when Frederick responded quite favourably to the pope's protest on behalf of the Dominicans—to the extent (says Tocco, c. 8) of having Thomas's brothers placed under arrest—the friars should have thought it best to let the matter drop. They 'decided that it was wiser not to take the matter to law, and in this they were encouraged by the fact that the young brother was showing himself firm . . . and true to his vocation' (Walz, p. 36).

It is natural to suppose that the friars' appeal to the pope would be made through their Master General, John the German, whether or not he had been actually present at the abduction, as Tolomeo and Gerard de Frachet say and Mandonnet confidently asserts. He was certainly at Bologna for the General Chapter before the end of May 1244. Elected Master General at the General Chapter at Paris in 1241, John was the third to hold this office after St. Dominic, succeeding to St. Raymund of Peñafort (1238–40), who himself succeeded Bd. Jordan of Saxony. John was perhaps especially suited to negotiate between pope and emperor: the *Vitae Fratrum* says of him, 'hic fuit multum notus in curia papae et eciam domino Frederico' (*ed. cit.*, p. 333); and Mandonnet has suggested that his election at Paris in 1241 was in response to pressure from Gregory IX, who desired, as the Dominican Master General, a man more acceptable to Frederick than St. Raymund had been. As a German, John was the emperor's subject. See Mandonnet, *op. cit.*, VIII, no. 31, pp. 20–4. For Frederick II's relations with the Dominican Order, consult Huillard-Bréholles, *Historia diplomatica Friderici II*, v (Paris, 1852ss., pp. 1088–1100; VI, pp. 479–80).

17. Tocco, cc. 8–9. Calo, c. 6. These authors tell us what books Thomas studied in prison: the Bible, the *Sentences* of Peter Lombard (this may be only conjecture), and parts of Aristotle's *Organon* (implied by Tocco's statement that Thomas 'is said' to have written a treatise on Aristotle's 'Fallacies', i.e. the *De sophisticis elenchis*—a work which Thomas may well have studied in prison; but it is disputed whether his extant *opusculum*, the *De fallaciis*, could have been written as early as this; cf. Grabmann, *Die Werke*, pp. 348–53, 463, and Eschmann, *Catalogue*, p. 410). Thomas also had a breviary, said the divine office, and observed, as far as possible, 'all the laws of the Order' (de Frachet, see below, Section IV, p. 146). This study the young man was promptly turning into teaching, his first pupils being, apparently, his sisters (Canonisation Enquiry, LXII). We must not imagine Thomas as fettered in a dungeon; he was merely not allowed to leave the precincts of the castle and pestered, no doubt, to change his mind concerning his future.

One of his sisters—the eldest, says Tocco—was so affected by her brother's conversation that she decided to follow him into religion. She entered—almost at once, says Calo—the Benedictine convent of St. Mary at Capua; where, in a remarkably short time, perhaps by 1252, she was elected abbess. This election was disputed, but then confirmed by Innocent IV in 1254 (*Documenta*, ed. Laurent, pp. 541–4). Her name was Marotta, and she seems to have died between 1257 and 1259; see below, Note 52 and Appendix I.

It is just possible that about this time Thomas wrote the Italian sonnet printed below in Appendix II.

18. Tocco, c. 9. Calo, c. 6. Both these authors stress the tearing of Thomas's habit by his brothers and his persistent refusal to discard it; cf. Canonisation Enquiry, LXII, LXXVI. Still, he was not left in mere rags, which was just as well, since he remained captive for at least a year (see Note 21). The remedy, as Gui tells us (c. 8), was provided by his spiritual father, John of S. Giuliano.

19. II Corinthians, 12: 9.

20. Tocco, c. 10. Calo, c. 7. Canonisation Enquiry, LXI. This last is Tocco's deposition at the Enquiry, in which he says that he had the story from Robert of Sezze O.P. [not to be confused with Sessa, as Prümmer confuses these names in *Fontes*, p. 349 n. (*a*), although the Latin text clearly distinguishes 'Sitia' and 'Suessa']. On this Robert, see Taurisano, *Miscellanea*, p. 180. It seems odd that Tocco does not refer to Reginald of Priverno here, as he does elsewhere in his deposition (LVIII, LIX); for, if Gui and Calo are to be believed, no one but Reginald knew of Thomas's being girded by the angels—at least, not while the saint still lived. The rest of the episode, the attempted seduction and Thomas's vigorous counter-attack, may have become known in various versions before the death of the hero of it; though it is not in the *Vitae Fratrum* and Tolomeo ignores it. A garbled version of it is given by another Dominican author, Thomas of Cantimpré, in his *Bonum universale de apibus*; one of the

many anecdotes which give that curious work most of its interest. Cantimpré says (writing not later than the 1260s): '. . . et his omnibus nequius cogitantes [i.e. the brothers of St. Thomas] per quod possent juvenilem animum evertere, secum mulieres in carcere per tempus aliquod concluserunt. Qui, fortius quam prius, spretis illecebris, sic annis duobus vel tribus in carcere perduravit' (Book I, c. 20, Douai, 1605, p. 79). Cantimpré's details need to be taken with much salt, and J. A. Endres rejects the whole story as a coarse legend stemming from the visits paid to Thomas in prison by his sisters. But this is probably too sceptical a view; see Walz, p. 37.

I have mentioned (Note 16) Mandonnet's opinion that the seduction was attempted right at the start of St. Thomas's captivity, and so not later than May 1244 (*op. cit.*, VII, pp. 243–60). But there is this small difficulty: would Thomas have had a fire in his room, in south Italy, in May? Yet the firebrand is an essential part of the story. Walz mentions this objection as Pelster's, p. 199.

St. Thomas began to be called 'Doctor Angelicus' in the fifteenth century (Walz, p. 188; cf. *Xenia Thomistica*, III, p. 164). But Tocco, in his *Life*, naturally takes occasion from the dream described in this chapter to call Thomas 'puritate angelicus'.

21. Agreeing with Tocco, c. 11, and Calo, c. 8. Bartholomew of Capua has 'for more than a year' (Canonisation Enquiry, LXXVI), the *Vitae Fratrum*, 'almost a year' (ed. Reichert, MOPH, I, p. 201). We shall not be far out if we suppose that Thomas was free by the late summer or autumn of 1245 (cf. Walz, p. 40).

22. Tocco, c. 11. Canonisation Enquiry, LXXVI; this source—Bartholomew of Capua—is conclusive against Tolomeo (XXII, c. 21) and de Frachet (*Vitae Fratrum*, ed. Reichert, MOPH, I, p. 201), who say that no Dominican could visit Thomas in prison; for Bartholomew's informant was John of S. Giuliano himself, as he states *in loco*.

23. On the manner of the escape Gui repeats Tocco, c. 11. Tolomeo makes it more dramatic, XXII, c. 21. Conversely, Bartholomew (Canonisation Enquiry, LXXVI) and de Frachet (MOPH, I, p. 201) say that Thomas was simply let go. And he seems to have gone at first to Naples, though Tolomeo says Rome, which was certainly visited on the journey north which followed (Gui, c. 9).

24. Tocco, c. 12, and Calo, c. 8, agree with Gui that when Thomas left Italy between the middle of 1245 and the early months of 1246 he was bound for Paris and its priory school of St. Jacques, the intellectual centre of the Order. De Frachet agrees with this (MOPH, I, p. 201). On the other hand, Tolomeo takes Thomas straight from Rome to Cologne (XXII, c. 21); and, at the Canonisation Enquiry, Tocco relates the tradition in the saint's family that 'he was sent to study at Cologne' after his release (LXII). To Cologne he certainly went by 1248, but it seems more likely than not that he was at Paris first, and that he even spent the better part of three years there studying under St. Albert (so Mandonnet, *op. cit.*, VIII, pp. 490 ss.; followed by Chenu, *Intro-duction*, p. 12; and Grabmann agrees, *Thomas v. Aquin*, p. 14). True, the sources are silent about so long a first period in Paris, apart from a phrase in the letter of the Parisian faculty of Arts in 1274 (see below, Section V) boasting that Paris had the honour of having first reared and nourished Thomas ('. . . quae ipsum prius educavit, nutrivit et fovit'). Perhaps a better argument

in this sense is that before 1248 Paris was the only international house of studies (*studium generale*) in the Order and far and away its chief intellectual centre; and also that Albert was almost certainly there between 1245 and 1248. In 1248 the General Chapter at Paris set up four new *studia generalia* for the provinces of Provence, Lombardy, Germany, and England respectively. Cologne was the German one, and St. Albert its first regent [*Acta Cap. Gen.*, ed. Reichert, I (MOPH, III, p. 41)]; Albert would then have left Paris for Cologne in the summer of 1248, accompanied by young Thomas Aquinas. Yet, if this seems the more likely course of events, it is not accepted by all. Walz, pp. 44-7, somewhat hesitantly suggests what might be called the 'German' view of a longer period at Cologne—perhaps from 1245 to 1252—the view upheld also by two other German scholars, by Fr. Pelster in our own day, and the great Denifle in the last century; though Grabmann, we have noted, is with the Frenchmen, Mandonnet and Chenu. If an English non-specialist may venture an opinion, I find the 'French' view the more probable—that Thomas studied under Albert at Paris between 1246 and 1248, before proceeding to Cologne under the same master.

As for the journey from Italy in 1245, Thomas may well have made it, as Tocco says (c. 12) in the company of the Master General, John, who had to be at Paris for the General Chapter held there in 1246. They probably took the sea route to France, for we are told that Thomas once experienced a storm at sea (Tocco, c. 38, Gui, c. 35), and all his later long journeys were certainly overland.

25. Tocco, c. 12. Calo, c. 8. St. Albert is called *dominus*, 'lord', by Gui, because he was later a bishop, being appointed to the see of Ratisbon (Regensburg) by Alexander IV in 1260; though, as Tolomeo rather humorously insists (XXII, c. 19), Albert got rid of the burden as soon as he could.

St. Thomas was more successful in evading high office in the Church, though he only did so by showing, more than once, something of that stubborn resolution to be a Dominican friar and nothing else whatsoever which had carried him through the opposition of his powerful family.

Albert is known to history as 'the Great', and, if anyone does, he deserves the epithet: but to his own age he was Albert 'the German' or 'of Cologne'. He was closely associated with Cologne through the school of philosophy and theology which grew up around him there, at the priory of Holy Cross (Walz, p. 48). It is as Albert of Cologne that St. Thomas introduces him to Dante in the *Paradiso* (x, 97-9):

> Questi che m'è a destra più vicino,
> frate e maestro fummi, ed esso Alberto
> è di Cologna, e io Thomas d'Aquino.

'He who stands nearest me on the right was both my brother and my master: he is Albert of Cologne, and I, Thomas of Aquino.'

An outline of St. Albert's career is given below, in Section III, Note 2.

26. Tocco, c. 12. Calo, c. 8. Cf. Walz, pp. 51-2. The best introduction to the literary resources and technical procedure of the medieval schools in the thirteenth century is probably the brilliant work of M. D. Chenu: *Introduction*

à l'étude de S. Thomas d'Aquin, especially pp. 66–170. I have already, in my Introduction, drawn attention to the notable silence, or near-silence, of our sources on the major part played by St. Thomas in the Aristotelian movement, in that winning for the Greek what Chenu calls 'droit de cité dans la Chrêtiente' (p. 175). In this work Aquinas extended very greatly, especially in theology and metaphysics, the preparatory labours of Albert.

It is clear that Denys, the pseudo-Areopagite, only interests Gui incidentally here; yet his assimilation into St. Thomas's mind—so strongly affected by the very dissimilar thought of Aristotle—is a fact of the deepest interest, as Chenu brings out forcibly in his section on Denys, *op. cit.,* pp. 192–6. We have what is probably an autograph of a *reportatio* made by St. Thomas of St. Albert's commentaries on Denys (see G. Thery, in AOP, I (1930), pp. 15–86; Dondaine, *Secrétaires de S. Thomas,* pp. 19–20). Albert's Commentary on the *Divine Names* has been recently edited by F. Ruello in *Traditio,* xii (1956), pp. 231–314. N.B. a *reportatio* was not the result of a dictation. A good deal of dictating was done, and we know that much of St. Thomas's work was dictated (see Dondaine, *op. cit.* and *infra* Note 77), especially his later work. But a *reportatio* was a reproduction of a master's lecture or series of lectures, made *post factum* by one of the students, working no doubt on notes (Dondaine, *op. cit.,* p. 15). Some works ascribed to St. Thomas are in fact 'reports' of this kind, e.g. the Commentary on St. John, which we owe to Reginald of Priverno.

27. Tocco, c. 12. Calo, c. 8. Thomas was still an 'undergraduate' when this disputation took place, not yet a Bachelor, *baccalaureus* (see Note 28). It happened presumably at Cologne, in the Dominican school. The *Quaestiones disputatae,* which preserve for us so much of the scholastic thought of the time, were much more important affairs. Still, Albert was there as the presiding Master who alone had the right to cast a thesis into its final form and answer all the objections raised against it—the act of 'determining', *determinare.* Hence his protest—but prompted, it is clear, by admiration, not irritation—at his pupil's having apparently forgotten himself so far as to take the Master's place, 'locum determinantis', instead of sticking to the subordinate's job of discussing and answering objections in a provisional way, 'locus respondentis'. On the terms used here and the history of the scholastic *quaestio,* see Chenu, *Introduction,* pp. 73–81; Mandonnet in *Rev. Thomiste,* xxiii (1928), pp. 267–9.

Walz and others have argued from this chapter, and Tocco's corresponding c. 12, that already in Cologne Thomas may have been a Bachelor *lector,* lecturing under St. Albert: but this surely is excluded by the first sentence of the next chapter—see Note 28.

Tocco tells us that Albert at this time gave a course on Aristotle's *Ethics,* discussing points of doctrine raised by the text ('. . . cum quaestionibus'), and that Thomas carefully wrote out his notes on the lectures, i.e. 'reported' them. This would not, of course, be his own Commentary on the *Ethics,* written fifteen or twenty years later.

28. Gui's terms distinguish between the state of a mere pupil, such as Thomas had been hitherto ('tempore studii quo in *audiendo* magistrum . . . insudavit') and that of a Bachelor, *baccalaureus.* Once possessed of the latter degree a man had to lecture; he would give courses on the *Sentences* of Peter Lombard and (in a summary or elementary way, *cursorie*) on Holy Scripture;

doing so under the general direction of a theological Master, *magister in sacra pagina*: see Chenu, *Introduction*, pp. 207, 226ss.

SS. Thomas and Albert had now spent six or seven years together as pupil and master. Thomas's very impersonal cast of literary expression leaves us guessing at his feelings towards Albert or the extent to which he consciously acknowledged an intellectual debt to him. We know more about Albert's feelings, if we may trust the sources (Gui, c. 43, Canonisation Enquiry, LXXXII) which tell us of his grief over Thomas's death and of his journey in old age to Paris to defend him from accusations which Thomas could no longer rebut in person. We can be sure, of course, that the years they had passed together were immensely profitable to Thomas. Very different in natural genius and mentality, the two men were at one in their deepest aim, as the Church has recognised in canonising both, and as the Order to which they belonged will never forget. Dante, as he so often does, finds the right phrase, when his St. Thomas introduces Albert, standing by his side in heaven, as 'frate e maestro' (*Paradiso*, x, 98).

Separated now, in 1252, by the recall of Thomas to Paris to begin his lecturing as a Bachelor, they would meet occasionally again, but never for long: at the General Chapter at Valenciennes in 1259 and probably at Orvieto between 1261 and 1263, while Albert was at the papal Curia after resigning his bishopric (see Note 25).

Tolomeo, XXII, c. 21, and Thomas of Cantimpré, *Bonum universale*, I, p. 20, say that while still a student at Cologne Thomas was offered the abbacy of Monte Cassino by the pope—'as a favour to his parents', adds Tolomeo. There seems no reason to doubt that the offer was made, but Alexander IV could not have made it at this time, as Tolomeo says, since he was not pope until 1254; doubtless he is confused with Innocent IV (1243–54). The offer, if made, may well have been connected, as Tolomeo says, with the reduced fortunes of the d'Aquino family after the rebellion of some of its members against Frederick II: see Note 1, and *infra*, Note 82.

It was probably at Cologne that St. Thomas was ordained priest (Walz, pp. 53–4).

29. Tocco, c. 14. Calo, c. 9. The Master General, according to these sources, is still John the German, who held the office from 1241 to 1252. Tocco and Calo also tell us that John asked St. Albert to choose a new Bachelor for the school at Paris, but hesitated when Albert proposed Thomas. The latter's merits, says Tocco, 'were not yet known' to John; which seems odd if Master John and the young Thomas had really been travelling companions in 1244 and again in 1245 or 1246 (see Notes 15 and 24 above). Yet, as we have seen, there is evidence that the two had been on the road together, at least for a time. Did Thomas then only show John the 'dumb ox' side of his nature? The result, at any rate, was satisfactory, as we learn also from Tocco and Calo; for another eminent friar, Hugh of St. Cher, was called in by Albert to persuade the Master General to accept Thomas as a Bachelor for Paris. Hugh was the second Dominican to have a Master's chair in the theological faculty at Paris, and the first Dominican to become a cardinal (see *infra*, Note 9 to de Frachet's *Cronica* and AOP (1925), p. 189). John seems to have met Hugh in Germany in 1251 or 1252; and St. Thomas in

consequence was sent to Paris. But the initiative came from St. Albert (see Walz, pp. 59–61).

St. Thomas began to lecture at Paris in 1252, being in his twenty-sixth or twenty-seventh year. The striking impression he at once made on the University is conveyed by Gui, Tocco, and Calo in almost identical terms which have become famous; the crucial word, of course, is *novus*, 'new', repeated thrice by Gui and five times by Tocco. The lectures would have been biblical for one year, followed by a course of two years on the *Sentences* of Peter Lombard (Walz, pp. 65–6). The chief writings of Thomas at this period are the four books of commentary on the *Sentences* (see Supplementary Note *infra*, p. 81) and two philosophical *opuscula*, the *De principiis naturae* and the important *De ente et essentia* (see Grabmann, *Thomas v. Aquin*, pp. 27–32; cf. Tolomeo, XXII, c. 21).

These first years of Thomas's teaching at Paris coincided with a violent outburst of hostility to his own Order and to the Franciscans on the part of the secular (clerical) Masters in the faculty of theology. The details of this quarrel, which smouldered on for half a century, need not concern us here, though it must be emphasised that, for the Dominicans in particular, with their mission as theological teachers and preachers, it was a matter of life and death; without a secure footing at Paris they could not realise their ideal. St. Thomas was deeply involved in the controversy during both of his periods at Paris, in 1252–6 and again in 1269–72; and it had important effects on some aspects of his theological writing (Chenu, *Introduction*, pp. 229, 242, 292–3). On the quarrel in general, see D. L. Douie, *The Conflict between the Seculars and the Mendicants at the University of Paris in the 13th century* (Aquinas Papers, no. 23) and Walz, pp. 62–5; and cf. *infra*, Notes 5 and 6 to de Frachet's *Vitae Fratrum*. Tocco has a rather confused chapter (19) on the matter; so also Calo, c. 12. Gui does not mention it. Tocco and Calo bracket Siger of Brabant (whose great historical importance lies in the quite different field of philosophy) with the leader of the secular anti-Mendicants, William of St. Amour. Cf. E. Jallonghi in *Miscellanea*, pp. 213–22.

30. Tocco, c. 16. Calo, c. 10. Tolomeo, XXII, c. 21. St. Thomas received his licentiate in theology early in 1256, though he was not officially admitted to the corporation of Masters in the University until August 1257 (see Note 33). In 1256 he had been lecturing for two years on the *Sentences* at the Dominican school of St. Jacques (Walz, pp. 65–9, Chenu, *Introduction*, p. 229). There seems to have been a lull in the quarrel with the secular Masters. On 3 March 1256 Pope Alexander IV wrote to the chancellor of the University congratulating him on having given the licentiate to 'our beloved son brother Thomas of Aquino . . . a man of noble birth and evident integrity of character, who has amassed, by God's grace, a treasure of learning and science' (*Chartularium Univ. Paris.*, I, p. 307; also printed in *Documenta*, ed. Laurent, pp. 544–5).

In his *Cronica brevis* (*Fontes*, p. 257) Gui dates Thomas's licentiate in 1254, which is wrong, and makes him 'about thirty-one', which is right. Tocco merely notes that Thomas was under the usual age of thirty-five (*Chartularium Univ. Paris.*, I, p. 79). Obviously this four or five years' anticipation was a remarkable token of esteem.

31. Psalm 11 (Vulgate): 1.
32. Psalm 103 (Vulgate): 13.

33. One of the most popular stories about St. Thomas, and very well attested, being in Tocco, c. 16, Calo, c. 10, *Vitae Fratrum*, Part 4, c. 24 (MOPH, I, p. 216), the Canonisation Enquiry, XLIX, LX, and XCII. These last three testimonies each refer to a different source. No. XLIX is part of the deposition of Dom Peter of Montesangiovanni, one of the Cistercians from Fossanova who visited St. Thomas as he lay sick at Maenza in February 1274, and then rode back with him to Fossanova where he was presently to die. Dom Peter says that Thomas was persuaded to tell this story during the visit. In LX we are referred by William of Tocco to the saint's nephew, Thomas of Marsico (son of Theodora d'Aquino and Roger of San Severino), who himself had it from St. Thomas, 'ab ore dicti fratris Thomae'. Finally, XCII takes us to Paris, where the witness, a south Italian Dominican, Peter Capotto (or Cappucci), had heard it when the *Vitae Fratrum* was read out to the brethren there (we may recall that this work was approved in 1260 for circulation within the Order of Preachers, see Introduction, p. 16). It was at Paris, too, that Peter Capotto met the tradition that the old friar of St. Thomas's vision was St. Dominic (who, however, did not live to old age).

It is likely enough that Thomas was nervous before his first public performance as a Master in the University. Not only was he well below the normal age: there was also the persistent opposition of the secular Masters which was to provoke a vigorous intervention from the pope expressly in favour of St. Thomas and of his fellow-Mendicant, the Franciscan theologian St. Bonaventure (*Chartularium Univ. Paris.*, I, pp. 338–40; *Documenta*, ed. Laurent, pp. 551–4). In the event, these two saints had to wait until August 1257 for their official admission among the University Masters (Walz, pp. 71–2; cf. *Chartularium Univ. Paris.*, I, p. 366).

34. Job, 28: 11.

35. Tocco, c. 15. Calo, *proem*. I have not been able to trace this derivation.

36. This chapter follows a traditional pattern of scriptural 'examples': Gui has simplified Tocco's cc. 15 and 17; cf. Calo, c. 11.

37. II Peter, 1: 19.

38. Tocco, c. 22. Calo, c. 14. But the best account of this incident is in the deposition of Bartholomew of Capua, Canonisation Enquiry, LXXXVI. Bartholomew tells us that he learned of it from the Dominicans at Anagni, and adds a number of details, e.g. that the two Jews were father and son, and Romans, and skilled in Hebrew. Molara is south of Roma, on the Via Latina near Rocca di Papa. It was the scene of a later miracle narrated by Gui, c. 18, and Tolomeo, XXIII, c. 10. The present incident doubtless took place during St. Thomas's sojourn in central Italy between 1260 and 1268 (Walz, p. 111, says 1256, but this must be a misprint, the saint being then still at Paris). Cardinal Richard degli Annibaldi (who died in 1274, at the Council of Lyons) was an uncle of one of Thomas's Dominican friends, Annibaldo degli Annibaldi, who himself became a cardinal in 1262 after filling one of the two Dominican chairs of theology at Paris for the two years following St. Thomas's recall to Italy in 1259. Cardinal Annibaldo died in 1272 (see AOP (1925), p. 190; Walz, pp. 86, 95, 131). His theological work is briefly described by Grabmann in the chapter on the Italian Thomist school in *Mittelalterliches Geistesleben*, I, pp. 332 ss.

39. Tocco, c. 29. Calo, c. 16.

40. Tocco, c. 29. Calo, c. 16. The office for the new feast of Corpus Christi (1264) was written by St. Thomas at the behest of Pope Urban IV; see below, Note 17 to Tolomeo.

41. Tocco, c. 29. Calo, c. 16. The same is said by many witnesses at the Canonisation Enquiry.

42. From the *Te Deum*; cf. Tocco, c. 58; Calo, c. 28.

43. Tocco, cc. 17, 29, 48. Calo, c. 16.

44. Tocco, c. 30; cf. cc. 24 and 32. Calo, c. 17. In his c. 30 Tocco is surely recalling what Reginald of Priverno said to the Dominican community at Naples, on returning there from burying Thomas at Fossanova. The passage deserves to be quoted. St. Thomas (Tocco says) took no account of worldly riches, but

like Solomon asked for nothing from God but wisdom. Hence it may easily be believed, nay the fact is manifest, that it was through the merits of his prayer and piety that he received what he taught and wrote and dictated. This we have, too, from the mouth of brother Reginald, his *socius*, who was in his master's confidence and saw things that he did not reveal while the latter was still living. But after the death of his master, when Reginald returned to Naples from Fossanova, and resumed his lecturing (for he was a lector) he spoke thus, with many tears: 'My brothers, while my master lived he would not let me reveal the wonderful things I knew about him, among which was this, that his amazing knowledge was not an effect of human intelligence but of prayer. For always, before he studied or disputed or lectured or wrote or dictated, he would pray from the heart, begging with tears to be shown the truth about the divine things that he had to investigate. . . . And when any difficulty arose he . . . had recourse to prayer, whereupon the matter would become wonderfully clear to him. Thus, in his soul, intellect and desire somehow contained each other, the two faculties freely serving one another in such a way that each in turn took the lead: his desire, through prayer, gained access to divine realities, which then the intellect, deeply apprehending, drew into a light which kindled to greater intensity the flame of love.'

Reginald's testimony to the brethren at Naples is evidently what Tocco again refers to in Canonisation Enquiry, LVIII.

45. Tocco, c. 21. Calo, c. 13. 'Homilies' renders *collationes*. This was the name given to short sermons, often preached in the evening before supper; hence *collatio* came to be the name for supper itself—the light one taken on fast-days—in religious houses; see Mandonnet in *Miscellanea*, pp. 198–9. The *Collationes Patrum*, 'Homilies of the Fathers', are ascribed to Cassian in the prologue written by Humbert of Romans to de Frachet's *Vitae Fratrum*, ed. Reichert, MOPH, I, p. 4.

46. See Note 44.

47. Tocco seems to refer to this in c. 17: 'He wrote on all the epistles of Paul, which he valued above all writings, the gospels alone excepted; and while engaged on this work at Paris, he is said to have had a vision of the Apostle.' This special devotion of St. Thomas to St. Paul has been somewhat ignored, I think. It is one of the links between St. Thomas and St. Dominic; see Vicaire, *St. Dominique de Calaruega*, p. 224; cf. MOPH, xvi (1935), p. 146.

48. Tocco, c. 31. Calo, c. 17. Canonisation Enquiry, LIX. This last is part

of Tocco's deposition, from which we learn that he had it from Francis de Amore, vicar of the bishop of Nola, who himself had it from the *socius* Reginald; another indication of Reginald's importance in the tradition.

49. Tocco, c. 51. Calo, c. 26.

50. Tocco, c. 50. Calo, c. 26. But Tolomeo, who tells us that he was present at the incident, gives more details, XXIII, c. 10. See also Walz, p. 142.

51. Tocco, c. 45. Tolomeo, XXIII, c. 16. Tolomeo, as we should expect, gives more details, since the vision certainly took place in 1273 and at Naples, where he was in daily contact with St. Thomas. When Thomas left Paris for the last time in the spring of 1272, his place was taken, as Master in Theology, by his Bachelor, Romano de' Rossi Orsini (Walz, pp. 133–7). Romano, however, died by May 1273 (MOPH, III, p. 170). He was a Roman and nephew of that Orsini pope, Nicholas III, whom Dante treats so fiercely in *Inferno*, XIX. On his theology, see Grabmann, *Mittelalterliches Geistesleben*, I, pp. 340 ss., who considers him much more Augustinian than Aristotelian. The verse quoted is Psalm 47 (Vulgate): 9.

52. Tocco, c. 44. *Vitae Fratrum*, ed. Reichert, MOPH, I, pp. 215–16. The sister in question seems to have been the eldest, Marotta, who became abbess of Capua: see Note 17. Since she died in 1257–9, her first appearance to Thomas could have taken place before he left Paris in 1259; and we know that he spent a year or two at Rome in the following decade—1265–7. On Landulf and Reginald, see Note 1; cf. Scandone in *Miscellanea*, pp. 79–80, and Pelster in *Civiltà Cattolica* (1923), pp. 299–313.

53. Tocco, cc. 34, 44. That St. Thomas had a brother called, in Latin, 'Raynaldus' or 'Rainaldus' (which I render as Reginald, because *inter alia* this is the English name usually given to the saint's *socius* who is also 'Raynaldus' in the documents) is attested, not only by Gui and Tocco but also by Tolomeo, XXII, c. 20, and Bartholomew of Capua, Canonisation Enquiry, LXXVIII. All these sources mention his being put to death by Frederick II. Tolomeo says this apropos of Reginald's part in the ambush of the young Thomas at Acquapendente; in order, apparently, to advise the reader that Reginald was not a bad man at heart; he was to die in defence of the Church—cf. Tocco, c. 37, Calo, c. 20. The other sources take occasion from Reginald's end to stress St. Thomas's affection towards his kith and kin and his concern for Reginald's salvation. With all this, Reginald remains a shadowy figure. If Frederick had him killed, this must have been before the end of 1250, by which time the emperor himself was dead. Reginald was probably involved in a rebellion of a part of the southern aristocracy against Frederick in 1246, along with his brother-in-law William of San Severino (husband of Mary d'Aquino) and William's father, Thomas. The revolt was crushed, and William and Thomas were put to death. Another brother-in-law of Reginald and St. Thomas was also involved, but escaped to the papal states: this was Roger, count of Marsico, husband of Theodora d'Aquino. Reginald's death was evidently a cruel one (Gui says 'tormenta'), and in his saintly brother's opinion also unjust; cf. Canonisation Enquiry, LXXVIII; Tocco, c. 42. Is this Reginald the poet Rinaldo d'Aquino, familiar to students of early Italian literature? The point has been much disputed, but inconclusively. If this Reginald was not the poet, perhaps that honour belongs to one of St. Thomas's

nephews, a son of Philip d'Aquino—*if* Philip really was the saint's brother, for this again is disputed (see Scandone in *Miscellanea*, pp. 80–1). And there we had better leave the matter until some fresh information comes to light— only regretting that Reginald d'Aquino's attractive figure remains so indistinct. On the few essential facts, see Walz, pp. 4 and 40, and Appendix I below.

54. These three petitions are substantially the same as those mentioned by Bartholomew of Capua in the Canonisation Enquiry, LXXVIII. Bartholomew tells us that he heard of them from the Dominican John of Caiazzo, who is an important link in the tradition deriving from those friars who had personally known St. Thomas (cf. Canonisation Enquiry, LXXVI); and in Canonisation Enquiry LXXV he is named as a cross-link between Reginald of Priverno and old brother Leonard of Gaeta—who himself had known the saint at Naples— concerning a miracle at Rome in the mid-1260s. John of Caiazzo was provincial of the Roman province after 1285, and a Preacher General; and was probably dead by 1300 (see Taurisano, *Miscellanea*, pp. 124–6).

Tocco in c. 63 seems to refer to the same incident as Gui does in this chapter, namely to a moment near the end of Thomas's life when he consoled Reginald (who saw that the end was near) by saying that he died happy. But Tocco seems also to confuse this incident with a conversation, recorded by Bartholomew in the Canonisation Enquiry, LXXVIII, in the course of which St. Thomas rather abruptly put a stop to Reginald's day-dream that a cardinal's hat was awaiting Thomas at the Council of Lyons at the end of the journey which they had just begun (they were still not far from Naples, on the road between Borgonovo and Teano). For Tocco in c. 63 makes Reginald deplore, not only his master's approaching death but his dying too soon to receive 'at the Council of Lyons . . . some great dignity that would give honour to the Order'. In short, there were two rather similar conversations: one referred to by Gui in this chapter and by Bartholomew in Enquiry LXXVIII, which was told the latter by John of Caiazzo; and another, apparently referred to by Tocco in his c. 63, and also mentioned by Bartholomew in Enquiry LXXVIII, but as reported to him by a certain Roffredo.

The gist, in any case, of St. Thomas's cheering reply to Reginald (as Gui reports it here) is wholly characteristic—the aversion from any dignity that might interrupt his work for the Church in the 'studium sapientiae' (cf. *Contra Gentiles*, I, c. 2); and his strong family affection governed by charity.

55. Ezekiel, 8: 3.

56. Tocco, c. 33. Calo, c. 17. Walz (p. 158) thinks that this happened in the last year of Thomas's life, after the shattering experience at Mass on 6 December 1273 (see Canonisation Enquiry, LXXIX). Advised to take a rest, St. Thomas went to stay for a little while with his sister Theodora at San Severino. He and Reginald could have gone by way of Salerno.

57. Tocco, c. 34. Calo, c. 18. The reference to the *tertia pars* of the *Summa theologiae* dates this incident, in all probability, to 1273, but to a time not later than 6 December, the feast of St. Nicholas, if it is true, as Bartholomew of Capua stated on oath (Canonisation Enquiry, LXXIX), that on that day Aquinas had the experience which ended his writing.

58. Tocco, c. 52 (not in Calo). Tocco's authority was 'brother Martin, a student from the Spanish province' of the Order, who was told of the incident

by an eyewitness and passed it on to Tocco when the latter called at S. Maximin on his way to the Curia (at Avignon) for the business connected with St. Thomas's canonisation; therefore in July–August 1318 (see Mandonnet in *Mélanges Thomistes*, p. 25). But the incident is not mentioned in the Canonisation Enquiry. Walz, p. 131, dates it, implicitly, during the second period of teaching at Paris, 1269–72.

59. Tocco, c. 43. Calo, c. 24. Tocco says that St. Thomas was now working on the *Summa theologiae*. St. Louis left Paris for the Crusade in March 1270, and St. Thomas had got back to Paris from Italy in the spring of 1269; hence the luncheon can be placed between these two dates, when we know that St. Thomas was dictating (the word is Tocco's, *dictabat*) the *secunda pars* of the *Summa*. On this ground Walz rejects the suggestion of the Leonine editors of the *Contra Gentiles* that Book III, c. 15, of that work (which ends with 'Per hoc excluditur error Manichaeorum . . .') was the piece on which Thomas was engaged when the king's invitation came; and he suggests that Tocco may have confused the Manichees with the 'monopsychistae' or the 'murmurantes' or even the 'Averroistae' (Walz, pp. 128–30).

This may have been the last meeting of the two saints: St. Louis died near Tunis on 25 August 1270.

60. Tocco, c. 43. Calo, c. 24. Tocco gives as his authority brother Raymund Etienne, O.P., of the Province of Toulouse and later archbishop of Ephesus (Walz, p. 151). Raymund got the story from the archbishop of Capua himself, Marino of Eboli ('Peter', in Gui's account, must be a mistake). Marino of Eboli is mentioned by one of the witnesses at the Canonisation Enquiry—the knight Nicholas Filimarini, XLIII—as a friend of Aquinas; and Tocco calls him a disciple. See also Tolomeo, XXIII, c. 9. The authorities do not identify the cardinal-legate. If the incident occurred at Naples it must have been in the last two years of the saint's life; which makes Gui's allusion to the *Contra Gentiles* unplausible, for that work, it is commonly thought, was finished by the mid-sixties.

61. Tocco, c. 29. Calo, c. 16. Both also place the incident at Naples and on Passion Sunday.

62. Tocco, c. 29. The versicle is sung in Compline during Lent.

63. Tocco, c. 47. Calo, c. 24. Neither adds anything to Gui. By far the best account of this deeply significant incident was given by Bartholomew of Capua at the Canonisation Enquiry, LXXIX. As his authority, Bartholomew names a Dominican of Anagni, John of Giudice, saying that this friar got the whole story 'particulariter et distincte' from Reginald of Priverno himself when the latter was on his death-bed. It is Bartholomew who tells us that the ecstasy took place on the feast of St. Nicholas (6 December; the year, 1273, may be inferred), while the saint was saying Mass in the chapel of St. Nicholas; and at S. Domenico in Naples. The visit to his sister Theodora at San Severino came a little later—as a holiday, Walz supposes; for clearly St. Thomas's condition was giving rise to anxiety at S. Domenico (Walz, p. 158). From Bartholomew too we get the saint's vivid phrase to Reginald, 'all I have written seems to me so much straw'.

This was all told Bartholomew (by John of Giudice) at Anagni, and 'before the lord Pope Boniface was captured'—a clear allusion to the well-known incident of 7 September 1303. Bartholomew repeated the story to the successor of Boniface VIII, the Dominican Bd. Benedict XI (1303–4). It was later, no doubt, that Bartholomew told 'William of Tocco and other Friar Preachers' (Canonisation Enquiry, LXXIX).

64. Tocco, c. 47. Calo, c. 24. Cf. *Summa theologiae*, 2a, 2ae, cxxv, 3 *ad* 1.

65. Tocco, c. 47. Calo, c. 24.

66. Tocco, c. 47. Calo, c. 24. The reference to the work on Boethius, *de Trinitate*, places this incident in the first period of teaching, as a Master, at Paris, probably in 1256 (Chenu, *Introduction*, p. 238; Grabmann prefers 1257–8, *Thomas v. Aquin*, p. 30).

67. Tocco, c. 47. Calo, c. 24. All three sources call Thomas 'miro modo passibilis'—'extraordinarily sensitive'.

68. Tocco, c. 48. Calo, c. 24. Cf. Canonisation Enquiry, LVIII. Since both Tocco and Gui tell us that St. Thomas only preached to the faithful in Italian—and South Italian at that—he presumably only preached in Italy. Tocco adds that St. Thomas could not learn any other language 'because of his almost continual abstraction', *propter continuum mentis raptum*. He probably thought in Latin. He liked sermons to be short; for then 'they are much more acceptable; because if they are good, they are heard the more eagerly, and if they are bad, the boredom does not last long', *In Epist. ad Hebraeos*, lect. III *ad fin* (quoted by Mandonnet in *Miscellanea*, p. 211).

69. Romans, 15: 18.

70. Tocco, c. 53. Calo, c. 26. Canonisation Enquiry, LXXV. Tocco and Calo say that St. Thomas was preaching in St. Peter's; the witness at the Enquiry, Leonard of Gaeta, O.P., says St. Mary Major, and Walz (p. 94) accepts this, presumably because Leonard got the story from the lips of Reginald of Priverno who was an eyewitness. Leonard tells us that this was about thirty-five years before the Enquiry, i.e. about 1284.

71. Tocco, c. 24. Calo, c. 15. This remark, in all three accounts, is in *oratio directa*.

72. Tocco, c. 25. Calo, c. 15. Walz, following Mandonnet, thinks that this incident probably took place on the journey back from Central Italy to Paris in the latter months of 1268 (Walz, pp. 113–14; Mandonnet in *Xenia Thomistica*, III, pp. 9–40. In this article Mandonnet argued very cogently that St. Thomas could not have left Viterbo, where he was lecturing, before the second half of November; that he preached in Bologna on 2 December and in Milan a week later. The journey, on this reckoning, was very rapid; for Mandonnet holds that Thomas was already in Paris in January 1269—allowing him therefore but two months to march from Viterbo to Paris on foot, with the Alps in between.) The whole incident implies that St. Thomas was already famous and regarded with a certain awe by the general public; which would agree, of course, with a fairly late date.

73. Tocco, c. 26. Calo, c. 15. Tocco adds that the story was vouched for 'by those who were with him [Thomas] at Paris': he also presents the unfortunate 'new Master' in a slightly more sympathetic way than Gui, by quoting St. Thomas's words at the end of the dispute: 'Now you've got it right' (Fr. S. Bullough's rendering of the saint's 'modo bene dicitis', Walz, p. 132). Prümmer, *Fontes*, p. 99, n. 1, is inclined to identify the discomfited disputant

with John Pecham (later archbishop of Canterbury); but on no other grounds (that I can see) than a similarity between St. Thomas's bearing on this occasion and on that of the argument in public which he certainly had with Pecham and of which we are told in the Canonisation Enquiry, LXXVII. Walz, p. 120, dates this latter dispute 'probably' in Eastertide of 1270; but Pecham was then regent of the Franciscan school at Paris and therefore surely not the 'tyro' of the other dispute.

74. Tocco, c. 39. Calo, c. 21. The latter names the student to whom St. Thomas said this—Daniel of Angusta.

75. Daniel, 9: 23.

76. Tocco, c. 17. Calo, c. 22. Tolomeo, XXII, p. 24. This is the *Catena aurea*, as it came to be called. Urban IV (1261–4) laid the task on St. Thomas between 1261 and 1263; see Chenu, *Introduction*, p. 212, for the circumstances linking this 'Catena' with the polemical work intended to further reunion with the schismatic East, the *Contra errores Graecorum*. The section on St. Matthew was dedicated to Urban, the rest to the saint's friend, Cardinal degli Annibaldi (see *supra*, Note 38).

77. Tocco, c. 17. On St. Thomas's use of secretaries for dictation, see the masterly work of A. Dondaine, *Secrétaires de Saint Thomas*, Rome, S. Sabina (1956). This 'enquête austère', as the author calls it, is in the main a book for specialists; but anyone interested in St. Thomas would surely profit by some contact with it. Dondaine summarises his own conclusions thus: 'Les principaux résultats de l'enquête que nous venons de faire sont d'établir solidement le fait historique de l'existence d'un bureau de secrétaires de saint Thomas et de l'intervention de ceux-ci comme collaborateurs du Maître pour la publication, nous dirions l'édition, de ses écrits.' The phrase 'bureau de secrétaires' will not, perhaps, surprise a reader who has already reflected on the end of Tocco's c. 17, together with the many other references to dictation, 'dictare', in our sources (cf., as a single example, Bartholomew of Capua's words in Canonisation Enquiry, LXXVII). The later works of St. Thomas, including the *Summa theologiae*, were, in fact, dictated, not literally written, for the most part.

On the 'scriptor' named by Gui and Tocco, Evan Garnit, see Walz, p. 135, and Dondaine, pp. 202–3. It has been supposed he was an Irishman from Cork, on the strength of the variant 'Crocarensis' (for 'Corcagiensis') printed by Prümmer in his edition of Tocco (*Fontes*, p. 89). But 'Trecorensis', i.e. Tréguier in Brittany, is better attested; and both Tocco and Gui call the man 'brito', i.e. a Breton. Dondaine calls him a 'clerc séculier', i.e. not a Dominican, though probably in holy Orders. On the use of such 'externs' for secretarial work, by the thirteenth-century Dominicans, see Humbert of Romans, *De Vita Regulari*, ed. Berthier, II, pp. 267–8.

78. II Corinthians, 11: 29. On St. Thomas's attitude to sinners, see Tocco, c. 36, Calo, c. 19.

79. Tocco, c. 36. Calo, c. 19. These two sources particularise what Gui leaves vague, citing as witness to the spiritual charm of St. Thomas's company Eufranone della Porta, O.P., of Salerno. This friar was prior of S. Domenico in Naples in 1269 and must have known Thomas well in those last two years of his life (see Taurisano, *Miscellanea*, pp. 123–4). He was remembered by

Bartholomew of Capua, Canonisation Enquiry, LXXVI. He seems to have died in 1275.

80. Tocco, cc. 36, 37. Calo, c. 20. These authors link St. Thomas's charity to the poor with heredity: 'he was disposed to these virtues (compassion and liberality) by the ancient nobility of his family . . .'; and both then proceed to special praise of Thomas's mother, of his sister Theodora, countess of Marsico, and of her son Thomas, and finally of the saint's brothers.

81. Tocco, c. 42. Calo, c. 23. Canonisation Enquiry, LXXVIII. Walz, pp. 132-3, places this incident in the saint's last period at Paris, 1269-72. The 'students' with whom St. Thomas made the outing to St. Denis were not necessarily all Dominicans, nor even 'religious'. We know that he was popular in the faculty of Arts; see Section V.

82. Tocco, c. 42. Calo, c. 23. Tolomeo, XXII, 39. Cf. *supra*, Note 28. Clement IV was pope from 1265 to 1268. At this time St. Thomas, working at Orvieto, Rome, and Viterbo successively, was within easy reach of the pope; and was on excellent terms with Clement, as he had been with his predecessor, Urban IV. Tocco and Calo imply that Clement wished, through St. Thomas, to assist financially the d'Aquino family, who were still suffering from the effects of their rebellion—'pro causa Ecclesiae', our authors like to insist—against Frederick II; see *supra*, Note 53.

83. Tocco, c. 38, cf. 66. Calo, c. 21. Canonisation Enquiry, XV, XIX, XLII. From these sources we get a general impression of the build and appearance of St. Thomas. Phrases like 'nobile corpus', 'virilis robore', suggest that he was both handsome and robust as well as uncommonly large. Note that although tranquilly studious in his habits and having the fine sensibility which normally accompanies great intelligence, St. Thomas lived very hard and was capable of exertions that would seem prodigious today. Every friar in the thirteenth century had to be prepared to tramp the roads of Europe (and what roads!) for weeks or months on end. And St. Thomas's record was as good as most: 1245, from Naples to Paris (apart from a stage by boat); 1248 and 1252, from Paris to Cologne and back; 1259-60, from Paris back to Italy; in the following years, frequent moves from city to city in the peninsula; 1268-9, the furious winter march from Viterbo to Paris; 1272, all the way back from Paris to Naples. And always, or nearly always, on foot: by the rules of the Dominican Order it was a serious fault to use a horse for a journey, 'except with permission or in extreme necessity' (*Constitutiones Antiquae Ord. Praed.*, Dist. I, c. 22; text in ALKM, ed. Denifle, I, p. 208; cf. Mandonnet, *Rev. Thomiste*, VII, pp. 530ss.). St. Thomas, we can be sure, observed this rule strictly: when we do hear of him 'riding' from Maenza to Fossanova (Canonisation Enquiry, XLIX) he was a very sick man indeed. The allusion, here, to his bearing in stormy weather gains in force perhaps if we remember that Aquinas was by profession a poor man and that, when caught by such weather out of doors, he had to foot it to the nearest shelter, carrying his own luggage.

As for details, we may note the exceptional height and erect carriage; the dark complexion remembered by the Cistercian lay-brother Nicholas (Canonisation Enquiry, XIX); the delicate sensibility ('tenerrima complexio in carne', says Tocco, c. 38; cf. Note 67 above); the corpulence ('corpus . . . grossum, pingue et magum', Tocco, c. 66); the partial baldness (Canonisation Enquiry, XVI, XIX, XLVI).

84. Tocco, c. 54. Calo, c. 26. Canonisation Enquiry, LXXXVII.

85. Tocco, c. 56. Calo, c. 27. Tolomeo, XXIII, c. 8. Canonisation Enquiry, VIII, XIX, L, LXXVIII, LXXIX. At the Chapter of the Roman province, held at Florence in 1272, Aquinas was entrusted with the organisation of the new theological *studium* or school at Naples (MOPH, XX, p. 39; the text does not mention Naples, but this city, with Orvieto, had been chosen three years previously as the site of a new *studium*—see *ibid.*, p. 36—and it was to Naples that the saint at once proceeded after the chapter). The general Chapter of the Order also met at Florence in 1272, and it is probable that St. Thomas, just returned from Paris, attended it; and, if so, it is possible that Dante Alighieri, then seven years old, may have seen him round about S. Maria Novella. The work to be done at Naples was evidently the reason, or one of the reasons, for the recall of St. Thomas from Paris, much against the wish of the University or at least of its younger and more numerous part, the faculty of Arts (see Section V). So Thomas went south to his homeland and Naples, where he spent the next year and a half. Then, early in 1274, came the summons from Pope Gregory X, ordering him to Lyons for the forth-coming Ecumenical Council. The chief subject to be deliberated was reunion with the Greek Catholics, and Thomas was told to bring his treatise, *Contra errores Graecorum*. In poor health he set out from Naples, accompanied as usual by Reginald, in January or early February (Walz, pp. 160ss.; Mandonnet, *Miscellanea*, p. 202; Grabmann, *Thomas v. Aquin*, pp. 23–5). After Capua they must have taken the Via Latina by Teano and Borgonovo, for Bartholomew gives details of a conversation *en route* between those places (Canonisation Enquiry, LXXVIII and *supra*, Note 54). Then a slight uncertainty intervenes; we know the travellers reached Maenza near Priverno, which suggests that they turned down to the coastal road (Via Appia) and through Formia and Terracina; besides, the Bull of Canonisation says that St. Thomas took the 'via maritima' (*Fontes*, ed. Laurent, p. 522). He could still have done this even if, as there is reason to think, he wrote to the abbot of Monte Cassino from the vicinity of the abbey (Scandone, *Miscellanea*, p. 31, rejects this letter as spurious on supposed internal evidence, but later authorities allow its authenticity; see Grabmann, *Die Werke*, pp. 377–8, 465; Eschmann, *Catalogue*, p. 418). The diversion to Maenza, the home of St. Thomas's niece Frances, wife of Annibaldo de Ceccano, was made because the saint badly needed a rest. They reached the castle in the latter part of February: Lent had begun. On Annibaldo and Frances de Ceccano, see Scandone, *Miscellanea*, p. 81; Walz, pp. 108–9, 149; and Appendix I.

86. II Kings (II Samuel) 23: 15–17. Tocco, c. 56, and Calo, c. 27, say that Thomas ate none of the herrings after all. Walz, p. 163, thinks that he did eat some, in view of Canonisation Enquiry, L; but see *ibid.*, IX: 'noluit comedere'.

87. Tocco, c. 57. Calo, c. 27. St. Thomas stayed about a week at Maenza; during this period he was visited by some Cistercian monks from Fossanova (about six miles away) whose names have been recorded (Canonisation Enquiry, XLIX). Thomas's condition was now serious, and, feeling the approach of death, he asked to be taken to that monastery: 'if the Lord is coming for

me now', he is reported to have said, 'I would rather He found me in a house of religious than among seculars' (Canonisation Enquiry, VIII). Concerning the following two weeks at Fossanova, the last of his life, many details are recorded. Monastic communities have long memories; besides, the death of Aquinas was—even allowing for exaggerations—evidently accompanied and followed by many miracles. At the first and principal Canonisation Enquiry, which opened at Naples on 21 July 1319, thirteen monks of Fossanova gave evidence, of whom five had already entered the monastery when the dying saint arrived there forty-five years previously. Much of this testimony has to do with miracles that followed St. Thomas's death, but there is a good deal also about the circumstances of his arrival at the abbey, his conduct during sickness, and when receiving the Last Sacraments. The most interesting testimonies, from the biographical point of view, are those of Abbot Nicholas (VIII), of Dom Octavian (xv), of the lay-brother Nicholas (XIX), of Dom John of Adelasia (XXVII), of Dom Peter of Montesangiovanni (XLIX–L). These sources fill out the spare accounts of the three Dominican biographers: Tocco, Gui, and Calo. Tocco himself was an important witness at the Enquiry (LVIII–LXV).

On Fossanova and its community at that time, see Fedele and Serafini in *Miscellanea*, pp. 187–94 and 223–92. The church and part of the abbey buildings are now used by Conventual Franciscans who run a boys' school there. The great Gothic church—a strikingly 'northern' building to find so far south—and the cloisters are well worth a visit.

The commentary on the Canticle, mentioned here, is not extant (Grabmann, *Die Werke*, pp. 254–5, 461; Eschmann, *Catalogue*, p. 395).

88. Tocco, c. 58. Calo, c. 28. The following numbers in the Canonisation Enquiry refer to the piety of St. Thomas on his death-bed: VIII, xv, XIX, XXVII, XXXV, XLIX, LXXX. Of these testimonies, four are given by eyewitnesses: Abbot Nicholas (VIII), Octavian of Babuco (xv), Nicholas of Priverno (XIX), and Peter of Montesangiovanni (XLIX–LI)—all monks of Fossanova, and already such in March 1274, when St. Thomas lay dying in the room provided for him by the abbot. Nos. VIII, xv, XIX, and XXXV convey only a general impression of a holy death, but in XXVII, XLIX, and LXXX we are given two important details, also mentioned, and with emphasis, by the Dominican biographers: the saint's profession of faith in the Real Presence and his submission of his writings to the judgment of the Roman Church. It will be noticed that only one of our four eyewitnesses, Dom Peter, vouches for these details; but Peter is an important witness; he tells us more than the other monks who took part in the Enquiry, and he particularly insists on his status as an eyewitness (see especially LI: 'dixit quod . . . continue morabatur et assistebat dicto fratri Thomae dum jaceret infirmus in dicto monasterio, et in mort ipsius similiter astitit obsequiose'). Moreover, we know that Reginald of Priverno, the chief source of the Dominican tradition concerning St. Thomas, was present (see XLIX, *inter alia*). Tocco, the chief transmitter of the tradition, refers explicitly to Reginald as his source (LVIII). Finally, Bartholomew of Capua (LXXX) draws together both lines of tradition, the Dominican and the Cistercian; for he stated at the Enquiry that he was a frequent visitor at Fossanova, precisely because of the memories of St. Thomas which lingered

there (LXXX), and also that he was an eager listener to the older generation of Dominicans who had known the saint (LXXVI and *passim* to LXXXVI).

It seems proper thus to insist a little on the elements of the tradition concerning St. Thomas's last hours. What appears most clearly is his faith in the Real Presence, and, only less emphatically, his submission of judgment, as a theologian, to the Church. Both of these points were stressed in the Bull of Canonisation issued on 18 July 1323 (*Fontes*, ed. Laurent, p. 523).

Tocco, Gui, and Calo agree that St. Thomas joined in the prayers at the Last Anointing. There is a slight difference as to the date of the death: Gui (with Canonisation Enquiry, x) says that Thomas died in the morning of 9 March 1274 and in his fiftieth year; Tocco and Calo make the date 7 March, Tocco adding that it was the fourth year of the pontificate of Gregory X, the saint being in his forty-ninth year (c. 65).

89. Tocco, c. 62. Calo, c. 30. Frances, countess of Ceccano, came over from Maenza; see Appendix I and Note 85.

90. Tocco, c. 62. Calo, c. 30. Gui's 'aside' on the loud lamentations—'more patriae' (which I render rather freely)—is a slightly French addition, perhaps.

91. Tocco, c. 63; cf. c. 27. Calo, c. 30. Canonisation Enquiry, XLIX and LVIII.

92. Tocco, c. 63. A well-deserved tribute to the faithful Reginald; the most intimate companion of St. Thomas in his daily Dominican life ('domesticus et continuus socius', says Bartholomew of Capua). Reginald is, after all, our chief source of knowledge of the saint; on him generally, see Taurisano in *Miscellanea*, pp. 118–20, and on his place in the 'Thomist school', Grabmann, *Mittelalterliches Geistesleben*, I, pp. 332 ss.

93. Tocco, c. 59. Calo, c. 29.

94. Tocco, c. 60. Calo, c. 29. But Tolomeo's account of this 'vision' is the most interesting because he was at S. Domenico in Naples when it happened, and 'three days later' heard, with the rest of the community, of St. Thomas's death (XXIII, c. 9). With this mention of St. Paul cf. Note 47 above.

95. Canonisation Enquiry, LXVII. Not in Tocco or Calo. No. LXVII occurs in the deposition of Anthony of Brescia, O.P., who was told of the tears shed by St. Albert at the time of Thomas's death by that other Albert (of Brescia) who had the vision of SS. Thomas and Augustine together in glory, which is recorded in the office for the feast of St. Thomas (Canonisation Enquiry, LXVI). Bartholomew of Capua adds an interesting, if sadly sketchy, account of the veteran Albert's activity in defence of his old pupil's doctrine which 'was being attacked in Paris' in the years immediately following St. Thomas's death (Canonisation Enquiry, LXXXII). Bartholomew's source was a Dominican, Hugh of Lucca, then studying under Albert at Cologne and later Provincial of the Roman province; see Taurisano in *Miscellanea*, p. 180.

96. Tocco, cc. 61, 66, 67. Calo, cc. 29, 31. Canonisation Enquiry, chiefly VIII, XV, XX, LI, LII. The miracles in question are as follows:

(1) The restoration of sight to the sub-prior of Fossanova, John of Ferentino; see the account of Peter of Montesangiovanni, an eyewitness (LI). This took place shortly after the saint's death, before the washing of the corpse. (2) Seven months later St. Thomas appeared in a dream to the prior of Fossanova, James of Ferentino (Tocco and Calo say the abbot, but the witness of Abbot Nicholas,

no. VIII, is explicit against them; and cf. XIX). In this dream Thomas chided the prior for having had his body removed from its first resting-place, before the high altar, and taken secretly to the chapel of St. Stephen; and he ordered its return to the original position. This order the prior then carried out, with the following results: on opening the grave in St. Stephen's chapel the monks (3) smelled a strong and sweet fragrance, and (4) found the body incorrupt and its clothing intact; whereupon they carried it back solemnly to the high altar and sang the Mass as for a Confessor, *Os justi*, since a requiem Mass now seemed to them inappropriate.

The reason for that first and secret transference to St. Stephen's chapel was, of course, that the monks—at least those in authority—feared to lose the body unless they concealed it. Later, the prior's conscience was troubled (the dream playing its part) and the body was taken back to its first position. The Dominican biographers are, naturally, critical of these proceedings. The body, they insist, was only entrusted to the monks for the time being, 'sub deposito', and Gui adds that after the funeral Reginald of Priverno had had a legal instrument drawn up to guarantee its recovery by the Dominicans; moreover, that St. Thomas himself had expressed the desire that his body should be given back to his religious brethren as soon as possible, and taken to Naples (Gui, c. 45).

A few facts may be added regarding the later fortunes of the body. In January 1276, little more than a year after the replacement of it in front of the high altar, Peter of Tarentaise, a Dominican, became pope (Bd. Innocent V). The anxiety to which this event gave rise at Fossanova led the monks, according to Bartholomew of Capua, to dig up the body again, secretly, and remove and conceal the head (Canonisation Enquiry, LXXX). This story may be true in part, but the decapitation, on this occasion, is doubtful, for we learn, on equally good authority, of two later disinterments at neither of which was the corpse found headless. The first of these was in 1281 or 1282, when Dom Peter of Montesangiovanni, recently elected abbot, caused the body to be dug up again and put in a 'more honourable place' on the Gospel side of the high altar and under a stone slab. Dom Peter himself stated this at the Enquiry nearly forty years later (LII); and he added that the body was found still fragrant and intact, except that part of the right thumb was missing; but he said nothing about the head (*ibid.*). The loss of the thumb seems to be explained by the statement of another witness (LXXXIX) that Reginald of Priverno had taken one of Thomas's thumbs—presumably before the funeral in 1274—and given it to Hugh de Billom, bishop of Ostia and later a cardinal (see AOP, XVII (1925), p. 335). Then another exhumation seems to have taken place in 1288 and to have been due to the desire of St. Thomas's sister, Theodora of San Severino (see Appendix I and Notes 63 and 80), to have one of her brother's hands (Gui, c. 48, Tocco, c. 68, Canonisation Enquiry, XX). And at this exhumation the body was found apparently in the same state as in 1281 or 1282, complete with the head (XX). Theodora's son, Thomas, count of Marsico, later gave that hand to the Dominicans at Salerno (Tocco, c. 68), where Tocco and Thomas of Aversa saw it in 1317 or 1318 (Canonisation Enquiry, XCV; cf. XLVI).

If the monks ever did remove the head, this may have been in 1303 when another Dominican, Bd. Benedict XI, was elected pope (though he, too, lasted only a little while, dying in 1304 to the sorrow, probably, of Dante among others). But it is likely that another event took place about this time which would have made decapitation somewhat pointless, namely the boiling of the body to remove the flesh from the bones. Tocco, witnessing at the Enquiry (LXV), said that he saw 'some of brother Thomas's bones' in a chest at Fossanova in 1319, and later an eyewitness of the final translation of the saint's remains to Toulouse in 1368 (by order of Pope Urban V) stated that it was commonly believed in his time that the monks of Fossanova had boiled the body so as to preserve it 'in parvo loco', and he described the bones as 'of a reddish colour, looking as if by boiling or some other change effected by heat they had been violently detached from the flesh' (C. Douais, *Les reliques de S. Thomas d'Aquin*, p. 84; quoted by Mandonnet in *Mélanges Thomistes*, p. 18, n. 2). At all events, most of this much-tried corpse seems to have reached Toulouse in 1368 and remained with the Dominicans there until the Revolution, after which it was transferred to the church of S. Sernin, where it still lies. The cathedral of Naples, however, claims to have a bone of the left arm, and the church of the Minerva at Rome the right arm.

97. Tocco, c. 67. Calo, c. 31. This insinuation, that the monks were reluctant to make the miracles known, is also found in the deposition of Bartholomew of Capua (Canonisation Enquiry, LXXXI). And yet, after all, the abbey of Fossanova was well represented at the Enquiry in 1319; an *amende honorable*.

Supplementary Note. Concerning the date of St. Thomas's Commentary on the *Sentences*, see the valuable article by M. B. Crowe in the *Irish Theological Quarterly* for October 1957 (vol. XXIV) which only came to my notice as I was correcting the final proofs of this book. Fr. Crowe holds that Thomas may have started his two-year course of lectures on the *Sentences*, as a Bachelor at Paris, in the autumn of 1253, though the more usual opinion says 1254. In that case the biblical course would have run from 1252-3, as I have implied in Note 29, p. 68 *supra*. But Fr. Crowe's chief concern is with the problem raised by Tolomeo's reference to a second draft of Bk. I of St. Thomas's Commentary on the *Sentences* (Tolomeo XXIII, c. 15; see the relevant Note 40, p. 145 *infra*), and on this matter Fr. Crowe favours the more usual view that Bk. I as we have it represents the saint's original work and not a revision made in the 1260s.

II

From the First Canonisation Enquiry[1]

(NAPLES, AT THE ARCHBISHOP'S PALACE; 21 JULY TO
18 SEPTEMBER 1319)

I. These are the minutes of the Enquiry into the life, morals and miracles of brother Thomas of Aquino of worthy memory, a friar of the Order of Preachers and Doctor of Sacred Theology, conducted by the reverend Fathers and Lords, by the grace of GOD, Humbert Archbishop of Naples and Angelo Bishop of Viterbo, assisted by the worthy Lord Pandulf Savelli, Papal Notary . . . these persons being specially deputed to this task by our holy Father and Lord Pope John XXII; there being present, throughout the whole Enquiry, Peter John of Rocco-Tarani of the diocese of Sabina, a public notary by Apostolic and Imperial Authority, and Francis of Laureto of the diocese of Penna, a public notary by Apostolic and Regal authority; being specially commissioned by the Lords Inquisitors to draft an exact report in writing of the proceedings of the Enquiry; the same being written by me, Peter, the notary aforesaid.

II–V. Preliminaries to the Examination of the Witnesses. On Saturday, 21 July 1319, William of Tocco, O.P., prior of Benevento, presents letters from the Pope to the archbishop of Naples and the bishop of Viterbo; in consequence of which, and in the absence of the papal notary Pandulf Savelli, their Lordships appoint Peter John of Rocca-Tarani and Francis of Laureto to take a record of the proceedings (II). There follows the text of the letter of Pope John XXII to the said archbishop, bishop and papal notary, formally introducing the cause of brother Thomas of Aquino and ordering the examination of witnesses (III). On Monday 23 July *litterae clausae* from the Pope are opened and read, in the presence of the archbishop and bishop, prescribing the mode of interrogation of the witnesses[2] (IV). There follow (i) a statement that, the archbishop being prevented by sickness from holding the Enquiry anywhere other than Naples, the witnesses have been cited to come before him in that city;[3] and (ii) the form of the oath to be taken by the witnesses (V).

Peter Grasso

VI. Peter Grasso of Naples, a knight and functionary in attendance on the king; about sixty years old. Having declared that he himself had received miraculous favours from the said brother Thomas of Aquino, he was called before the lords Inquisitors and took the prescribed oath to speak the simple truth on whatever he knows, whether by sight, hearing or other men's report, about the life and miracles of brother Thomas; also to answer all questions truthfully, taking no account of love or hatred, prayers, or bribes, favours or inducements of any kind whatsoever.[4]

First then, concerning the life of Thomas, the witness said that ever since he was a schoolboy he had always heard this religious spoken of as a man of holy life, and that many held him to have been a virgin from his mother's womb; and that every day he said Mass before anyone else, and that since his ordination it had been his custom, after his own Mass and before completely unvesting himself, to hear another Mass through—the other priest being already vested before his own Mass was ended. This Thomas always did before starting the day's work. Moreover, apart from the interruptions required by nature, he never wasted any time in idleness or worldly occupations but was always either reading, writing, dictating, praying, or preaching.

Asked how he knew this, the witness said, partly by common report, partly from the testimony of religious or of students, and in particular from Lord Bartholomew of Capua, Chancellor to the king of Sicily,[5] and from brother Reginal of Priverno (brother Thomas's *socius*) and brother James and other Friar Preachers whom he had heard from time to time talking of these things.[6] Moreover, brother James of Viterbo, of the Order of the Hermits and at that time archbishop of Naples, had once remarked to the witness (in a conversation which turned upon learning and learned men) that no one who did not follow closely the writings of brother Thomas should lay claim to full knowledge of theology, since he was the master in this subject. Asked where he had heard these things, the witness said, wherever he had passed any length of time and particularly in the city of Naples.[7]

VII. Asked about miracles worked by brother Thomas, the witness gave the following account of one. He had been afflicted with a complete paralysis of his right arm, so that he could not even raise his hand to comb his own hair or tie a scarf under his chin without help. This continued for about ten months until, in the Lent of 1316, he happened to be journeying to Rome, and, coming into the neighbourhood of Terracina, he turned aside to visit the grave of brother Thomas at the abbey of Fossanova. He had been told that Thomas lay buried there, and it had crossed his mind that perhaps the merits of the holy man might help to cure his arm; indeed he soon began firmly to believe that he would be cured. So, with two companions—Nicholas Filmarini and Henry Caracciolo, both knights of Naples like himself, and both eager to visit the tomb[8]—he turned aside to Fossanova, leaving the other travellers to continue their journey to Rome. And entering the monastery courtyard, he met a monk who directed him towards Thomas's grave, pointing to it from some way off. It lay, the knight says, to the left of the high altar, covered with a sort of carpet. This he had removed, and then, kneeling on the ground and facing the grave, he prayed in these words: 'Lord God, who art wonderful in thy saints, through the merits of this thy saint restore strength to my arm.' Then he lay down flat on the grave; and at once he felt his arm grow stronger. For a while a kind of numbness remained about the joints as though the muscles were still sluggish; but this too had vanished by the end of the same day. Next morning he found his arm restored to perfect health; not a trace of the paralysis remained.

Asked for dates, he said that the paralysis began in May 1315 and continued until May of the year following, when the cure took place. Asked about the place and witnesses, he answered as above.

Nicholas, Abbot of Fossanova

VIII. On Tuesday, 24 July, at Naples in the archiepiscopal palace, the venerable Nicholas, abbot of the Cistercian monastery of Fossanova, was called before the Inquisitors and took the oath in the form stated above.

He said that in the time of Pope Gregory X of happy memory, brother Thomas, while on his way through the Campagna on the way to the Council of Lyons, fell ill at the castle of Maenza which belonged to the lord Annibaldo of Ceccano;[9] and his condition worsening, he was heard by several people to say: 'If the Lord has chosen this time to come for me, I had better be found in some religious house.' So he got himself carried to Fossanova, about six miles distant from the castle; and there he lay sick for about a month. And on arriving at the monastery door he was heard to say (so it was reported to the witness): 'Haec requies mea in saeculum saeculi, hic habitabo quoniam elegi eam'. And while he lay ill there the monks, much impressed by his reputation for holiness, used themselves to carry in faggots from the wood for his fire; for they thought it hardly fitting that animals should render this service to such a man. But when Thomas saw them doing this he would struggle to his feet, protesting, 'Who am I that holy men should bring me my fire-wood?'

Asked how he knew this, the witness said that he was there at the time, and saw and heard for himself. He added that he saw brother Thomas receive the sacraments of the Church, with much fervour and reverence and tears, lying there with the sickness that caused his death. Asked about the time—the year, month, and day—the witness said he could not remember, except that it was in Lent. Asked who else was present when he saw and heard these things, he named Peter of Montesangiovanni and Octavian of Babuco, monks of Fossanova and both still alive. There had been many other witnesses, monks of the community, who were now dead.[10]

Asked what else he knew about Thomas's life, he said he had always heard him spoken of as a man of great virtue, pure and holy, who said Mass every day when he was in good health and was always occupied in study or prayer; a virgin, too, from his mother's womb. These things he had learned from the aforesaid Peter of Montesangiovanni, who got them from Thomas's confessor, and was himself personally acquainted with Thomas.

Asked about miracles—whether he knew of any worked through the merits of Thomas, either before or after death—the witness said that when Thomas died his body was buried at first before the high altar, but then the monks, fearing it might be taken from them, transferred it secretly to St. Stephen's Chapel in the same abbey-church. But about seven months later Thomas appeared in a dream to a brother James, who was prior at the time, and said: 'Take me back where I was at first.' So they took him back, with due solemnity. (This dream was and still is commonly talked about in the monastery.) And when the tomb was opened a delicious fragrance came out, filling all the chapel and cloister: whereupon the community sang the Mass *Os justi meditabitur sapientiam*, etc., in honour of Thomas as of a saint;

7

they thought the Mass *Pro defunctis* hardly suitable for such a man.

All this the witness knew because he was there and saw it for himself; it happened about seven months after Thomas's death; but he could not be sure of the month or the day. Asked who were present, he said 'the whole community'. . . . Asked who had called him to the place where the fragrance was smelt, he said he himself smelled it; it drew him to where the tomb was.[11]

IX. Asked if he knew of other miracles attributed to brother Thomas, the witness said that he had heard of many; and in particular that when Thomas lay sick in the castle of Maenza and was urged to eat something, he answered, 'I would eat fresh herrings, if I had some.' Now it happened that a pedlar called just then with salted fish. He was asked to open his baskets, and one was found full of fresh herrings, though it had contained only salted fish. But when the herrings were brought to Thomas, he would not eat them.[12]

The witness spoke too of a Master Reginald, a cripple, who was cured at the tomb of brother Thomas.

Asked how he knew of these two miracles, he replied that that about the fish he had from brother William of Tocco, prior of the Friar Preachers at Benevento,[13] who himself had it from several people at Maenza, where the event occurred. The other story he had from brother Octavian (mentioned above) who averred that he had seen it happen. And in the monastery these miracles were common knowledge.

Nicholas of Fresolino

X. On the same day, at the same place, Nicholas of Fresolino, a monk of Fossanova, was called as witness and took the oath. . . . Touching the life and morals of brother Thomas, the witness said that he had always heard that he was a holy man . . . and that he himself was present when brother Thomas came from Maenza to Fossanova. Brother Thomas was ill; and while he lay sick in the monastery he received the Lord's Body and the other sacraments with much devotion and tears. But as the witness was only a novice at the time, he has no knowledge, he says, of other details; except that he has heard from brother Peter of Montesangiovanni that when Thomas entered the abbey he said, 'Haec requies mea', etc. Asked as to when this happened, the witness said it was forty years ago and in February; and that Thomas died on the ninth of the month following, before the end of Lent. . . .[14]

Octavian of Babuco

XV. On Wednesday, 25 July, in the same place brother Octavian of Babuco in the Campagna, priest and monk of Fossanova, took the oath in the prescribed form. . . . He averred that the said Thomas was a man of pure and holy life, chaste, temperate in food and drink, diligent in prayer, fasting and study; that in prayer he shed tears; that he was most charitable, compassionate and humble, full of devout wisdom in his dealings with God and man. Asked how he knew all this, the witness said that he had known brother Thomas and spoken with him and done him services from time to time, and seen him say Mass and shed tears at the communion. Asked how long he had known Thomas before his death, he answered 'about four and a half years'.

Asked where he had seen and conversed with him and done him services, the witness said it was in the castle of Maenza, whither Thomas often came to visit a kinswoman of his,[15] and also at Fossanova. Asked if he was sure that Thomas had persevered in holiness to the end, the witness answered that he was. Asked how he knew, he replied as before. Asked how long it was since Thomas's death, he said, 'about forty-six years'. He added that he had seen Thomas arrive at Fossanova from the castle of Maenza (where he had been taken ill) and stop in front of the choir in the abbey-church where he said, 'Haec requies mea', etc. The witness was present at the time and heard the words spoken. Asked who else was present, he said that besides himself there was brother Peter of Montesangiovanni, who was still alive, and many other monks of the same monastery whose names he could not remember.

Brother Thomas (the witness continued) was patient in his sickness, always gentle and no trouble to anyone. Asked if he had received the Sacraments during his illness, the witness said he had heard from other monks of the abbey that he had done so, and with reverence and devotion and many tears. Asked whether this was the illness that Thomas died of, he answered that it was.

Asked where the body of Thomas was buried, the witness said it was placed in front of the high altar of the abbey-church, but that it lay there only one day, for in the following night it was removed by some of the monks and buried in the chapel of St. Stephen; where it remained for about seven months, being finally taken back to the place in front of the altar. Moreover, when it was exhumed it was found to be intact and very fragrant, which caused the monks to carry it back to the former grave, chanting in procession. And next morning the Mass for a confessor, *Os justi*, was sung by the monks. Asked how he knew all this, the witness said he was present at the transporting of the body and at the Mass, which he sang along with the other monks. Asked who was the priest who celebrated, he said he could not remember.[16]

Asked about Thomas's appearance, the witness said he was a tall man and stout, with a bald forehead; and that he seemed about fifty when he died.

Nicholas of Priverno

XIX. On Thursday, 26 July, at the same place, Nicholas of Priverno, a lay-brother at Fossanova, was called as a witness, and, having taken the oath in the form described, was asked first concerning the life of brother Thomas of Aquino. He answered that he had seen Thomas lying ill at Fossanova, whither he had come from the castle of Maenza, where he had broken the journey he was making towards Lyons in order (the witness had been informed) to take part in the Council held in the time of Gregory X. It was since that date that the witness had heard of the holiness of Thomas and of his constant virginity; he had not seen or known him before. But he saw him, during that stay in the monastery, always humble, kindly and patient, never upset or annoyed in those last days of his life. . . . The witness had been told that Thomas had been invited to the Council because he was thought to be one of the wisest and best men in the world.

He said, too, that he had heard that when Thomas first entered the choir of the abbey-church he exclaimed, 'Haec requies mea', etc. Asked who had told him all this, the witness said he had heard of Thomas's holiness from brother James of Ferentino,[17] at that time prior of the monastery, and from many others of the same community whose names he could not remember. . . . Asked when he saw Thomas ill in the monastery, he said it was about forty-five years ago. He remembered him as a big stout man, with a dark complexion and bald. As for his age, he had seemed to the witness about fifty or sixty.

XX. Being asked whether he knew of any miracles worked by brother Thomas, either while still alive or after death, the witness said that a long while—about seven months—after Thomas's death, when his body was taken from the chapel of St. Stephen to the grave in front of the high altar, the witness saw the body intact and smelled a strong and sweet scent that came from it. And later, about fourteen years after Thomas's death, the grave was reopened at the request of one of his sisters, the Countess Theodora, who desired a relic of him; and one of the hands from the body was given to her. And the body was still intact and very fragrant.[18]

Asked how he knew these things, the witness said he was present and saw them and smelled the fragrance both times. Asked about the times, he answered as before; but he could not recall the exact month or day. Asked who was present, he said that at the first opening of the grave nearly the whole community was there: they carried the body in procession with the cross and holy water and all solemnity; but at the second exhumation when the hand was given away, he named only brother Peter of Montesangiovanni, then abbot of the monastery, as present.

Peter Francisci

XXII. On the same day, at the same place, brother Peter Francisci . . . a lay-brother at Fossanova was called as witness and took the oath. Asked about brother Thomas's way of life, he said that in the monastery and at the castle of Priverno and in all that region there was a common opinion that Thomas was a saint; but that he never knew the man himself, being too young ever to have seen him.

Asked concerning miracles, the witness said that before he entered religion he used to work as shoemaker for the monks in a workshop by the monastery. One day while taking a rest in that place he thought he would get up and have a drink; but just then a hairy man appeared by his bed and gripped his feet, pressing them down on the bed, and said, 'Don't move, I will bring you some water.' So he, thinking this was one of the monastery servants, answered, 'Very well, fetch me some water.' The hairy man then went out and soon returned with water cupped in the palms of his hands, and said, 'Drink!' But when the witness looked at the man he now seemed to have taken the form of a dog, excepting his face, which was still human, but hairy and terrible; and he gave out a horrible stench, so that the witness was terrified, and hid his face, crying, 'Go away, I will not drink!' And in that fear he lost almost all his strength, and could not speak all that day, and his hands and fingers became rigid, with the thumb of the right hand drawn back against his arm and the fingers of the left hand bent over so tightly that he could not straighten them at all. His feet too had become heavy, numb, and powerless. Indeed his whole body was rigid and motionless.

In this condition he was carried to his mother's house at Priverno, where he lay for eight days and got no better, though his mother tried all sorts of remedies. Finally someone suggested that he should be carried to the grave of brother Thomas. His mother took this advice and had him taken to the grave and laid on it. And a little while later he suddenly got up completely cured of the contraction and rigidity and able to walk about freely and praise God for his cure. Then he continued for a time working in the monastery as a layman; until, a year later, he took the religious habit. And ever since he has enjoyed good health, as he does now.

Asked about the time—the month and day—of the miracle, he said he could not remember except that it was harvest-time. Asked who was present, he said that brother Gregory from the castle of St. Stephen,[19] a monk and priest of the monastery, was there, and also a Frenchman called Pierrot, a monastery servant now dead; besides his mother, who had come with him, but, being a woman, had to remain outside the abbey gates. She was delighted on hearing of the cure and returned to Priverno praising God; and ever afterwards, in thanksgiving to God and to brother Thomas, she made it a rule to fast for three successive days at the time of year when the miracle had occurred.

Leonard of Priverno

XXVI. On the same day, in the same place, brother Leonard of Priverno, a lay-brother of the monastery, was called as witness and took the usual oath. Asked first about the life of brother Thomas, the witness said that while still in the world and since his entry into religion—in all about forty years now—he had heard brother Thomas spoken of as a holy man; he knew nothing else in particular about him.

Asked about miracles . . . the witness replied that at the time when brother William of Tocco and his *socius*—Friar Preachers both and engaged in the enquiry concerning Thomas—were staying at the abbey of Fossanova[20] they had the use of two mules to carry them about, and these had to be shod; and the witness, being a blacksmith, was required to see to this; and being bored by the work, this thought came into his mind: 'How these Dominicans pester and plague us with their brother Thomas! If he was really a saint why doesn't he work a miracle to settle the matter? And then these friars would leave us alone!' Now he had no sooner said this to himself than he felt a terrible pain in the right arm: and it became motionless so that he could not even lift his hand to his mouth. And so it remained until the following day; but then, remembering his evil thought, his conscience reproved him; and, going to the grave of brother Thomas, he laid his paralysed arm on it and remained there, praying for an hour; after which the arm suddenly became well again, so that on the following Monday he was able to resume his work; and from that time on he very gladly shod mules for the Friar Preachers.

Asked about the time—the month and day—the witness said that it happened in June of this year; the paralysis began on a Saturday between noon and vespers, and was cured at the tomb of brother Thomas on the Sunday morning following. Asked who was present at the cure, he said 'nobody'; but his assistants at the smithy saw him when paralysed and afterwards cured. Their names are James of Sonnino and Leo of Priverno.

Asked if he knew of any other miracles, the witness said he had heard that God had worked many others through brother Thomas, but that he knew nothing of them in detail, being only a novice in the monastery. His own cure, he added, was common knowledge in the monastery and the neighbourhood.

John of Adelasia

XXVII. On the same day, in the same place, brother John of Adelasia of Priverno, priest and monk of Fossanova, was called as a witness and took the oath. Asked about brother Thomas's way of life, he replied that many religious had told him (indeed it was everyone's opinion) that this Thomas was a holy man all his days, devoted to prayer, his mind absorbed in the things of God; that he was always a virgin; and that he said Mass every day; and that when dying he received the Lord's Body with great reverence and devotion, after saying these words: 'I have written much on the holy Body of Christ, and now I leave it all to the judgment of the holy Roman Church.' When he received Extreme Unction brother Thomas himself made the responses.[21]

Asked for his authorities for these statements, the witness named brother Nicholas, now the abbot of Fossanova, brother Peter of Montesangiovanni, a former abbot, and a Friar Preacher, brother Richard, who is a nephew of that brother Reginald who was for long Thomas's *socius*. . . . Asked where he had heard the things he reports, the witness said it was partly in his own monastery, partly at Anagni, and in other places.

Henry Caracciolo

XL. On Monday, 30 July, at the same place, the noble lord and knight Henry Caracciolo of Naples was called as witness and took the prescribed oath. Asked concerning brother Thomas's life and habits, he said he had often heard men speak of this religious as very upright, pure and holy, as a great contemplative and man of prayer; and that he said his Mass daily and then assisted at another (or if impeded from celebrating himself, he would hear two Masses); after which he always studied; so that all his life (apart from time given to bodily needs) was passed in reading, writing, or prayer. Asked for his authorities, the witness named brother John of Naples, a Dominican and Master in Theology,[22] brother William of Tocco, also a Dominican, and Lord Bartholomew of Capua, and many others.

James of Caiazzo

XLII. On Tuesday, 31 July, in the same place, brother James of Caiazzo, a Friar Preacher, was called as witness and took the oath.[23] Asked concerning the life of brother Thomas, the witness said he himself had seen Thomas—a contemplative man, unworldly, absorbed in heavenly things; a great lover of solitude; very upright, too, and chaste and temperate, so that he never demanded special food, being content with what was served to him. . . . Each day he said Mass and then heard one; after which he would pray or study or write. Asked how he knew all this, the witness said that he had known Thomas. Asked where, he mentioned Naples and Capua. Asked about Thomas's appearance, the witness said he was a big man with a bald forehead. Asked how long it was since he had seen Thomas, he said it seemed about forty-five years, and that Thomas could have been about forty-six when he (the witness) saw him first.

Asked about miracles, the witness said he had heard of many worked through the merits of brother Thomas, especially of cures in various places. Asked where he had heard of these, he mentioned Naples and Capua and other places 'on both sides of the Alps'.[24] . . . His informants were many, both religious and men of the world, but especially Lord Bartholomew of Capua.

Peter of San Felice

XLV. On the same day, in the same place, brother Peter of San Felice, a Dominican, was called as witness and took the oath.[25] Asked first about the life of brother Thomas, the witness said he was a very good man, both in himself and in his dealings with others, whom he desired to be even as he was. Humble and patient, he was never heard to use haughty or aggressive speech against anyone. He was a great contemplative, continually busy with prayer, study, or writing . . . absorbed in the thought of God. At meal-times he was content with whatever was put before him—if indeed he noticed it at all. Asked how he knew these things, the witness said that he had lived in the same community with Thomas for a year as one of his students. He had also heard the like from many fellow Dominicans, especially from Reginald of Priverno and Benedict of Montesangiovanni.[26] Asked where he had seen brother Thomas, he answered, 'In his cell and in the choir at Naples, and teaching and preaching.' He added that Thomas was tall and stout with a bald forehead.

Conrad of Sessa

XLVII. On the same day, in the same place, brother Conrad of Sessa, an old Friar Preacher and a priest, was called as witness and took the usual oath.[27] Asked first about brother Thomas's way of life, the witness said that he was a holy, clean-living man —peaceful, abstemious, humble, devout, tranquil, and contemplative. His chastity was reputed to be virginal. Temperate in food and drink, so that he never asked for anything special. Unconcerned about his clothes. Every day he either devoutly said Mass himself or heard Mass, sometimes twice over; and apart from the time required for rest he was always either reading, writing, praying, or preaching. Asked how he knew all this, the witness said that he knew Thomas personally and lived with him for several years at Naples and Rome, and at Orvieto in the time of Pope Urban of happy memory,[28] at whose command brother Thomas wrote his commentaries on the four Gospels. Asked whether this account of Thomas's life was true for the whole period in which the witness was acquainted with him, he said that it was. . . . Asked how long it was since he had first seen and known Thomas, he said it was sixty-two years ago; he himself being now seventy-seven—and indeed he looks no younger.

Peter of Montesangiovanni

XLIX. On Wednesday, 1 August, brother Peter of Montesangiovanni, an old monk of Fossanova and a priest, was called as witness and took the oath.[29] . . . He said he had known brother Thomas for a long while and in several places . . . in the castle of St. John at Marsico, at Naples and at Maenza, and at Fossanova itself. Asked how long he had known him, he said for ten years in all; they used to meet from time to time, and he always saw Thomas following the same way of life, right to the day of his death when the witness was able to minister to him.

He added that while Thomas was on the way to the Council of Lyons, in obedience to Pope Gregory X of happy memory, he called at the castle of Maenza in the diocese of Terracina, and, being rather tired, stayed there a few days. And brother James of Ferentino, the prior, at that time, of Fossanova, with the witness and brothers John of Piedemonte and Fedele (also monks of the monastery) went to see brother Thomas at Maenza. This visit lasted four or five days, in which time they saw him say Mass with great devotion and tears. . . .

Four days later brother Thomas rode over from Maenza to Fossanova with the said prior and monks and his own companions; and on entering the monastery, he said these words in the parlour: 'Haec est requies mea in saeculum saeculi,' etc. And while in the monastery his condition grew worse, but he bore it most patiently; and received the sacraments of the Church reverently and devoutly, and especially the Body of Christ. . . . Before receiving Christ's Body, he said in the presence of the whole community of monks and many Dominicans and Friars Minor, many beautiful things concerning it, and in particular this: 'I have taught and written much on this most holy Body and on the other sacraments, according to my faith in Christ and in the holy Roman Church, to whose judgment I submit all my teaching.' And having received the Body, he lingered on for three days and then fell asleep in the Lord. And a Friar Preacher who had for long been confessor to brother Thomas, preached at the funeral and said before them all: 'I have heard this holy man's general confession, and I bear witness that he was as pure as a five-year's-old child; he never felt the corruption of the flesh.'[30] . . .

L. Asked if he knew of any miracles worked by Thomas in life or death or after death, the witness narrated the following which happened during that stay at Maenza. Thomas's health declined while he was there, and his *socius*, seeing his weakness, begged him to take some food: whereupon Thomas said, 'Do you think you could get me some fresh herrings?' The *socius* replied, 'Oh, yes, across the Alps, in France or England!' But just then a fishmonger called Bordonario arrived at the castle from Terracina with his usual delivery of sardines; and the *socius* (Reginald of Priverno) asked him what fish he had and was told 'sardines'. But on opening the baskets, the man found one full of fresh herrings. Everyone was delighted, but astonished too, because fresh herrings were unknown in Italy. And while the fishmonger was swearing that he had brought sardines, not herrings, brother Reginald ran off to tell Thomas, crying, 'God has given you what you wanted—herrings!' And Thomas said, 'Where have they come from and who brought them?' And Reginald said, 'God has brought them!'

Asked for his authority for this story, the witness said that the event took place within the four days that he himself spent at Maenza, along with the prior and the other monks mentioned above. He was present and saw everything and also ate some of the herrings—as also did brother Thomas himself and all the company, including Thomas's niece the Countess Frances (who was wife to Annibaldo de' Ceccano, lord of Maenza) and many other persons both secular and religious.[31]

. . . Asked who were present at the event, he mentioned himself and his prior and John of Piedemonte, and brother Fedele of Tuscany, and Reginald of Priverno, and an attendant on brother Thomas called James of Salerno.[32] Asked if these men were still living, he said 'no'; he was the only one left. Asked why he happened to be then at Maenza, he said he had gone

with his prior, under obedience, to visit brother Thomas. . . .
Asked how he knew that the fish were herrings, he said that he
had seen salted herrings at the papal court at Viterbo, so that
he knew herrings when he saw them. Besides, brother Reginald,
who had eaten fresh herrings in the countries across the Alps,
declared that these were herrings too. Asked how they had been
cooked, he answered that some were boiled and some fried.

LI. Asked if he knew of any miracle worked by Thomas at the
time of his death or afterwards, the witness said that while the
corpse still lay in the bed in which he had died, and before it
was washed, the then sub-prior of the monastery, John of
Ferentino, who had lost his sight, was about to kiss the dead
man's feet—as they all were doing because of his holiness—when
it was suggested to brother John that he should lay his eyes
against the eyes of Thomas. So he did this; and at once he
recovered his sight fully and clearly.[33]

Asked how he knew this, the witness said that he was present
and saw this happen, in fact he was one of those who advised
brother John to do as he did. Asked about the time—the month
and day—he repeated that it was the day on which Thomas died,
though he could not recall the exact day of the week nor the
month. . . . Asked who else was present, he mentioned Francis,
bishop of Terracina (of worthy memory), and the aforesaid
brother Reginald, and four or five Friars Minor and many Friar
Preachers and monks and lay-brothers of the monastery, to the
number, in all, of about a hundred. . . . Asked who had called
him to see this miracle, the witness said that no one had called
him; he had been continually at brother Thomas's bedside as he
lay ill and was there when he died, ministering to him; in fact
he was standing just beside the dead body; and he remained
there afterwards, with some other monks, to wash it. So he saw
the whole thing. Asked then what words brother John had used
when he laid his eyes on Thomas's, the witness said he had not
heard; the brother had prayed mentally. Asked how long he had
seen this man suffering from loss of sight, he said for twenty days,
during which time he could not recognise people and was
unable to read. Asked how long he had known brother John
subsequently enjoying the use of his eyes, the witness said
that thenceforth for thirty years he saw him enjoying good
sight.

LII. . . . The witness added that after Thomas had been buried seven months in the chapel of St. Stephen, he was exhumed and taken to a place before the high altar, where they buried him again. But when they exhumed him a sweet smell came out of the grave and filled all the chapel and even the cloister. And the clothes in which the corpse was wrapped were whole and entire, as was the corpse itself, except that the tip of the nose was missing. And some of the monks, in order to make sure of that fragrance, came and put their noses right down on the body and so assured themselves that the sweetness came from the body and its clothing. . . .

Then after seven years, the witness himself having now been elected abbot, he had the body again exhumed and transferred to a more honourable place, namely to the left of the altar (as one approaches it) and under a tombstone raised above ground-level. And in this disinterment also the same sort of fragrance was experienced, and again the body and its wrappings were found whole and undecayed, except that a part of the thumb of the right hand had gone. . . . Asked how he knew all this, the witness said that he was present at both translations of the body, and the second one he himself ordered, as abbot of the monastery. Asked concerning the times—the days and months—he said the first translation was seven months after brother Thomas's death, and the second one seven years after the first. The months and days he could not recall exactly, they were so long ago now. . . .[34]

William of Tocco

LVIII.[35] On Saturday, 4 August, in the same place, brother William of Tocco, an old Friar Preacher and priest, and prior of Benevento, was called as witness and took the oath. . . . Asked first about Thomas's life, the witness said that he had seen him writing on the *De generatione et corruptione*, which was, he thinks, the last of Thomas's philosophical works.[36] He had also heard him preaching and lecturing. Many people came to hear him preach. He was a sweet-tempered man, humble and gentle; free from all worldly ambition; very pure and chaste, so that it was commonly believed that he had always been a virgin, and this was maintained by brother Peter of Sezze, the procurator of the Dominicans at Anagni, in a sermon preached at Thomas's funeral in which he (Peter) revealed that he had heard the dying man's general confession.[37] In short, the entire life of Thomas was spent in prayer and contemplation, in writing or dictating, lecturing, preaching, or conducting disputations. And he never fussed about his meals or required anything special in food or clothing.

Again, the witness said, on the authority of Reginald of Priverno, that Thomas's knowledge was not acquired by natural intelligence, but by the influence of the Holy Spirit: all his writing began with prayer, and in all his difficulties he had recourse to prayer, with many tears; after which he never failed to find his mind cleared and his doubts resolved. This the witness had heard himself from brother Reginald, who had declared the same publicly in the Schools, saying (and he wept as he said it) that Thomas had forbidden him to tell anyone of this during his lifetime.[38]

LIX. For example, there was the occasion (of which the witness had heard from Francis de Amore of Alatri, vicar of the bishop of Nola, who had it from Reginald of Priverno) when Thomas was commenting on Isaiah, and, coming to a passage which baffled him, he prayed hard and fasted many days, begging God to show him what the text meant. And after some days Reginald heard Thomas speaking one night in his room with someone. Then the voices ceased, and at once Thomas called to his *socius* to light a candle and fetch the commentary on Isaiah and write to his dictation. So Reginald wrote for a while, until that hard text was explained; and then Thomas said, 'Son, go and rest now.' But Reginald got down on his knees and begged with tears to be told who that was with whom Thomas had been speaking. Then Thomas, himself weeping . . . revealed that God in His mercy had sent the blessed Apostles Peter and Paul to teach him. . . . But he added: 'In God's name, I command you never to disclose this as long as I live.'[39]

Asked for his authority for all he had said so far, the witness said that he had seen and known Thomas; they had been together at Naples at various times. He had also spoken with many religious and laymen who had personally known him, and in particular with brother Reginald, the *socius*, and with Lord Bartholomew of Capua.

LX. Asked concerning miracles worked by brother Thomas, in life or after death, the witness gave the following as an example of those commonly remembered among the Friar Preachers.

Once, at Paris, Thomas, on rising in the morning, found that one of his teeth had grown in a way that hindered him in his speech. He had to conclude a public disputation that morning; so there was nothing for it, he thought, but to set himself to prayer. So he went and prayed, and after a while the tooth fell into his hand. He showed it to Reginald; and afterwards he used to carry it about as a reminder of God's goodness to him.

This story, the witness said, he had from Lord Thomas of San Severino, count of Marsico, who was a nephew of brother Thomas,[40] and also from brother Tolomeo, the bishop of Torcello, who is now in the Curia with the cardinal-bishop of Sabina, and who was once a student under brother Thomas, and has written much about his holiness.[41] The witness had this and other stories from brother Tolomeo when they met at the Roman Curia in the previous August. The count's report he thinks he had in November 1316. . . .

He added that brother Tolomeo told him that once when Reginald, Thomas's *socius*, was ill with recurrent fever, brother Thomas took some relics of St. Agnes, which he wore hanging from his neck, and placed them on Reginald's chest, praying meanwhile to St. Agnes; and at once Reginald was cured. The witness heard this also at the Roman Curia, and at the same time as the previous story.[42]

Again, he said that it was commonly stated by old friars of his Order—and he heard the same from the said lord count—that when brother Thomas was to become a Master in Theology, an old friar appeared to him as he was praying, to assure him that he would certainly receive the degree and that for the inaugural lecture he must take as his text, 'Rigans montes de superioribus suis, de fructu operum tuorum satiabitur terra.' The said lord count got this from the lips of Thomas himself, as he told the witness.[43]

LXI. Again, the witness said that, returning from the Curia in late December of the previous year, he passed through Anagni, where he met brother Robert of Sezze, a well-known Dominican theologian and preacher.[44] This Robert told the witness what his uncle (a certain brother Stephen, a worthy religious) had told him concerning Thomas's imprisonment in the castle of Montesangiovanni, when his brothers abducted him from the Order and tried, unsuccessfully, to make him discard his religious habit and, with it, all his good intentions; and of how his brothers sent a pretty girl to his room to allure him to sin; and of how Thomas, seeing her and feeling the first effect of her presence in himself, snatched a log from the fire and indignantly drove her out, and then, with the tip of the log, marked a cross on the wall in a corner of the room; and then prayed long and with tears to God that no carnal impulse might ever corrupt his mind or body. And so praying, Thomas fell asleep; and in sleep he saw two angels come to him. . . . And they bound his loins, saying: 'In the name of God we bind you with a chastity that will resist every temptation.' And he cried out with the pain of that binding, and so woke up; but to no one would he disclose the cause of that cry; until later he revealed it, with many other things, to his *socius* for the love he bore him.[45]

LXII. Next, the witness gave an account of what he had been told by the Lady Catherine, a niece of brother Thomas and mother of Lord Roger of Morra, while staying at Marsico with the count of that place. He had gone there in the course of his enquiry about the miracles which God had worked through Thomas, undertaken at the order of the provincial of Sicily[46]— the information, once collected, having then to be submitted to the pope. Lady Catherine, an old and devout lady, told the witness—in the presence of a judge and a notary and sworn witnesses—that she had heard from Thomas's mother, Lady Theodora, how one day a hermit . . . came to the castle of Roccasecca and said to her: 'Rejoice, my lady, for the child you bear is a son whom you will call Thomas; and you and your husband will have a mind to make him a monk of Monte Cassino, but God has disposed otherwise, for he shall be a Preaching Friar, with no equal in his day for learning and sanctity.' And in fact (Lady Catherine went on) the boy was brought up at Monte Cassino, and then went to Naples, where he joined the Dominicans. And, his mother wishing to see him, he was pursued by his brothers to the priory of Santa Sabina at Rome; and later captured by them (who were serving under the Emperor Frederick) and sent back to his mother, still wearing the religious habit. And he was kept a prisoner until his brothers returned, meanwhile resisting every attempt to deprive him of the habit. And in prison he studied much and taught his sisters. And at last his parents and brothers, overcome by his constancy, gave him back to the Order; whereupon he was sent to study at Cologne.

Asked who received this testimony, the witness said it was made before the count of Marsico and his wife, the Countess Suana, and many of their household whose names he does not remember. Asked when this took place, he said 'last year'—in February, he thinks, but he cannot recall the day.[47]

LXIII. Again the witness said that while waiting at Fossanova for the bishop of Viterbo—whom the Pope had appointed one of the committee to enquire into the miracles of brother Thomas —on the day before the bishop's arrival a monk of that monastery, Dom Peter of Fondi (who was himself required as a witness in the case), said to the witness: 'Brother William, I can't go to Naples, the gout in my feet is too bad; but I am praying to our saint; perhaps he will help me.' But as he seemed to get no better, the witness also prayed for him with tears. And when the witness came again to the cloister where the sufferer was seated, he found the latter quite cured and walking about. And the next day he could ride off with the others to Naples. Asked when this happened, the witness said, 'on 17 July'. Asked who was present, the witness said the monk had been alone with his pain and his complaints when the words reported were spoken; but everyone knew of the sickness and also of the cure; though whether the others paid any attention to either, he could not say.[48]

Again, during his stay at the monastery, said the witness, a woman came called Stefania de Rocca, from the castle of Sonnino, who was all swollen with dropsy. She came to the gate and begged for some relic of brother Thomas for whom she had conceived a devotion and through whose merits she believed she might be cured. . . . The witness went out to her with a number of the monks and some relics of Thomas; and when they had all prayed together there, he touched her breast with the relics. And on her way home she found herself cured of her disease; and sent her son back to inform the witness and the monks. And many people since have told the witness that she was perfectly cured from that day on. This happened, he said, on 12 June of this year.

LXIV. Again, on the next day of the same month and year, while the witness was in the monastery guest-house, a poor

8

woman came from Carpeneto, called Mary de Nicolao; who declared before many there that she had been a paralytic, and while in this state she used to come and glean in the monastery fields, so far as she could, all trembling as she was. And the lay-brothers advised her to make a vow to brother Thomas—he would cure her. So she vowed to bring a lighted candle to his grave; and at once she was cured. The witness did not know the names of the lay-brothers concerned. Then there was Nicholas de Leone of Sonnino who was seized with such a pain in the hip, while working in a field alone, that he thought he would never get back to his house. But remembering the many miracles worked by God at the tomb of brother Thomas, . . . he vowed there and then to visit the tomb, barefoot and with a stone hanging from his neck; and at once he was quite cured; and the next day came and told the witness of this. Asked who else was present at the miracle, the witness said 'nobody—the man was alone in the field'. But Richard of Fondi, the sacristan, saw Nicholas come to fulfil his vow, with the stone hanging from his neck. This happened on 16 July of this year.[49]

LXV. Again, the witness described the case of Nicholas Massimo of Priverno. This man had been struck on the right arm so violently that the bone was broken; and though the wound had healed, the bone remained broken, and Nicholas could not use his arm. But he allowed himself to be persuaded to make a vow to brother Thomas to pardon all his enemies and to bring a waxen arm to the saint's tomb. And having carried out this promise, he went to sleep; and on waking up, he knew that he was cured and began to bend his arm and work with it. . . . And the witness, wishing to see the matter for himself, sent for Nicholas; who came to the tomb and, baring his arm, showed it to the witness who touched it with his hand and was able (he thought) to feel the break in the bone. This happened, he said, in March of this year; he could not remember the day. Asked who else was present, he said that when Nicholas made the vow only his wife was present.

Again, there was Peter Balie of Priverno, whose sight gradually weakened for the space of ten years, until he was quite blind. He got himself led to the tomb; and, praying there and making a vow, he rose up with his sight fully restored. Asked when this happened, the witness said it was in the same year that Thomas died, but the month and the day he did not know. Nor did anyone remember who was present on the occasion; Peter himself told the witness about it, when they chanced to meet at the gate of Priverno.[50]

Finally, the witness said that when he arrived at Fossanova he went to the sacristy and asked Richard the sacristan to show him the chest containing some of brother Thomas's bones. . . . And when he opened the chest a strong scent came out of it, unlike any odour in nature. On his asking the sacristan about this the latter swore by the altar that he had not put anything on the bones to make them smell. They always had that scent. And the witness added that one experiences more or less of the scent according to the degree of one's devotion. He saw these relics first in the octave of Easter this year, and afterwards many times until he left the monastery on 15 July.[51]

Anthony of Brescia

LXVI. On the same day, at the same place, brother Anthony of Brescia, a Dominican priest and student in the priory at Naples, was called as witness and took the oath. . . . He said that he had heard from Nicholas of Marsillac—a Friar Preacher and formerly chaplain and counsellor to the king of Cyprus, and before that a student under brother Thomas at Paris (where he lived in the same house with Thomas for a long time)[52]—that brother Thomas was a holy and upright man, and in particular a lover of poverty; for example, he wrote the *Summa contra Gentiles* on small bits of scribbling paper, since he had no other writing material.[53]

Asked about miracles . . . the witness said that he had often heard from brother Albert of Brescia, a lector at Brescia and a saintly man, that Thomas's holiness had been shown by miracles. This Albert was an ardent Thomist and would often say, in the course of his lectures, 'Dear brothers, I know that this man is a great saint in heaven.' So, having heard this many times, the witness and another student one day begged Albert to tell them why he was so sure of what he asserted. Brother Albert, being adjured in the name of God to explain his words, at last spoke as follows:

> My dear sons, I am, as you know, an enthusiast for Thomas of Aquino's doctrine. I have always marvelled at his having attained to such wisdom and holiness so quickly; and I used often to pray to our Lady

and Saint Augustine that his actual glory might be revealed to me. Now once as I knelt at our Lady's altar and prayed more fervently than usual, and continued praying, there appeared to me—awake as I was and praying—two venerable and radiant figures. One was wearing a mitre; the other, who wore the Dominican habit, had on his head a golden and jewelled crown and around his neck two necklaces, one of gold and the other silver, and on his breast a great jewel that lit up the church; his cloak too was woven with gems, but his tunic and hood were white as snow.

Amazed by this sight, Albert fell at the feet of those figures, begging to be told their names. Then the mitred figure said to him:

Brother Albert, why this astonishment? Your prayer has been heard. I am Augustine, Doctor of the Church; I am sent to declare to you the doctrine and glory of Thomas of Aquino, here at my side. For he is my son indeed, who faithfully followed the apostolic teaching and my own, and so illuminated the Church. To this these jewels bear witness, and particularly the gem on his breast which signifies the purity of his intentions as defender and declarer of the Faith. The other gems signify his many books and writings. He is my equal in glory, except that in the splendour of virginity he is greater than I.

The witness and the other student whom brother Albert told of this were forbidden by him to reveal it to anyone, unless a Canonisation Enquiry should be undertaken concerning Thomas's miracles. Asked who were present when Albert made this statement, the witness said there was no one but himself and his companion, a brother Giannino of Brescia now dead. The statement was made nine years ago, in January (he could not recall the day), and in brother Albert's cell. [54]

LXVII. The witness also said that he had heard from the same brother Albert that, when Thomas died, the lord Albert the German, being then at table in the refectory (it was during Lent) suddenly began to weep; and, on the prior asking him the reason, Albert said to the prior and all the community: 'I have sad news for you; brother Thomas of Aquino, my child in Christ and a light of the Church, is dead. This God has revealed to me.' The prior took note of the time, and later verified that it indeed coincided with the time of Thomas's death. . . . [55]

The witness added the following statement made to him by brother Nicholas of Marsillac, counsellor and chaplain to the king of Cyprus, a learned and holy man who had been a pupil of Thomas in Paris. This Nicholas said: 'Brother Anthony, I was with brother Thomas at Paris, and I declare before God that I have never known such a lover of purity and poverty. For instance, he wrote the *Contra Gentiles* on scraps of paper, though he certainly could have had good writing paper if he had asked for it; but it was like him to pay no heed to trifles.' Asked when these words were said to him, the witness answered that it was thirteen years ago, in September, but he could not recall the day. Asked who else was present, he said that brother Peter of Mantua was there, and several others whose names he has forgotten. Asked about the place, he said it was in the Dominican school at Nicosia, on the island of Cyprus.[56]

John di Blasio

LXX. On Monday, 6 August, in the same place, the lord John di Blasio, a judge of Naples in the service of Her Majesty Queen Mary of Sicily, was called as witness and took the oath. . . . He said that he had known brother Thomas for five years and more, meeting him in the refectory and in his cell; besides having heard him preach from time to time over a period of ten years, including the whole of one Lent when he preached on the text *Ave Maria, gratia plena, Dominus tecum*. He preached with his eyes shut and his mind in heaven.[57]

And one day, while visiting Thomas in his cell, the latter went out on to an open terrace. Then the witness saw a devil, in the form of a black man clothed in black; and Thomas also saw it, and rushed at it with his fist raised and struck it, crying, 'Why do you come to tempt me?' Whereupon the devil vanished. . . . Asked how he knew it was a devil, the witness said that on another occasion he had seen it in a crystal, when an exorcism was being performed to recover a book which had been stolen from a student; and it was the same devil which he saw appear to Thomas. Asked about the time of day, he said it was about nine in the morning. Apart from himself and Thomas and the devil, no one else was present. This happened at Naples, on a sort of terrace by Thomas's cell.[58]

Bartholomew of Capua

LXXVI. On Wednesday, 8 August, his excellency Lord Bartholomew of Capua, Chancellor and Protonotary of the kingdom of

Sicily, was cited as witness and took the prescribed oath.[59] Asked what he knew—and how he knew it—of the life and miracles of brother Thomas of Aquino of revered memory . . . the witness described the sources of his knowledge as follows.

When as a mere lad he came to the University of Naples, he began often to visit the Dominicans in that city; and so became acquainted with brother John of Caiazzo, a man of some eminence and a good scholar, who had known brother Thomas very well and been his pupil both at Paris and in the kingdom of Sicily. In those days there were also other Friar Preachers in Naples of much distinction and learning and religious dignity, such men as Eufranone of Porta, James of Manzano, Troiano, Matthew of Castellammare, Hugh of Maddaleno, and John of San Giuliano. This last-named friar, a very old man of great virtue and humility, was commonly supposed to have received brother Thomas into the Order.[60]

From John of Caiazzo and John of San Giuliano, as well as from common report, the witness learned that the father of brother Thomas, who was a powerful nobleman, sent his son as a child to Monte Cassino with a view to his eventually becoming abbot of that monastery.[61] Well, Thomas grew up an example to all, and then, at the University of Naples, where he took the Arts course, he surpassed all his companions in study.[62] And, his judgment maturing very quickly, he entered the Order of Preachers while still a boy in years.[63] The Friars, fearing Thomas's father, took measures to get the youth out of the kingdom and safely on the road to one of their centres of study; but his father's influence caused him to be captured and imprisoned in one of the family castles, where he was kept closely guarded for more than a year. His father tried to make him put on the habit of a monk or a layman's dress, but in vain. . . .[64] Meanwhile Thomas had begged and obtained from his brothers, when his imprisonment began, a Bible and a breviary. The Bible he then studied so deeply that he understood most of it by the time of his release. This happened when his father at last understood that nothing could shake the lad's constancy; so he yielded to the prayers of his wife and set his son free. . . .[65] And that constancy and purity of young Thomas in prison, brother John of San Giuliano never tired of praising, according to the witness.

LXXVII. Again, the witness declared that it was commonly believed by those who had known Thomas, and especially by the Dominicans already named (men of considerable authority), that the Holy Spirit dwelt in him. For the expression on his face was always so lively, sweet, and gentle; he was so entirely detached from the world; always studying, lecturing, or writing for the good of his fellow Christians. From brother John of Caiazzo we know that Thomas was always the first to rise in the night for prayer; and when he heard the others coming to pray, he would at once retire to his cell. The witness himself often saw Thomas—and he saw him as often as possible—and he seemed always recollected and untrammelled by this world. Common report said he was a virgin clean and pure. . . . No one ever heard him say an idle word. In scholastic disputations—so often the occasion for intemperate flights of language—Thomas was always gentle and humble, never windy-worded or pretentious. Even at meal-times his recollection continued; dishes would be placed before him and taken away without his noticing; and when the brethren tried to get him into the garden for recreation, he would draw back swiftly and retire to his cell alone with his thoughts.

Again, the witness heard from the above religious, or some of them, and from others, and in particular from Nicholas Fricia[66] —who used to attend brother Thomas's lectures and hear Mass daily at the Dominican church—that very early in the morning Thomas would say his Mass in the chapel of St. Nicholas,[67] after which . . . he heard another Mass, and then, taking off his vestments, at once began his teaching. This done, he would set himself to write or dictate to his secretaries until the time for dinner. After dinner he went to his cell and attended to spiritual things until the siesta; after which he resumed his writing. And so the whole of his life was directed towards God. It was the common view . . . that he had wasted scarcely a moment of his time.

The witness, who was several years at Naples when Thomas was there, and was a frequent visitor at San Domenico, never remembers having seen Thomas outside the cloister, except once in the afternoon and another time at the royal court at Capua, whither he had gone (as the witness was told) to deal with some matter affecting the well-being of his nephew the count of Fondi.[68]

Again, the witness said he had been told by several Friar

Preachers, whose word could be relied on, that at Paris once when Thomas was conducting a disputation at which the Franciscan John Pecham (later archbishop of Canterbury) was present, the latter attacked Thomas in a pompous and over-bearing way, whereas Thomas remained unalterably humble, gentle, and courteous.[69] Such was always his way in disputations, however sharply and shrewdly contested they might be.

LXXVIII. The witness further reported his having heard from one who lived on intimate terms with Thomas (the same John of Caiazzo) that it was his constant prayer to God to keep him from all ambition and always a simple friar; and also that he might be shown what had become of the soul of his brother Reginald whom the Emperor Frederick—unjustly as Thomas believed—had put to death. These prayers were answered: it was shown him that his status would not be altered nor his soul defiled by worldly pride, and that his brother's name was in the Book of Life.[70]

While on the way to the Council of Lyons, in obedience to Pope Gregory X . . . and going down from Teano to Borgonuovo, Thomas chanced to bang his head against a tree that had fallen across the road, and was half stunned and hardly able to stand. Reginald of Priverno, his companion, ran up at once and asked him whether he was injured, and Thomas answered 'not much'. (There were present also William, then dean and later bishop of Teano, and Roffredo, William's nephew who was later dean.) Then Reginald thought he would provide (as he hoped) a little relaxation; so he said to Thomas: 'Master, you are going to the Council where much good will be done for the whole Church and for our Order and for the Kingdom of Sicily.' And Thomas replied, 'Please God, that will be so.' Then Reginald took another step, saying: 'And you and brother Bonaventure will be made cardinals—an honour for the two Orders!' To which Thomas answered, 'I can serve the Order best as I am.' But Reginald insisted: 'Father, I am not thinking of *your* advantage but of the common good. . . .' But Thomas cut him short: 'Reginald,' he said, 'you may be quite sure that I shall go on exactly as I am.' All this was repeated to the witness by his friend Roffredo, who was there and heard everything, as did the bishop of Teano.[71]

Once Thomas was returning to Paris from St. Denis with a

number of brethren, and when the city came into view they sat down to rest a while. And one of the company, turning to Thomas, said: 'Father, what a fine city Paris is!' 'Very fine,' answered Thomas. 'I wish it were all yours,' said the other; to which Thomas replied, 'Why, what would I do with it?' 'You would sell it to the king of France, and with the money you would build houses for Friar Preachers.' 'Well,' said Thomas, 'I would rather have Chrysostom on Matthew.' This story, the witness said, he had from—among others—brother Nicholas Malasorte of Naples, who had been an adviser to the French king and a particular friend and pupil of his own; he told it when he came on a mission from the same king of France to King Charles II of noble memory . . .; saying that it was well known in Paris.[72]

LXXIX. The witness went on to recall that while brother Thomas was saying his Mass one morning, in the chapel of St. Nicholas at Naples, something happened which profoundly affected and altered him. After Mass he refused to write or dictate; indeed he put away his writing materials. He was in the third part of the *Summa*, at the questions on Penance. And brother Reginald, seeing that he was not writing, said to him: 'Father, are you going to give up this great work, undertaken for the glory of God and to enlighten the world?' But Thomas replied: 'Reginald, I cannot go on.' Then Reginald, who began to fear that much study might have affected his master's brain, urged and insisted that he should continue his writing; but Thomas only answered in the same way: 'Reginald, I cannot—because all that I have written seems to me so much straw.' Then Reginald, astonished that . . . brother Thomas should go to see his sister, the countess of San Severino, whom he loved in all charity; and hastening there with great difficulty, when he arrived and the countess came out to meet him, he could scarcely speak. The countess, very much alarmed, said to Reginald: 'What has happened to brother Thomas? He seems quite dazed and hardly spoke to me!' And Reginald answered: 'He has been like this since about the feast of St. Nicholas—since when he has written nothing at all.' Then again brother Reginald began to beseech Thomas to tell him why he refused to write and why he was so stupefied; and after much of this urgent questioning and insisting, Thomas at last said to Reginald: 'Promise me, by the living God almighty and by your loyalty to our Order and by the love you bear to me, that you will never reveal, as long as I live, what I shall tell you.' Then he added: 'All that I have written seems to me like straw compared with what has now been revealed to me.'[73]

So Thomas, leaving the countess very sad, returned to Naples; and then set out for the Council to which he had been summoned. And on the way, at the castle of Maenza in the Campagna, he fell ill of the sickness of which he was to die. And several years later brother Reginald, too, fell mortally ill; and when near to death he declared to brother John of Giudice (this old man, born at Anagni, was much respected in the Order for the integrity of his character) clearly and in detail what has been said above. And brother John in turn repeated it all to the witness, when the latter was staying as a guest at the Dominican priory at Anagni, a little while before Pope Boniface was captured; and the witness declared it all, as soon as he could, to brother William of Tocco and to other Friar Preachers, and later to Pope Benedict XI of blessed memory, who was in Rome at the time and heard it all with intense interest and great joy.[74]

LXXX. The witness added that when Thomas began to feel seriously ill he asked to be carried from Maenza, where he then was, to the abbey of our Lady at Fossanova: which was done. And on entering the monastery, ill and weak, he clung with his hand to the doorpost, saying: 'Haec requies mea in saeculum saeculi, hic habitabo quoniam elegi eam.' . . . And in the monastery he lay ill many days. And he desired to receive the body of our Saviour; and when it was brought to him, he greeted it on his knees with wonderful expressions of praise, reverence, and adoration. 'I receive You,' he said, 'the price of my soul's redemption, the food of my pilgrimage. For love of You I have studied and kept vigil and worked and prayed and taught. Never have I spoken against You, unless it was in ignorance. And I don't wish to insist on my opinions; but if I have said anything amiss, I leave it all to the correction of the Roman Church.' A little later he died and was buried near the high altar of the abbey church—a marshy spot because it is not far from the monastery garden where a stream runs (which they use to turn a wheel there), making the whole place damp, as the witness himself has carefully and frequently observed.[75]

About eight months later there came a rumour that the Dominican Peter of Tarentaise had been made pope and that he wished the body of brother Thomas transferred to one of the greater churches of his Order. So the monks of Fossanova, fearing to lose the body, selected three of their number who dug it up one night and cut off the head, which they hid in a secret place in a corner of a chapel behind the choir. The witness knows the chapel well. The monks argued that if they had to lose the body, they might at least keep the head. And the witness heard from brother Peter of Montesangiovanni and from another monk (a Sicilian, he says, and at that time sub-prior) that the body was found entirely incorrupt, with all the hair still on the head. The only part missing was one hand, which the countess of San Severino had. There was also a dent near the tip of the nose as if a mouse had bitten it. The body had a good smell.[76]

These facts have been commonly remembered and repeated at Fossanova for many years now. The witness has often heard them mentioned both there and elsewhere; for his devotion to this holy man has often caused him, when travelling to the Roman Curia on business from his lords the kings of Sicily, to turn off the straighter road through the Campagna and go down towards the coast and put up at the monastery of Fossanova. . . .[77]

LXXXI. He added that he had heard it stated publicly that one year when the town of Priverno—which lies one or two miles from the monastery—was afflicted by a dangerous epidemic, the sick used to come in crowds to the tomb of brother Thomas and be cured. It was also, he said, very commonly asserted that the monks kept quiet about many of the miracles worked by God through Thomas, because they feared to lose the custody of his body.[78]

He said, too—what many Dominicans had told him—that Thomas's *socius* Reginald, lecturing after his master's death, had called God to witness that when Thomas met with intellectual difficulties he used to go to the altar and stay there a while weeping and sobbing, and then return to his cell and his writing.[79]

He said, too, that the brethren had told him that one of Thomas's favourite recreations was to walk round the cloister alone with his head held high. The witness himself had often seen him walking thus round the cloister of San Domenico.

Another point he mentioned was that when Thomas was told

of the death of his nephews or other relatives, he made no sign or expression of grief, but cheerfully and calmly saw that Masses and prayers were said for them, and himself prayed for them. . . .

LXXXII. Brother Hugh of Lucca who had been the Dominican Provincial in Tuscany and was a friend of the witness (they used to meet at Anagni first, and then at Lucca, when the witness was on his way to Provence) told the latter of the distress of brother Albert when he heard the news of Thomas's death. Albert had been Thomas's master; and he wept much when news came that his pupil was dead, and afterwards whenever he was reminded of him, calling him the flower and beauty of this world. Indeed the brethren were troubled by so much sorrow in Albert and thought his many tears a symptom of senile weakness. And when, later, it was rumoured that Thomas's writings were being attacked at Paris, Albert said he desired to go there to defend them. This did not please the brethren; Albert was an old man, the journey would be a long one; and especially they feared that, were Albert to go to Paris now, his authority and reputation there would suffer, since he was now in decline and his memory and general intelligence were not what they had been. So for a while they managed to dissuade him. But finally Albert—who was also an archbishop or bishop—decided that he would go, come what might of it; such noble writings must be defended! So he went to Paris, with brother Hugh (so the latter told the witness) as his *socius*. And after their arrival, there was a general assembly of masters and students at the Friar Preachers' school, and Albert spoke from the chair on the text: 'Quae laus vivo, si laudatur a mortuis?'; making this mean that it was Thomas who was alive and the others who were dead, and proceeding to praise and glorify Thomas in the highest terms. He was ready, he said, to defend the shining truth and holiness of Thomas's writings before the most competent critics.

Then brother Albert . . . returned to Cologne, still accompanied by brother Hugh. And once returned, he caused all Thomas's writings to be read out to him in a definite order; after which, at a solemn assembly convened for the purpose, he pronounced a great panegyric of Thomas, ending with an assertion that the latter's work had put an end to everyone else's, and henceforth to the end of the world all other men's labour would

be to no purpose. And, as brother Hugh told the witness, Albert
could never hear Thomas named without shedding tears.[80]

LXXXIII. Again, the witness referred to some words of brother
James of Viterbo of holy memory, doctor of sacred scripture and
archbishop of Naples, who had been both a father and friend to
him, and who had once remarked to him that, in all sincerity
and in the Holy Ghost, he believed that our Saviour and Master,
for the enlightenment of the world and the Catholic Church,
had sent out first the Apostle Paul, and then Augustine, and
finally, in our own day, brother Thomas—who himself would
have no successor until the end of time. And the same brother
James also repeated to the witness a tribute spoken by Giles of
Rome, the Augustinian theologian; who used often to say to him
at Paris, in the course of conversation: 'James, if the Dominicans
desired to keep a monopoly of knowledge and leave the rest of
us in darkness, all they need to do would be to refuse to let us
see the writings of brother Thomas.'[81]

From the same brother James the witness then quoted the
following observation on the writings of Thomas: that we find
in them a quality of the normal and universal—and this not only
in the truth which they convey to the mind, but also in their
clarity of expression, and in the way they elucidate difficulties,
and in their pedagogical method which leads the reader so
rapidly to an all-round understanding of the matter in hand.
Always they show the same breadth and normality; never anything peculiar or eccentric.[82] And brother James added that, for
his part, he never wished to read any other man's writings after
tasting the sweetness of brother Thomas's; which he firmly
believed (as he very often told the witness) were the product of
spiritual meditation inspired by the Holy Spirit, rather than of
mere human intelligence. Hence when he first came to Naples
and was able to visit San Domenico, he had himself taken to
the cell which had been Thomas's and, being shown where
the master's desk had stood, he immediately knelt down in the
presence of the brethren, saying: 'I have come to worship at the
place where his feet have stood.'

With regard to the supernatural inspiration of Thomas's
writings, the witness himself is convinced (so far as he can judge)
that the opinion given above is true; and this for several reasons:

In the first place, it does not seem possible for a man using merely human powers to have written so many great works (see the list below) in so short a time; considering that Thomas died (according to the usual view) in his forty-eighth year and was always scrupulous in his recitation of the divine office and in reading and prayer.[83] Secondly, because while many of the writings of great saints and doctors have been attacked and demolished after their death, those of Thomas, though certainly attacked since his death by many critics, including some eminent ones, have, in fact, notwithstanding such attempts to discredit them, lost none of their authority with the passage of time; on the contrary, their influence has continued to spread more and more, even reaching (so the witness has been told) as far as barbarous nations.[84] And everywhere they are winning enthusiastic adherents. Thirdly, these writings can be read with ease and profit by everyone, according to his mental capacity. Hence we find even laymen and people of modest intelligence desiring to possess copies of them.[85]

LXXXIV. The witness went on to say that throughout the kingdom, and especially among the nobility and with men of virtue and education, the virtues, doctrine, and holiness of brother Thomas enjoyed a very great reputation; and in general it might be said that the majority of good and intelligent people in the kingdom is persuaded that he was a man chosen by God, a splendid teacher, a virgin pure and intact, a humble, devout and entirely unworldly religious.

He added that having for some years been in the habit of reading Thomas's works, he happened to remember one day that somewhere in one of them he had read that what was customary among Christian people should be taken as binding in law. But when he looked for this text he could not find it, though he searched diligently for several days whenever he had leisure to do so. Finally he knelt down and asked Thomas himself to show him where it was; then he opened the *Secunda secundae*, and there it was under his eyes—he did not have to turn a page —in the section on fasting.[86] And so it was, he had found, in all his needs; brother Thomas never failed to help him, according to the degree of his faith.

LXXXV. The witness then made the following list of work, composed by Thomas.[87]

LXXXVI. The witness went on to say that when he was a guest of the Friar Preachers at Anagni, the prior, Nicholas of Sezze, told him of the Christmas that brother Thomas kept with Lord Richard of worthy memory, cardinal deacon of Sant' Angelo, at Molara. This cardinal was very fond of Thomas and knew him well. Now when Thomas arrived at Molara, as the cardinal's guest for that Christmas, he found two Roman Jews there, also invited for the feast—a father and his son, rich men and both learned in the Hebrew tongue. And the cardinal said to Thomas, in the presence of the Jews: 'Brother Thomas, say some of your good and holy words to these hardened Jews'; and Thomas replied that he would gladly say what he could, if they cared to listen.

Thomas and the two Jews then withdrew to a chapel in the castle, where they remained a long time arguing and discussing; and Thomas answered all their questions. Finally, when the Jews seemed to be quite satisfied with his explanations, Thomas said: 'Go and think over these points, and tomorrow let us meet here again, and you will tell me frankly if you still have any doubts.' Well, the next day—which was Christmas Eve—the Jews and Thomas met again in the same place, and Thomas spoke to them for a while. And then the voices of all three were heard singing together, 'Te Deum laudamus' . . .; on hearing which the cardinal, who had the gout and could not walk, got himself carried to the chapel with his chaplains and servants; and all of them, Thomas, the Jews, the cardinal, and his company, continued together singing the 'Te Deum' to the end. Then the Jews were baptised. And to celebrate the occasion the cardinal sent invitations to Rome, to many noble friends of his, that they should come to Molara in festal array to rejoice together over this sudden conversion. The Jews, for their part, told the cardinal that as soon as they had entered the chapel with Thomas, and heard him begin to speak, they felt entirely changed, so that only with difficulty could they find any objections to his arguments.[88]

John Coppa

LXXXVII. On Thursday, 9 August, at the same place, John Coppa, a notary of Naples, was called as witness and took the oath. . . . He said that brother Thomas was an entirely good and holy man. Asked how he knew this, he answered that he had seen Thomas and lived with him continuously at the

Dominican priory at Naples for about one year; and that he was commonly regarded as a saint. Through the Lent of that year the witness saw and heard him preach on the Lord's Prayer, taking each time a part of the prayer as his text. There was such a devotion to him at Naples that almost the whole city came to every sermon.[89]

Asked about miracles, the witness said he could speak of one. For one day he and his brother—a Friar Preacher called Bonfiglio—visited brother Thomas when he was lying ill in his cell; and during the visit the witness saw a very bright star come in through the window and hang over Thomas's bed. It stayed there a short time and then vanished. Asked how he knew this, the witness said he was in the cell and saw the star. Asked when this happened, he said it was in the same year that Thomas died, about forty-five years ago, he thinks. Asked who was present, he said brother Bonfiglio was there and that he saw the star too. . . . Asked whether this Bonfiglio were still alive, he said he was not. Asked about the size of the star, he said it measured about a foot and a half across. . . . It was like the stars in the sky, with rays and a great brilliance; and it hung over the bed for as long as one might say a 'Hail Mary' slowly. It was silvery-white in colour.[90]

John of Gaeta

LXXXVIII. On the same day, at the same place, John Zecca-denario of Gaeta, a doctor of canon law, was called as witness and took the oath. . . . He said that Thomas had been a man of very pure and holy life, chaste, upright, contemplative, and abstemious. Asked how he knew, the witness said that he had seen and known Thomas and heard him preach several times at San Domenico in Naples;[91] and what he has said about Thomas was just the common opinion on him. . . . Asked when all this was, he said, 'forty-five years or more'. He added that many old men had told him of miracles which God had worked and continued to work through the merits of brother Thomas. He knew nothing else in particular.

John of Boiano

LXXXIX. On Saturday, 11 August, John of Boiano, an old Friar Preacher and a priest, was called as witness and took the oath. . . . Asked about the life of brother Thomas, he said that he was a completely spiritual man; each day he said his Mass, and then heard another, or sometimes two, and then was continuously occupied with reading, writing, praying, or preaching. He spent little time eating or sleeping. He was humble, temperate, and chaste. Asked how he knew all this, the witness said he had seen and known Thomas at San Domenico in Naples, and so was able to judge for himself (besides being told by older members of the Order) that such was the tenor of Thomas's life to the end.

Asked about miracles, . . . the witness said that fifteen years after the death of brother Thomas he went, as prior of Durazzo, to the Provincial Chapter of the Friar Preachers at Anagni, where he was shown a thumb taken from one of Thomas's hands. This thumb had been given by Reginald of Priverno, the usual *socius* of brother Thomas, to the lord brother Hugh, the bishop of Ostia. The hand itself was in the possession of the lady countess, Thomas's sister. The thumb (said the witness) was whole and healthy; in fact, it seemed fresh, with the skin, nail, flesh, bones, and colour, like the thumb of a living man. . . .[92]

Peter Caracciolo

XC. On the same day, in the same place, Lord Peter Caracciolo of Naples was called as witness and took the prescribed oath. Asked about the life and ways of brother Thomas, the witness answered that he knew no more than what was commonly said, that Thomas was a holy man.

Asked about miracles . . . he answered that once when he was staying with Lord Thomas Dentiti at Naples, the latter's grandmother, Lady Constance Fanisari, and some other ladies fell to talking about the ways of various religious; and Lady Constance mentioned brother Thomas; and praising his holiness, she described how she had once seen his mother holding him—then but a child—in her arms. The little boy, she said, was clothed in the usual way, and his mother started to take off his clothes in order to wash him. And just then the child stretched out his hand and picked up a piece of paper from the floor, and clutched it tightly. And when his mother tried to take it away he cried, but when she let him keep it he was quiet. And wishing to see what was written on the paper, his mother found these words, 'Ave Maria, gratia plena', etc. But she gave him his bath still clutching the paper; there was no other way to keep him quiet.

9

Asked who were present when Lady Constance told this story, the witness said that he was there himself, and several other ladies whose names he cannot remember. It was about eight years ago, at the time when Pope Clement V was holding the Council of Vienne.[93]

Peter Capotto

XCII. On Monday, 13 August, at the same place, brother Peter Capotto of Benevento, a Friar Preacher, was called as witness and took the oath. . . . He said he had heard from many senior members of the Order, who had known brother Thomas and lived continuously with him, that he was a humble, chaste, devout man and very contemplative; that he said Mass each day and then heard another; that he confessed every morning before Mass; that he was most temperate, never minding what he ate or even noticing it, so detached and absorbed he was in contemplation; and that so he continued to the end.

Asked from whom and where he had heard these things, the witness said he had them from many of the older friars and in diverse Provinces of the Order—to wit, at Naples, where he had been a student for ten years, at Florence, where he spent two years, at Bologna, where he was for a time, at Montpellier, where he studied for three years, and at Paris, where he spent two years. Asked for the names of those older friars, he mentioned Raymund Severi, then the sub-prior at Montpellier, who had been several years a student under Thomas at Paris and used to hear his confession each morning before Mass. Raymund told the witness that Thomas never confessed to having had a carnal thought. The witness added that while he was a student at Paris it was the custom in the priory there to read aloud, at fixed times, paragraphs from a book called *Vitae Fratrum*. And from that reading he learned, among other things, that when Thomas was told to prepare himself to receive the degree of Master in Theology, he wondered what text he should take for his inaugural address; and that while he was in his cell wondering, a venerable figure, white-haired and in the Dominican habit, appeared to him and said: 'Why are you perplexed? Take this: *Rigans montes de superioribus suis, de fructu operum tuorum satiabitur terra.*' And Thomas agreed that this was a good text. . . . The witness added that the Dominicans at Paris commonly said that the venerable figure was St. Dominic.[94]

Thomas of Aversa

XCV. On the same day, in the same place, brother Thomas of Aversa . . . a Friar Preacher, was called as witness and took the oath. . . . He said that, being a young man, he only knows what is generally said in the Order, and also by the faithful generally, to the effect that brother Thomas was a man of holy life.

Asked whether he knew of any miracles, he said that, going once to Salerno with brother William of Tocco, he wanted to see the hand of brother Thomas which the count of San Severino had given to the Dominicans of that city. So he asked the sacristan to show it, but when he saw it and did reverence to it, he was surprised and disappointed because he smelled none of the fragrance that he had supposed it gave off. But he did reverence again, and then he smelled the fragrance distinctly. . . . And he kissed the hand.

Asked to describe the smell, he said he could not, exactly, but that it was very sweet and pleasant. Asked when this happened, he said 'more than eighteen months ago, during Advent'. Asked who was present, he said there was nobody there except brother John of Aversa, a lay-brother and at that time sacristan. . . .[95]

NOTES TO THE CANONISATION ENQUIRY

1. The events preceding and leading to this Enquiry have been outlined in my Introduction: the commission to William of Tocco and Robert of Benevento from the Chapter of the Sicilian Dominican province, in the autumn of 1317, to make an inventory of miracles attributed to the intercession of Thomas of Aquino; the consequent activities of William and his companion, their interrogation of members of the saint's family, their securing of petitions for the canonisation from the Queen Mother and other notables of the kingdom, their journey to Avignon in July 1318, to submit this material (which included a draft of Tocco's *Life* of Thomas) to the pope; and the favourable reception accorded them by the latter, who officially introduced the cause, on 13 September, by letters instructing Humbert Montauro, archbishop of Naples, Angelo Tignosi, bishop of Viterbo, and Pandulf Savelli, papal notary, to conduct the Enquiry and hear the witnesses.

2. The witnesses were interrogated separately and privately ('semoti et in secreto', *Fontes*, ed. Laurent, p. 273): hence Tocco could not make use of their depositions for his biography. That this—like Gui's and Calo's—has so much in common with the depositions is partly due to their common source, the

older generation of Dominicans who had known St. Thomas (cf. Tocco's own deposition, LVIII, with XLVII or LXXVI), but still more to the fact that Tocco had already interviewed many, perhaps most, of the witnesses while preparing the ground for the canonisation; and of course much of what they told him went into his book. Cf. Mandonnet, *Mélanges Thomistes*, pp. 30–1.

3. Tocco seems to have wished the Enquiry to begin its work at Fossanova, where or whereabouts most of the *post-mortem* miracles had occurred, and where a number of the older monks, who might be expected to find it hard to travel elsewhere, still remembered St. Thomas's brief stay with them forty-five years before. Tocco himself spent more than three months of the summer preceding the Enquiry at Fossanova (see LXIII–LXV). But in the event the aged archbishop of Naples could not manage the journey to the abbey (*Fontes*, ed. Prümmer, p. 149). Later on, in November 1321, a second Enquiry was in fact held at Fossanova; it concerned itself entirely with *post-mortem* miracles, and so offers no directly biographical material.

4. This formula will be shortened or omitted henceforth.

5. The most informative of all the witnesses and a main source for the biography of St. Thomas; see below, LXXVI–LXXXVI. Born at Capua *c.* 1248, Bartholomew studied at Naples while St. Thomas was there as regent of studies at S. Domenico, 1272–4. From 1278 he taught civil law at Naples. In 1290 he was with King Charles II at Paris, a useful contact with the Parisian tradition concerning St. Thomas. In 1294 he became protonotary of the kingdom of Sicily, and in 1296 the king's *logotheta* or lord chancellor (see Taurisano, *Miscellanea*, pp. 155–8; Walz, p. 147). Bartholomew is named as an authority by four other witnesses: Peter Grasso (VI), Henry Caracciolo (XL), James of Caiazzo (XLII), William of Tocco (LIX).

6. 'Brother James' is James of Caiazzo, O.P.; see XLII. Reginald of Priverno is the closest companion of Aquinas during his life in religion; his name is everywhere in our sources.

7. See LXXXIII and Note 81, below.

8. Both these gentlemen witnessed at the Enquiry: Filmarini's statement (XLIII) is omitted from this book; Henry Caracciolo's is below, XL.

9. See Gui, c. 37 (Note 85).

10. See XV, XIX, LXXX. Gui, cc. 38, 39 (Notes 87, 88).

11. See LII. Gui, c. 45 (Note 96).

12. See L. Gui, c. 37 (Note 86).

13. See LVIIIss.

14. Gui, cc. 38, 39 (Notes 87, 88).

15. This is Frances, wife of Count Annibaldo de Ceccano, whom Tocco (c. 56) and Gui (c. 37) call St. Thomas's *neptis*, niece; see Appendix I, *infra*. Scandone identified her with the daughter of a brother of the saint called Philip (*Miscellanea*, p. 81).

16. Gui, c. 45 (Note 96); and LII.

17. See XLIX. Gui, c. 44 (Note 96).

18. Gui, c. 48 (Note 96; cf. 53, 79).

19. A witness at the Enquiry, no. XXIV (omitted from this book).

20. See above, Note 3. Tocco stayed at Fossanova from early April to mid-July 1319.

21. Gui, c. 39 (Note 88).

22. John of Naples, a distinguished friar, regent of the Dominican *studium* at Naples; he bore witness at the Enquiry (XLVIII), but said little of biographical interest. In 1316, in a public disputation at Paris, John had maintained that the teaching of St. Thomas could be taught at Paris in respect of 'all its conclusions' (see Introduction, p. 4; cf. C. Jellouschek in *Xenia Thomistica*, III, pp. 73–104). This presupposed the condemnation of 1277 and the subsequent controversies; a condemnation which had seemed to many—and was intended by some—to include in its scope some specifically Thomist theses. Cf. Taurisano, *Miscellanea*, pp. 159–63; Grabmann, *Mittelalterliches Geistesleben*, I, pp. 374–84.

23. Cf. above, VI.

24. '. . . in pluribus aliis locis ultramontanis et citramontanis'—the phrase may refer to brother James's activities as ambassador for Charles II of Anjou (according to T. Valle, *Compendio degli più illustri padri della Provincia di Napoli*, Naples, 1651, p. 83; cited by Taurisano, *Miscellanea*, p. 178).

25. See Taurisano, *Miscellanea*, p. 178. Little is known of brother Peter; a survivor from the Naples community which knew St. Thomas, he is one of many witnesses to the importance, in the tradition, of Reginald of Priverno.

26. Another little-known figure (cf. Taurisano, *Miscellanea*, p. 179).

27. Another survivor presumably from the Naples community of 1272–4; but he had evidently known St. Thomas in the sixties also (Taurisano, *Miscellanea*, p. 179).

28. Urban IV (1261–4). Since St. Thomas returned from Paris to Italy certainly not before the autumn of 1259—and taught at Orvieto, 1261–5— brother Conrad's implicit statement that he had first seen the saint in 1257 must be a lapse of his ageing memory; see Walz, pp. 81–2.

29. See *supra*, VIII, *infra*, LXXX; and Notes to Gui's *Life*, 87, 88.

30. Cf. Gui, cc. 38, 39, 41 (Notes 87, 88, 92).

31. This is the most detailed account of the miracle of the herrings; cf. above, VIII and IX; Gui, c. 37 (Notes 85, 86).

32. No doubt a Dominican lay-brother. The custom of allowing Masters in Theology the services of a special attendant 'was gradually acquiring the force of law' in the Order, says Walz, p. 144. This James was such an attendant, though perhaps only for the journey. Another was Bonfiglio Coppa, when Thomas was ill at Naples in 1273 (Tocco, c. 54).

33. Gui, c. 44 (Note 96). Sub-prior John of Ferentino should not be confused with Prior James of Ferentino, mentioned in XLIX and XIX.

34. Gui, cc. 45–7 (Note 96).

35. On William of Tocco, see Introduction, pp. 6–8.

36. Cf. Grabmann, *Die Werke*, pp. 276, 461; Notes to Tolomeo, 16 and 31.

37. In his *Life* Tocco says that the preacher was Reginald of Priverno (c. 63), as do Gui (c. 41) and Calo (c. 20). The Cistercian Dom Peter (XLIX) says 'quidam frater Predicator qui fuerat longo tempore . . . fratris Thomae confessor'. This was Reginald, not Peter of Sezze. Tocco corrected his error before writing the final draft of his *Life*, in consequence of a vision; see Introduction, p. 8.

38. Cf. LXXXI. Gui, c. 15.

39. Gui, c. 16 (Note 48).

40. The miracle of the tooth is in Gui, c. 17. In the course of his enquiries preliminary to the canonisation of St. Thomas, Tocco twice visited Marsico in the Abruzzi, to see Thomas of San Severino, the son of the saint's younger sister the Countess Theodora; once in November 1316, and again in February 1318 (see LXII). The piety and the devotion to the Order of Preachers of Theodora and her son Thomas are warmly praised by Tocco, c. 37, and Calo, c. 20; see Note 80 to Gui's *Life*. Mandonnet in *Mélanges Thomistes*, p. 21, dates Tocco's first visit to Marsico in 1317, but this was corrected by Walz in *Xenia Thomistica*, III, p. 122.

41. Cf. Tolomeo, XXIII, cc. 8 and 10. Tocco met Tolomeo in Avignon (at the Curia, as he goes on to say) in July–August 1318. Tolomeo was writing his *Historia Ecclesiastica* in that city between 1313 and 1317 (so B. Schmeidler, introducing his edition of Tolomeo's *Annales* in *Monumenta Germaniae Historica: scriptores rerum Germ.*, new series, vol. VIII). Tolomeo was made bishop of Torcello in 1318, being then about eighty.

42. Cf. Tolomeo, XXIII, c. 10. Gui, c. 18 (Note 50).

43. Gui, c. 12 (Note 33).

44. See Taurisano, *Miscellanea*, p. 180.

45. Gui, c. 7 (Note 20).

46. According to Taurisano, *Miscellanea*, p. 147, this is probably the Robert of San Valentino, O.P., who presided at the provincial Chapter of the province of Sicily at Gaeta in 1317 as vicar for the Master General. It was this Chapter that commissioned Tocco to prepare the ground in view of the canonisation; see Walz, *Xenia Thomistica*, III, pp. 105 ss.

47. Lady Catherine de Morra was a daughter of William of San Severino and St. Thomas's sister Mary; and so a first cousin of Thomas of San Severino, the son of the saint's younger sister Theodora (*supra*, Note 40), though a good deal older than he; indeed in 1318, when Tocco met Lady Catherine, she was over seventy and 'comme la mémoire de la famille' (Mandonnet in *Mélanges Thomistes*, p. 22). Cf. Scandone, *Miscellanea*, pp. 64–6. The events recalled by Catherine are in Gui, cc. 1, 3–8 (Notes 2–23).

48. Dom Peter of Fondi's deposition at the Enquiry (XXXV–XXXIX) has scant biographical interest.

49. These two and many other miracles are recorded in the Supplement to Tocco's *Life*, *Fontes*, ed. Prümmer, pp. 145–60.

50. See above, Note 49.

51. This incident is not mentioned elsewhere by Tocco. But cf. Note 96 to Gui's *Life*.

52. A remarkably early witness to St. Thomas's life in the Order; through Anthony of Brescia and Nicholas of Marsillac we touch his first period as a Master at Paris, 1256–9, the period of the QQ. *de Veritate* and on the *de Trinitate* of Boethius. Cf. Walz, p. 76.

53. The *Contra Gentiles* was, according to Dondaine, 'almost certainly' written at Paris as far as Book III, ch. 45 (*Secrétaires de S. Thomas*, p. 92, n. 25). It was finished in Italy by 1264. This detail of the wretched paper used for that masterpiece is repeated in LXVII, where we learn that Anthony of Brescia heard it from brother Nicholas at Nicosia in Cyprus in September 1305 or 1306.

54. This incident took place, then, in January 1310 at Brescia. It is recorded in the Office for the feast of St. Thomas. It is given by Gui, c. 51, but not by Tocco.

55. Gui, c. 43 (Note 95).

56. See above, Note 53.

57. One of three allusions in the Enquiry to St. Thomas's sermons at Naples in the last year of his life, by men who heard him preach them; the other witnesses concerned being John Coppa (LXXXVII) and Peter Brancazio (XCIII). All three were laymen. Di Blasio recalls sermons on the 'Hail Mary', Coppa and Brancazio on the 'Our Father'; but all three say that they were preached in Lent. Mandonnet has shown that this must have been the Lent of 1273 and that there is good reason to hold that the saint's Lenten course for that year included homilies on the Creed, the 'Our Father' and the 'Hail Mary'. He would have preached, briefly, every day, the course extending from Sexagesima to Holy Week. See Mandonnet, 'Le Carême de S. Thomas d'Aquin à Naples (1273)' in *Miscellanea*, pp. 194–211. Di Blasio's mention of 'ten years' seems a gross error.

58. Cf. Tocco, c. 55.

59. See above, Note 5.

60. On the seven Dominicans mentioned in this paragraph see Taurisano, *Miscellanea*, pp. 120–6. Bartholomew is now (1319) in his late sixties; with these names of friars his memory goes back fifty years, to the Naples of 1265–75. Within this decade fell St. Thomas's period as regent of studies at S. Domenico. Those friars were associated in time and place with him. John of Caiazzo was later Provincial of the Roman Province and died after 1294. Troiano, a Neapolitan, was in his prime earlier, being Provincial in 1260–2 (Walz, p. 90) and Procurator General of the Order before 1269 (see *Documenta*, ed. Laurent, p. 571). Eufranone della Porta of Salerno was prior at Naples in 1269 and attended several General Chapters (see Note 79 to Gui's *Life*). For John of San Giuliano, see Gui, cc. 5, 8 (Note 11). Little is known of the three other friars named here (Taurisano, *Miscellanea*, p. 126, n. 1).

61. Gui, c. 3 (Note 5).

62. Gui, c. 4 (Note 9).

63. Gui, c. 5 (Note 11).

64. Gui, c. 6 (Notes 14, 15).

65. Gui, cc. 7, 8 (Notes 16–23).

66. A layman, apparently. For John of Caiazzo, see Note 60 above.

67. A detail we owe to Bartholomew; see below, LXXIX.

68. This is Richard, eldest son of Roger dell'Aquila, count of Traetto and Fondi, and St. Thomas's sister (or niece) Adelasia. Count Roger died in 1272, leaving St. Thomas as his executor; in which capacity the saint intervened, not only to settle the transmission of his dead relative's property and to pay his debts, but also to have the wardship of his four young nephews transferred from the royal procurator of 'Terra di Lavoro' (to whom the king, Charles I of Anjou, had entrusted them) to another brother-in-law, Roger, count of Marsico, the husband of Theodora d'Aquino (*Documenta*, ed. Laurent, pp. 575–9; Scandone, *Miscellanea*, pp. 67–76; Walz, pp. 153–4).

69. See Note 73 to Gui's *Life*.

70. Cf. Gui, c. 22 (Note 54).

71. Cf. Gui, c. 37 (Note 85). Bartholomew adds the names of Dean William and his nephew Roffredo. The party also included the lay-brother James of Salerno (see above, L, and Note 32).

72. Gui, c. 34 (Note 81). Bartholomew adds his authority's name, Nicholas of Malasorte, O.P. Charles II was king of Naples and Sicily, 1289–1309; the king of France must, then, be Philip the Fair, 1285–1314.

73. Gui, c. 27 (Note 63). In Bartholomew's account—the best we have of this sublime moment—there is a *lacuna* after 'Then Reginald, astonished . . .'; but probably we lack only some mention of a decision on the part of Reginald or St. Thomas to visit Theodora of San Severino. Only Bartholomew tells us that the vision happened at Naples, Tocco, Gui, and Calo placing it at San Severino. Perhaps the continuance of the saint's trance-like condition led to the two places being confused.

74. The series of witnesses is revealingly clear: Reginald (first hand) to John of Giudice, John to Bartholomew, Bartholomew to Tocco. Note that here Bartholomew is closer to the event (and such an event!) than even Tocco. Reginald is thought to have died, perhaps at Anagni, *c.* 1290 (Taurisano, *Miscellanea*, p. 120). Little is known of John of Giudice. He must have informed Bartholomew *c.* 1300–3, since Boniface VIII was 'captured' by William Nogaret, representing Philip the Fair, and Sciarra Colonna, on 7 September 1303. Pope Benedict XI (Nicholas Boccasini) was a Dominican and is 'beatified'.

75. Gui, cc. 37–40. Cf. VIII, X, XV, XIX, XLIX, etc. The stress on the swampiness of the soil is intended, of course, to show that the incorruption of St. Thomas's body was miraculous.

76. Here Bartholomew diverges slightly from the main tradition about the exhumations, as outlined above, in Note 96 to Gui's *Life*. Bartholomew alone speaks of an exhumation occasioned by the election of Bd. Innocent V (Peter of Tarentaise, O.P.) in January 1276; and of a decapitation which followed. This story is doubtful for four reasons: (*a*) Innocent V began to reign in 1276, not, as Bartholomew implies, before the end of 1274. (*b*) Bartholomew says nothing of the exhumation which certainly took place late in 1274, seven months after the saint's death. This suggests that he mistakenly associates this exhumation with the election of Innocent V. (*c*) We have eyewitness assurance that in 1281 or 1282 and later, in 1288, St. Thomas's body was re-exhumed and found whole and entire except that a thumb was missing. (*d*) Bartholomew is obviously vague as to the date of the removal of the saint's hand at the request of Countess Theodora; this happened fourteen years after St. Thomas's death, not, as Bartholomew implies, within the same year. For an outline of what really happened, according to the evidence, see Note 96 to the *Life* by Gui.

77. A feature of all Bartholomew's deposition is his great personal devotion to St. Thomas.

78. Cf. Gui, c. 46 (Note 97).

79. Gui, cc. 15, 16 (Note 44).

80. Cf. LXVII; Gui, c. 43. But of Albert's journey to Paris to defend his former pupil's teaching we learn only from Bartholomew: see Note 95 to

Gui's *Life* and Note 2 to Tolomeo. Hugh Borgognoni was several times prior of the Dominicans at Lucca and in 1299 provincial of the Roman province; he died in 1322; see Taurisano, *Miscellanea*, p. 180.

81. Bd. James of Viterbo and Giles of Rome were both Augustinian friars and both notable theologians, particularly the latter. Bd. James took his Master's degree at Paris in 1293, and in 1302 was appointed to the see of Naples by Boniface VIII; he died *c.* 1307. Giles of Rome is one of the great scholastics of the thirteenth century: born *c.* 1243, he taught in the faculties of arts and theology at Paris, becoming involved, as a keen follower of St. Thomas, in Bp. Tempier's condemnation of 1277—so much so, apparently, as to delay his becoming a Master in Theology until 1286. Giles was General of his Order in 1292, and in 1296 became archbishop of Bourges. He died at Avignon in 1316.

82. We shall see from Tolomeo (xxiii, c. 9) that in the first decades of the fourteenth century, St. Thomas was already being called 'doctor communis' at Paris; cf. Note 27 to Tolomeo. Bartholomew's report of the tribute of James of Viterbo is worth giving in Latin: '. . . in scriptis ipsius inveniuntur communis veritas, communis claritas, communis illuminatio, communis ordo et doctrina cito perveniendi ad perfectam intelligentiam'.

83. The speed of St. Thomas's literary production astonished his contemporaries; cf. Tocco, c. 17, Calo, c. 11, Gui, c. 32, Tolomeo, xxiii, c. 15.

84. Perhaps an allusion to Greek translations of St. Thomas (*Fontes*, ed. Prümmer, p. 385, note *a*). Walz, p. 170, takes this passage as a quotation from James of Viterbo, but in the text it does not appear so.

85. It is relevant to recall that Dante was a contemporary of Bartholomew; see especially *Paradiso*, x–xiii, for the poet's devotion to St. Thomas.

86. 2a, 2ae. cxlvii. 5 *ad* 3.

87. Bartholomew's list is more complete than Tolomeo's (xxiii, cc. 12–15). I omit it in order to save space and also because it would call for a more expert commentary than I could provide. Eschmann notes that 'the chronological indications of Bartholomew, as far as they go, are today accepted against those of Tolomeo of Lucca', *Catalogue*, p. 391. For information on the dates and circumstances of St. Thomas's works, the reader may consult the following Notes in this book: on Gui's *Life*, Notes 26, 29, 59, 77; on Tolomeo, Notes 12, 13, 16, 20, 21, 31–40. My authorities are chiefly Grabmann and Eschmann, and, being nothing of an expert in this matter, I limit myself to briefly reporting their conclusions.

88. Gui, c. 14 (Note 38).

89. See above, Note 57. John Coppa was perhaps a youth who did odd jobs in the house, 'un jeune serviteur de la maison', as Mandonnet says in *Miscellanea*, p. 203.

90. Gui, c. 36 (Note 84).

91. See above, Notes 57 and 89.

92. Little is known of John of Boiano, O.P. He was prior of Durazzo *c.* 1289, and later of Bari (Taurisano, *Miscellanea*, p. 180). He is our only informant that Reginald removed one of St. Thomas's thumbs—presumably before the first burial, March 1274; see Note 96 to Gui's *Life*.

93. A homelier version of the episode than we find in the biographers

(Tocco, c. 3, Calo, c. 2, Gui, c. 2). This conversation would have taken place *c.* 1311.

94. Peter Capotto, O.P.—or Cappucci, as Taurisano calls him, *Miscellanea*, p. 180—was from Benevento. A much-travelled man, like so many early Dominicans. Raymund Severi is also mentioned by Tocco, c. 27, as a witness to St. Thomas's purity, and with more details than are given by Capotto: Raymund was seven years with Thomas at Paris (presumably 1252–9), and they confessed to one another frequently; cf. Walz, pp. 76–7. The passage of the *Vitae Fratrum* referred to is IV, c. 24, section 8 (MOPH, ed. Reichert, p. 216). Cf. Gui, c. 12 (Note 33).

95. Taurisano, *Miscellanea*, p. 180, adds nothing about Thomas of Aversa, O.P. This young friar's visit to Salerno with Tocco was presumably late in 1317, before Tocco's visit to Marsico early in 1318; cf. LXII. Tocco, c. 50, confirms the gift of this hand to the Dominicans of Salerno by Thomas of San Severino, whose mother, the saint's youngest sister Theodora, obtained it at Fossanova in 1288; see Note 96 to Gui's *Life*; and above, Note 40.

III

From the 'Historia Ecclesiastica' of Tolomeo of Lucca

(VOL. XXII, CC. 17–25 AND C. 39)

17

. . . In this pope's time,[1] two great teachers flourished in the Order of Preachers; not that there were not others also famous for learning and virtue; but the pre-eminence of these two must allow them a special place in this narrative.

18

One was brother Albert the German, a man of noble achievement and great integrity as a servant of God in the Order. He was the most distinguished Master of his age, both for the width and variety of his knowledge and for the excellence of his method as a teacher. He has left us commentaries on the whole of Aristotle's logic and natural philosophy. On all that has to do with the experimental knowledge of nature Albert always wrote with extraordinary lucidity. He was also a theologian and wrote on the four books of the *Sentences*. In another work he discussed questions of natural science, classifying these as philosophy and as far as possible treating them in a philosophical way, while harmonising the philosophy with theology. He also explained a good deal of the Bible—the Gospels, the Epistles of Paul, the major and minor Prophets, the books of Solomon and Job. He began a *Summa* of theology, but got no farther than the first two volumes on the divine nature and the emanation of creatures.[2]

19

He was made bishop of Ratisbon in the duchy of Bavaria, a very honourable post; and for a while he submitted to the labours which this involved. But the episcopal office in Germany brings with it some excessively military occupations (no bishop is consecrated there without a sword), so that after a time, comparing his former peaceful state with the bondage in which he now found himself, Albert resolved not to rest until he had got the pope to accept his resignation. This he obtained, in fact, quite easily, being a very persuasive speaker; besides, of course, there was his great reputation for learning, and learning would clearly be the first thing to suffer amid those swords and lances.[3] His resignation once accepted, Albert chose to reside in the house of studies at Cologne, where he resumed his work as a lecturer and continued so for the rest of his life, about eighteen years; during which time he trained up many good scholars and wrote some of the works mentioned above. At last in 1280 he peacefully died, being already past his eightieth year. Although his scientific activity (and let this be a warning to others!) had declined a good deal from about three years before his death, owing to the failure of his memory—which hitherto, by a special grace, had been uncommonly powerful—this in no way impaired the piety with which he vigorously persevered in all the duties of a religious.[4]

20

The other great Master was brother Thomas of Aquino, himself a pupil of brother Albert. Brother Thomas was of noble birth, the son of a great lord of the kingdom of Apulia;[5] and he was nurtured in the manner befitting his rank. Some members of his family were put to death by Frederick, for their fidelity to the Church; but the family recovered under Charles.[6] As a boy Thomas was brought up by the black monks at the abbey of Monte Cassino, as is the way with noble youths of that region (for example, Maurus and Placid); and it was in the monastery that he took his first—and very promising—steps in logic and natural science; having always a private tutor in attendance on him, in the manner of the nobility in that part of the world.[7] When he had turned sixteen, however, he became a Friar Preacher and donned the habit that he was to wear with such purity and innocence for about thirty-two years.[8] But at first he had much to suffer at the hands of his relatives. For when the Master General of the Order (brother John the German, a world-famous man in his day) was conducting brother Thomas from Naples, where he had joined the Order, towards Paris, and they were beginning to cross Tuscany, they came upon Frederick himself, camped at one of his fortresses called Acquapendente. Now serving under Frederick was one of Thomas's brothers, the lord Reginald, a man of no small worth and at that time of high standing in Frederick's court, though later the emperor had him put to death. No sooner had Reginald heard that his brother was in the neighbourhood (Frederick meanwhile pretending not to know what was about to happen) than he took Peter of Vineis with him and some men at arms, and went and violently separated his brother from the Master General, and, forcing him to mount a horse, sent him off with a strong guard to one of the family castles in the Campagna called San Giovanni.[9]

21

There he remained a long time, hard pressed to throw off the habit of the Order; but neither threats nor coaxing nor anything else could make him waver in his holy purpose. No Friar Preacher was allowed access to him. However, through some persons in his confidence, he managed to arrange for some of the brethren to come under the castle wall on a certain night; his plan being to escape down a rope. And so it was done. And the friars had horses ready waiting to take Thomas to Rome.[10] Thence he went to Cologne, to brother Albert, and remained there a long time, in the course of which he was offered the abbacy of Monte Cassino by Alexander, as a favour to his parents who had by now been expelled from the kingdom; but he refused the offer.[11] At Cologne he learned much from others, though in any case his natural spontaneous intelligence—in which and the power of judgment he has had no equal—enabled him to discover much for himself. After this he went to Paris, being now twenty-five years old, and lectured on the *Sentences*. At Paris he received his 'contract', i.e. his licentiate in theology; and before becoming a Master he had written on the four books of the *Sentences*, and also some smaller works: one, which begins 'Domine ecce inimici tui sonuerunt', against William of Saint Amour; one on quiddity and being; a third on the principles of nature.[12]

22

After taking the degree of Master he wrote the Questions *de Veritate*; and then, as a Master now of three years' standing, returned to Italy in the pontificate of Urban IV (with whom our narrative must now concern itself).[13] His writing continued very fruitfully; and all this time, as we know from those who were with him at Paris, his mind was so continually engaged with every sort of problem, both active or purely speculative, that he seemed almost to live in a trance. He so devoted all his energies to God's service as to be utterly detached from this world even while dwelling in it.[14]

Let this suffice about brother Thomas in connection with the pontificate of Innocent IV—who was pope when he entered the Order—and with that of Alexander IV—under whom his qualities already revealed themselves so brilliantly. What remains to be told of him—and there is much indeed that is memorable—I reserve to my chapters on the three subsequent pontiffs. . . .

23

In the year 1261 (which was 2031 *ab urbe condita*) Urban IV began his pontificate, being elected on the feast of the Beheading of John the Baptist. He reigned three years and one month, after which the see was vacant for another five months. A Frenchman from the city of Troyes, he was Patriarch of Jerusalem at the time of his election, and had to come from overseas to take up office. At two ordinations he created two cardinals, the one his nephew the lord Anicherius, the other a Friar Preacher, brother Annibaldo, a nephew of the lord Richard degli Annibaldi. This brother Annibaldo was a Master in Theology, a very humble, sincere, and saintly man whom brother Thomas loved dearly. The writings on the *Sentences* ascribed to him are really only an abbreviation of brother Thomas's work.[15]

24

When, for definite reasons, brother Thomas had to be recalled from Paris, he did a great deal of literary work for Pope Urban; and this particularly in two ways. First, he wrote an exposition of the Gospels, combining passages from diverse authorities in such a way that they all seemed the work of one author—a task requiring considerable skill on the compiler's part, not to speak of the help of the Holy Spirit whose instrument he so admirably was. At this time, also, brother Bonaventure was flourishing in the Order of the Friars Minor; he was a Tuscan and a Master in Theology, of whom I shall have more to say later. Pope Urban had wished brother Bonaventure to write glosses on two of the Gospels, but when the latter pleaded his occupations as Minister General, the work was entrusted to our holy teacher, brother Thomas. And at this time Thomas—now directing the house of studies at Rome—also wrote commentaries covering the whole field of philosophy, both moral and natural, but with particular attention to ethics and mathematics, which he treated in a very striking and original way. The *Contra Gentiles* and the Questions *de Anima* also belong to the period of Urban's pontificate, besides the commentary on Job and various other minor works.[16]

By order of the same pope, brother Thomas also composed the Office for Corpus Christi—the second commission from the Pope to which I referred above. This Corpus Christi Office Thomas composed in full, including the Lessons and all the parts to be recited by day or night; the Mass, too, and whatever has to be sung on that day. An attentive reader will see that it comprises nearly all the symbolic figures from the Old Testament, clearly and appropriately relating them to the sacrament of the Eucharist.[17]

25

To this Office the Pope attached a large indulgence, available *in perpetuum* to all who should take part in it. The Office was later approved by Clement V in 1310, at the Council held at Vienne on the Rhône. . . .[18]

[The next few chapters are mostly concerned with the expedition to Italy of Charles of Anjou and the wars that followed. Chapter 28 notes the virtues of Pope Clement IV, who succeeded Urban IV in 1265 and died in 1268: he was buried in the church of the Friar Preachers (whom he 'loved much', notes Tolomeo) at Viterbo. Tolomeo returns to St. Thomas in Chapter 39.]

39

It was under this pope (Clement IV) that the fame of our brother Thomas shone out most gloriously. Clement wished to make him archbishop of Naples, with in addition the abbacy of St. Peter *ad Aram* in the arch-diocese, the revenues of which came to almost as much as the archbishopric itself; but Thomas declined both offers.[19] At this time he wrote the *Summa*, dividing it in three parts. The first part treats of natural theology and the natures of things, starting with the divine essence and going on to created beings. The second is moral theology, itself divided into two volumes: the first, called the *prima secundae*, treats of moral philosophy in a general way; the second, which we call the *secunda secundae*, is chiefly concerned with virtues and vices, and is all grounded upon and set out with texts and arguments from the philosophers and the authorities of the holy doctors. The third part of the *Summa*, and its fourth volume, we call Sacramental, since it deals with the sacraments and with the Incarnation of the Word; or it may be called the Conclusion, either as being the last part to be written or because the whole work comes to its conclusion in it. These three parts, then, of the *Summa* were written by brother Thomas almost entirely within the period covered by the pontificate of Clement IV and the vacancy that followed his death (which lasted two years and nine months; Vincent, however, says three years, because he includes a nine-months' 'vacancy' after Gregory had in fact been elected and had come to Viterbo).[20] During this period Thomas also wrote the Questions *de Spiritualibus Creaturis, de Malo,* and *de Virtutibus.*[21]

(VOL. XXIII, CC. 1, 2; 8–16)

I

So in the year of our Lord 1271, Gregory X was elected to the Chair of Peter. He reigned (if we count from the start of his effective use of authority, not from the actual election) four years and ten days. A Lombard of the family of the Visconti of Piacenza and an archdeacon of Liège, he was away on a pilgrimage to the Holy Land at the time of his election; but, on getting word of this—from Viterbo, where the cardinals were gathered—he returned by sea and crossed the kingdom of Apulia. King Charles went to meet him at Capua. Then he came to Viterbo, where the cardinals were, accepted the papacy, and went to Rome to be crowned and consecrated.[22]

2

He created some worthy cardinals, including two Masters in Theology: one, a Friar Preacher, brother Peter of Tarentaise, archbishop of Lyons and later bishop of Ostia; a truly pious and learned man who for a long while had been regent of studies in the theological faculty: the other, brother Bonaventure of the Friars Minor, also a Master in Theology as well as Minister General of his Order; a very gracious and gifted Tuscan with a fine command of language. Bonaventure wrote commentaries on the *Sentences* and on parts of the Bible—the books of Solomon and Job and the Epistles of Paul. Gregory made him bishop of Albano. . . .[23]

8

It was about this time that that famous teacher, brother Thomas of Aquino, departed to God. Summoned to the Council by the lord Gregory, he left Naples, where he was regent of studies, and was on his way through the Campagna when he fell seriously ill; and, there being no Dominican house in the neighbourhood, he turned aside to a great Cistercian abbey called

Fossanova which lay within the patronage of a kinsman of his, the lord of Ceccano. During his stay in the abbey the sickness grew worse, until the day came when he passed from this world to Christ; his mind fervent, his soul and body adorned with that purity which had ever invigorated his life in the Order. He was one of the best men I have known, and I knew him well: I have often heard his confession and we lived together for a long time on familiar terms; besides which, I was his pupil.[24]

There are accounts of many miracles having occurred at the place where he died, God choosing to manifest his holiness in this way. And therefore his relatives, who are powerful people in the Campagna, have not allowed his body to be taken away; indeed, on hearing that his brethren in the Order were trying to obtain the body, they hid it; although it had been very honourably interred in the sanctuary of the high altar of the abbey church.[25]

9

The monks of the abbey, and the Friar Preachers who were there at the time, tell us that when brother Thomas felt the approach of death he first devoutly pronounced the Creed, and then summarised his own doctrine—what he had taught and written in defence of the Faith and for the instruction of the faithful.[26] And let me say here that this man is supreme among modern teachers of philosophy and theology, and indeed in every subject. And such is the common view and opinion, so that nowadays in the University of Paris they call him the 'doctor communis' because of the outstanding clarity of his teaching.[27] Nevertheless, for greater security, and because he too—as blessed Augustine said of himself—was a mere man and therefore fallible, and also out of reverence for the Roman Church and a desire to give it honour, brother Thomas now submitted his works to the judgment of that Church, as the Catholic and Apostolic faith requires. And he repeated this submission several times; after which, he slept in the Lord.[28]

And while this was taking place a certain holy brother from the Abruzzi, then at Naples, had a vision concerning brother Thomas. He seemed to see the venerable teacher in his chair at Naples lecturing to a distinguished audience which included the lord Martin, archbishop of Capua and formerly a vice-chancellor of the Roman Church; who was also a doctor of both canon and civil law, yet a good philosopher too. There was also present Matthew, archbishop of Salerno, a man adorned with both sacred and secular wisdom; besides a great number of clerics and religious. Into this company suddenly blessed Paul came; he entered by the door, very suitably attended, and greeted everybody. And our venerable teacher, recognising blessed Paul, did him due reverence; after which they engaged in conversation, and our teacher enquired of blessed Paul whether his explanations of the Epistles were in agreement with their author's meaning. To which the Apostle replied that those explanations were as adequate as was possible in this life, but that the time was approaching when brother Thomas would understand their meaning perfectly. Then he took Thomas by the hem of his cloak and led him away. And seeing this in his dream, the aforesaid brother began to call out, 'Help, brothers! Help!' Then, waking up, he gave a clear account of his vision. And three days later a messenger arrived from the Campagna to tell us of the death of our father and master.[29]

10

I ought to mention a sign of his holiness which I myself saw. On one occasion when he and I were travelling together from Rome, he chose to turn aside to Molara, the dwelling of the lord cardinal Richard; and there both he and his *socius*, brother Reginald, fell ill—he of the tertian fever and Reginald of a recurrent fever. Reginald was dangerously ill; the critical symptoms had appeared and the cardinal's doctors took a very serious view of the case. Then the holy master took some relics of blessed Agnes which he was bringing from Rome (having a devotion to that saint) and gave them to Reginald, telling him to place them on his body and have perfect confidence. Reginald did so, and was cured, although the doctors had given him up. To commemorate the event brother Thomas decided to arrange that every year, when the feast of St. Agnes came round, the brethren should celebrate it with special solemnity and a good dinner. This they did in that same year; but next year brother Thomas himself passed away to God. He died in his fiftieth year (though some say his forty-eighth), having been twenty years a Master in Theology.[30]

I I

It was under the pope whose reign I am narrating at present that he wrote the last part of the *Summa*, which we call *sacramentalis* because it deals with the sacraments and the Incarnation of the Word—with those articles of the Creed, that is, which concern the humanity of the Word. But this part of the *Summa* was cut short by the writer's death. To this period also belong the Questions on the power of God and on creatures; and also, in the field of philosophy, the unfinished commentaries on the *de Coelo* and the *de Generatione*; and another, also unfinished, on the *Politics*. These works were, however, completed by his devoted disciple Peter of Auvergne, a Master in Theology and a notable philosopher, who was later the bishop of Clermont.[31]

As well as his many long works, the subject-matter of which called for an ample style of exposition, brother Thomas left a number of shorter writings composed on various occasions in reply to questions put to him by rulers and other persons. You may find these bound up in one volume, like the letters of Augustine. Here is a list of them in the usual order.[32]

I 2

De actionibus et operationibus occultis naturae: written for some knight across the Alps, and beginning 'Quoniam in quibusdam naturalibus corporibus'.

Utrum liceat uti judicio astrorum: written for brother Reginald, which begins 'Quia petisti ut tibi'.

De substantiis separatis: also written for brother Reginald, beginning 'Quia sacris angelorum solemniis'.

De principiis naturae: written for brother Silvester, which begins 'Nota quod quoddam potest esse, licet non sit'.

De sortibus (on whether one may cast lots): written for James de Burgo, beginning 'Postulavit me vestra dilectio'.

De ente et essentia: written before he became a Master, for his fellow-students in the Order. It begins 'Quia parvus error in principio'.

De rationibus fidei: addressed to the cantor of Antioch, beginning 'Beatus Petrus apostolus'.

Contra errorem Averrois circa intellectum humanum: which begins 'Sicut, omnes homines'.

De aeternitate mundi (whether this be possible): beginning 'Supposito, secundum fidem nostram'.

De expositione primae decretalis: addressed to the archdeacon of Trent and beginning 'Salvator noster'.

De articulis fidei et ecclesiae sacramentis: written for the archbishop of Palermo, which begins 'Postulavit a me vestra dilectio'.

Contra errores Gaecorum: written at the request of Pope Urban and beginning 'Libellum ab excellentia vestra'.

Responsiva super xxvi articulis: for the lector of Venice, beginning 'Lectis vestris litteris inveni'.

13

Determinatio quorundam casuum: addressed to the countess of Flanders and beginning 'Excellentiae vestrae litteras recepi'.

Responsiva quarundam questionum: written for brother John of Vercelli, Master General of the Order, which begins 'Reverendo in Christo patri'.

Responsiva to certain questions put by Gerard of Besançon, beginning 'Carissimi filii in Christo'.

De fide et spe: beginning 'Aeterni Patris Filius'.

Contra impugnantes religionem: beginning 'Ecce inimici tui sonuerunt'.

De regimine principum: written for the king of Cyprus, which begins 'Cogitanti mihi quid offerem'.

De motu cordis: beginning 'Quia omne quod movetur'.

De fato (whether fate exists): beginning 'Quaeritur de fato, an sit'.

Contra retrahentes a religione: beginning 'Christianae religionis'.

De elementis in mixto: on the mode of being of such elements, which begins 'Dubium apud multos'.

De absolutione et modo absolvendi: written for the Master General named above and beginning 'Perlecto libello'.

De perfectione vitae spiritualis: which begins 'Quoniam quidam perfectionis ignari'.

Quod lex amoris fuerit necessaria homini: beginning 'Tria sunt homini necessaria'. Note that this work is sometimes called the *Liber de praeceptis.*

14

Quod beata Virgo excedit angelos in plenitudine gloriae et gratiae: which begins 'Ave gratia plena'.

Expositio symboli: beginning 'Credo in unum Deum'.

De infantibus: which begins 'Quomodo circa naturam Verbi'.

De principio individuali: which begins 'Quoniam duo sunt potentiae cognoscitivae'.

De genere: beginning 'Quomodo omnis creatura'.

De natura materiae accusantis: which begins 'Quoniam omnis cognitio humana'.

De natura materiae: beginning 'Postquam de principiis'.

Besides all these minor works our author also wrote one on the Divine Names,[33] one on Boethius's book about happiness,[34] and one on the *Liber de Causis.*[35] He is also said to have compiled a concordance to his works.

15

Moreover, he gave an exposition of logic for the benefit of certain noblemen who were students in Arts, explaining modal propositions and fallacies—in all, a very clear introduction to the subject. He wrote, too, commentaries on the *Posterior Analytics* and the *Perihemeneias.*[36] What an output it all was! What a marvellous abundance of work produced in a lifetime that was relatively—compared with that of other doctors—so short!

Nor have we done yet. There are the Questions *de quolibet,*[37] which clear up many difficulties and are full of deep thought; and then, too, many useful writings in the form of notes taken by hearers of his lectures and later read and corrected by himself. Such are the glosses on all the Epistles of Paul, except *Romans*; for the notes on *Romans* (which I have seen and read) he wrote himself.[38] There is also the commentary on John, of which he wrote cc. 1–5; but the rest are students' notes revised by him. He also wrote on Isaiah, but this work is rare.[39]

Let this suffice on the venerable Master. (But let me add that while at Rome, and already a Master in Theology—it is a period I have touched on in an earlier chapter—he wrote a second version of the first part of his commentary on the *Sentences*: I saw this once at Lucca, but then someone took it away and I never saw it again.)[40]

16

Gregory X was still reigning when the troubles at Bologna between the Lambertazzi and the Geremei came to a head: the former, with their Ghibelline supporters, were banished from the city and almost completely ruined in 1273. So much for Gregory X and the chief things said and done in his time. He died, as the *Gesta Gallicanorum* says, and as I have already noted, on 10 January.[41]

In this pope's days flourished brother Romanus, a Friar Preacher, brother of the lord Mathew Rubeus and a nephew of Nicholas III; a man of great distinction in life and learning and a Master in Theology. It was he who succeeded to brother Thomas's chair at Paris; but in the following year he passed on to Christ, after which brother Thomas had a dream about him. And in his dream Thomas asked Romanus how things were with him, and the latter answered that things were well with him. Then Thomas asked him about the vision of the divine essence, whether it corresponded to what is written about it; to which brother Romanus, smiling a little, replied that the manner of it was nobler, and that brother Thomas would know this for himself before long. And with this he vanished. But the event proved him a prophet, for in the following year our glorious teacher departed to God. Thomas himself told me of this vision, and he seemed happy when he spoke of it.[42]

NOTES ON TOLOMEO OF LUCCA

1. Alexander IV (Rinaldo de' Conti); elected pope, 12 December 1254, died at Viterbo, 25 May 1261. He renewed the privileges of the Mendicant Orders, which Innocent IV had revoked; see Note 6 in Section IV (A).

2. St. Albert, the greatest *savant* of his time, was born at Lauingen in

Swabia, perhaps in 1206, but more probably before 1200 (this would agree with Tolomeo, who will tell us that Albert was past eighty at his death, which certainly took place in 1280). He became a Dominican while a student at Padua, probably in 1223. After teaching in Germany he held one of the two Dominican chairs of theology at the University of Paris, from 1245 at the latest. From 1248 to 1254 Albert was regent of the new *studium* at Cologne (see Note 24 to Gui's *Life*) with Thomas Aquinas as one of his pupils until 1252. He was provincial of Germany after 1254, and in 1259 took a leading part in planning the reorganisation of studies in his Order at the General Chapter of Valenciennes. In 1260 the pope made him bishop of Ratisbon (Regensburg) much against the will of the Master General, Humbert of Romans; but Albert was able to resign this charge in 1262. After a period of preaching in Germany he returned to the work of teaching in Dominican *studia*, being at Cologne again *c.* 1270. He attended the Council of Lyons in 1274, and two years later returned to Paris to defend the doctrine of St. Thomas against the anti-Aristotelian theologians, but failed to prevent the inclusion of some Thomist theses in Bp. Tempier's condemnation of 1277 (see Canonisation Enquiry, LXXXII, Note 80). Albert died at Cologne, full of years and honour, on 15 November 1280. He was canonised by Pius XI in 1931.

Tolomeo expresses himself rather vaguely about Albert's works, though rightly stressing, by implication, the enormous labours on the Aristotelian *corpus*, especially with regard to natural science. The work on the *Sentences* was written *c.* 1245. The 'other work' mentioned may be the early *Summa de creaturis* or perhaps the commentary on the *De causis*. On Albert's part in relating the Aristotelian notion of science to theology, see the pregnant essay of Chenu, *La théologie comme science au XIIIe siècle* (Bibliothèque Thomiste, 1943). The *Summa theologiae* was Albert's last work and, as Tolomeo notes, is unfinished.

3. Albert seems to have been an excellent bishop, if a reluctant one (see T. M. Schwertner, *St. Albert the Great*, pp. 101–19). Tolomeo's remarks on this episcopal interlude in Germany sound very Italian, and remind one of Petrarch's horror of the 'tedesca rabbia' (canzone, *Italia mia*).

4. In fact, Albert was not at Cologne for the last eighteen years of his life but for about ten years, with intervals elsewhere. Since he made a will 'sanus et incolumis' in January 1279, his decline may have set in later than Tolomeo says.

5. Cf. Gui, c. 1. The whole southern end of Italy was sometimes called Apulia (in Italian 'Puglia'); cf. Dante, *De vulgari eloq.*, I, x, 7; *Inferno*, XXVIII, 9.

6. Cf. Gui, cc. 20, 21 (Note 53); and *infra*, Note 2, on Section IV(A). 'Frederick' is of course the Emperor Frederick II, 1194–1250; 'Charles' is Charles of Anjou, brother of St. Louis IX; he won the kingdom of Sicily from Frederick's natural son Manfred by the battle of Benevento in 1266. This meant the end of the Hohenstaufen power in Italy, a fact most agreeable to the rulers of the Church, though they were to find Charles a 'tiresome' ally as Walz remarks, p. 110. As a Guelf, however, Tolomeo is inclined to see good in him.

7. Cf. Gui, c. 3 (Note 5); Walz, pp. 13–14. Tolomeo does not mention Thomas's period in the University of Naples.

8. Cf. Gui, c. 5 (Note 11). Tolomeo's dates are often vague. If we suppose that he knew St. Thomas died in 1274—the date given, unanimously, by Tocco, Gui, Calo, and the witnesses at the Canonisation Enquiry—then Tolomeo seems here to imply that St. Thomas entered the Order in 1242 or late in 1241; and that, being then sixteen, the saint was born not earlier than 1225 and probably in 1226. And in the next chapter he will apparently imply a birth-date as late as 1227, since he makes Thomas twenty-five on his return from Cologne to Paris, which we know to have been in 1252 (see Note 29 to Gui's *Life*). The earlier dates in Thomas's life are naturally the most disputed, but, by the usual chronology—birth, 1224–5, entry into the Order, 1243–4, the baccalaureate, 1252—Tolomeo makes Thomas one or two years too young at these last two occasions.

9. Cf. Gui, cc. 5, 6 (Notes 14–16); *Vitae Fratrum*, MOPH, I, p. 201. Tolomeo is with de Frachet in bringing John the German on to the scene already, whereas in Gui and Tocco he is not mentioned until after St. Thomas's release from prison when, as Tocco says, 'brother John . . . the Master General received him as a dear son in Christ, and took him to Paris and then to Cologne' (c. 12). On the death of Reginald d'Aquino, see Notes 52 and 53 to Gui's *Life*, and Note 2 in Section IV (A). For the passage running from 'For when' to 'Acquapendente' I adopt Mandonnet's correction of the text as printed in Muratori (*Rev. Thomiste*, VII (1924), p. 247, note 1).

10. Cf. Gui, cc. 7, 8 (Notes 17, 18, 20–3); *Vitae Fratrum*, MOPH, I, p. 201. Tolomeo is again with de Frachet in ignoring the attempted seduction which the other sources stress so much; and also in saying that no Dominican could visit Thomas in prison, against the 'Neapolitan' tradition concerning the visits of John of S. Giuliano, which passed through Tocco to Gui and Calo, and was expressed at the Canonisation Enquiry by Bartholomew of Capua. Tolomeo also omits Thomas's mother's part in the release (cf. Note 23 to Gui's *Life*).

11. Cf. Gui, c. 9 (Notes 24 and 28); c. 34 (Note 82). 'Alexander' is a mistake: Alexander IV only began his pontificate in 1254 when Thomas had already been in Paris two years; Innocent IV (1243–54) must be meant.

12. Cf. Gui, cc. 9 and 10 (Notes 25–7) for the period at Cologne; c. 11 (Notes 28, 29) for the transit to Paris; c. 12 (Notes 30–3) for the promotion to the Master's degree. Tolomeo naturally singles out the great commentary on the *Sentences* as the chief work of Thomas as Bachelor (1254–6). The work against William of St. Amour is the *Contra impugnantes Dei cultum et religionem* (1256), a refutation of William's anti-friar tract *De periculis novissimorum temporum*. The *De ente et essentia* may be Thomas's first written work, perhaps finished in 1254; it is dedicated to 'my brothers and companions', i.e. to his fellow-students and scholars at St. Jacques. The *De principiis naturae* was written about the same time and dedicated to 'brother Silvester'.

13. The 253 'questions' collected under the title *De veritate* are the major product of the years 1256–9. Tolomeo is again wrong here, for Alexander IV was still pope when St. Thomas returned to Italy towards the end of 1259. The slip may be due to the importance that Tolomeo attaches to the enlightened patronage of Urban IV—a pope whom the historians write off as a failure in politics, but to whom Christian culture owes far more than is commonly realised (see below, Notes 16 and 17). For Thomas's sojourn in

Italy in the 1260s, see Mandonnet in *Xenia Thomistica*, III, pp. 9–40 (in Latin; French translation, *Thomas d'Aquin, Lecteur à la Curie Romaine*, offprint, Rome, Vatican, 1924). In 1262 Thomas was made a 'Preacher General', an honour which entailed the obligation of attendance at the annual Chapters of the Roman province and consequently much travelling in central Italy as the Chapters moved from city to city (Orvieto, Perugia, Rome, Viterbo, Anagni, etc.).

14. Cf. Gui, cc. 15, 28, 32, which refer especially to the Parisian period, 1252–9.

15. On Cardinal degli Annibaldi, O.P., see AOP (1925), p. 190, and Note 38 to Gui's *Life*.

16. As often, Tolomeo's information is somewhat off-hand. What, for example, were the definite reasons ('ex certis causis') which brought Thomas to Italy in 1259? We are not told and scholars disagree (Walz, p. 88). Anyhow Thomas seems to have followed the Roman Curia from Anagni (1259–61?) to Viterbo and Orvieto (1261–5), and then, after an interval at his own province's *studium* at Rome, S. Sabina (1265–7), he returned to the Curia, under Clement IV, at Viterbo (1267–8). Tolomeo stresses the amount of work that Urban IV's patronage drew from St. Thomas. For the glosses on the Gospels, the *Catena aurea*, see Note 76 to Gui's *Life*. The philosophical work mentioned must be the great series of commentaries on Aristotle, beginning perhaps in 1265, for which St. Thomas now had the valuable co-operation of the Flemish Dominican Hellenist, William of Moerbeke, whom he seems to have met at Orvieto (Walz, pp. 103–5; Grabmann, *Mittelalterliches Geistesleben*, I, pp. 266–313; G. Verbeke, *Themistius, Commentaire sur le traité de l'Ame d'Aristote*, etc., pp. ix ss.). The *Contra Gentiles* was finished in 1264 (see Note 53 to Canonisation Enquiry). The extremely thorough *Quaestio disputata de Anima* may fall as late as 1269 (cf. Chenu, *Introduction*, p. 242) along with the commentary on Job (*ibid.*, p. 210).

St. Bonaventure (1221–74) had become Minister General of the Franciscans in 1257.

17. See Note 40 to Gui's *Life*; Tocco, c. 17. Tolomeo's is the only strictly contemporary witness to St. Thomas's authorship of the Corpus Christi office (Eschmann, *Catalogue*, p. 424): cf. Walz, pp. 97–8, and for references to studies touching the saint's sources and models, Chenu, *Introduction*, pp. 295–6.

18. Tolomeo is a year or two out; the Ecumenical Council of Vienne was held in 1311–12.

19. Cf. Gui, c. 34 (Note 82).

20. Clement IV began to reign in February 1265 and died in November 1268. Nearly three years followed before the election of his successor, Gregory X, on 1 September 1271; and another seven months before Gregory was crowned, on 23 March 1272. Tolomeo allows, then, about eight years for the composition of the *prima pars* and the two divisions of the *secunda pars* of the *Summa theologiae*; but in fact it was probably not begun before 1266. Tolomeo does not include the *tertia pars* in this period, for he will say (XXIII, c. 11) that it was written under Gregory X and left unfinished at Thomas's death—therefore 1272–4. Consequently, by 'three parts', where this phrase occurs the second time, I understand 'three volumes', in the sense

in which Tolomeo calls the *tertia pars* a fourth volume. The sentence in brackets is clearly corrupt as Muratori prints it, and is here altered to make sense. I do not know who 'Vincent' was; he could hardly be Vincent of Beauvais who died in 1264. For the date of the *Summa theologiae*, see Grabmann, *Die Werke*, pp. 296–301, 462; Eschmann, *Catalogue*, pp. 386–8.

21. It is notoriously difficult to date the *Quaestiones disputatae*: that on 'spiritual creatures' is generally placed in the Italian period, but most scholars date the other two mentioned here between 1269 and 1272; see Walz, pp. 93, 124; Eschmann, *Catalogue*, pp. 389–91.

22. Bd. Gregory X (Tedaldo Visconti) was elected on 1 September 1271, and crowned on 23 March 1272. He died at Arezzo, after the Council of Lyons, in January 1276. The king is Charles of Anjou, king of Naples and Sicily, 1266–85.

23. Peter of Tarentaise (Bd. Innocent V) is one of the great Dominicans of the thirteenth century. Born *c*. 1224, he taught theology at Paris from 1259 to 1264, and again from 1267 to 1269—an uncommonly long tenure of a Master's chair, as Tolomeo suggests. Peter was also twice provincial of his Order in France; and one of the committee of theologians, along with Aquinas and Albert the Great, who, at the Chapter of Valenciennes in 1259, recommended that philosophy be an essential part of the Dominican training. Gregory X made him archbishop of Lyons in 1272, and in 1273 a cardinal. He took part in the Council of Lyons in 1274, when it fell to him to preach the panegyric of St. Bonaventure who died in July of that year. On the death of Gregory (10 January 1276) Peter was elected pope (Innocent V), but he died only five months later. He was declared 'blessed' in 1898.

Bonaventura Fidanza, born in 1221 at Bagnorea near the lake of Bolsena (and now in Lazio, south of the Tuscan border), was the greatest Franciscan thinker of his age. He took the Master's degree, along with St. Thomas, in 1257, but in the same year his teaching was interrupted by election to the highest office in his Order, that of Minister General. Made a cardinal in 1273, he was at the Council of Lyons but died before it ended, on 14 July 1274. Dante glorifies him in the *Paradiso* along with SS. Thomas and Albert (cantos x–xiii). The commentary on the *Sentences* stemmed from his teaching at Paris, 1250–4. One may note that Tolomeo ignores Bonaventure's most lastingly famous works, the *Reductio artium ad theologiam* and the magnificent *Itinerarium mentis in Deum*. The latter was written on the holy mountain of the Stigmata, La Verna, Dante's 'crudo sasso' (*Paradiso*, xi, p. 106), in 1259.

24. Cf. Gui, cc. 37–9 (Notes 85–8). Tolomeo's personal acquaintance with St. Thomas is obviously important, but it could not have begun before the saint's return to Italy in 1259–60. They may have met between 1261 and 1265 at Viterbo or Orvieto, and were probably together at Rome, 1265–7. After St. Thomas's second return to Italy in 1272 he certainly travelled from Rome to Naples with Tolomeo (see below, c. 10). The final phrase renders 'ac ipsius auditor fui', which surely implies attendance at a full course of Thomas's lectures: this may well have been at S. Sabina, Rome, where the saint lectured in 1265–7; and Tolomeo also was probably his pupil at Naples, 1272–3. We know that Tolomeo completed the unfinished *De regimine principum*, probably between 1301 and 1303. According to Schmeidler (p. xxxi of his edition of the

Annales), Tolomeo returned to Tuscany in 1274 or not much later. In 1276 he was at the General Chapter at Pisa, and by about 1281 he was writing the anti-Imperialist tract *Determinatio compendiosa de jurisdictione imperii*, perhaps at the request of the Guelf government of his own city, Lucca (ed. M. Krammer in *Fontes Juris Germanici Antiqui*, Hanover and Leipzig, 1909).

25. Cf. Gui, cc. 42 ss. (Notes 96, 97); Canonisation Enquiry, LXXXI. But whereas our other sources lay this charge—implicitly at least—at the door of the monks of Fossanova, Tolomeo puts all the blame on the relatives of St. Thomas—a curious difference. It is not clear what the 'accounts' ('historiae') are to which he refers here. Prümmer's suggestion that this is a reference to some common source for all the early biographers of Aquinas (*Fontes*, p. 61) is carefully considered and rejected by Pelster, who himself proposes either Tolomeo's own *Annales* (*c.* 1306), which mention St. Thomas, or, as more probable, the *Flores Cronicorum* of Bernard Gui (*c.* 1315). Gui and Tolomeo were at Avignon together 1315–17 when the latter was writing his *Historia ecclesiastica* (see Pelster, *Die älteren Biographen*, etc., pp. 261 ss.).

26. Cf. Gui, c. 39 (Note 88).

27. Cf. Canonisation Enquiry, LXXXIII (Note 82). St. Thomas was called 'doctor communis' before 'doctor angelicus' (Walz, *Xenia Thomistica*, III, p. 164, note 4); and the older title was particularly emphasised by Pius XI in the encyclical *Studiorum ducem* (1923).

28. Cf. Gui, c. 39 (Note 88).

29. Cf. Gui, c. 42 (Note 94). On this archbishop of Capua (Marino of Eboli, not Martin), see Note 60 to Gui's *Life*. The archbishop of Salerno, Matthew della Porta, had a particular devotion to Thomas and the Dominicans, to whom he gave the site for a priory at Salerno in March 1272 (*Documenta*, ed. Laurent, p. 573). This passage, of course, proves Tolomeo's presence at Naples early in 1274.

30. Cf. Gui, c. 18 (Note 50); Walz, p. 142. For the phrase 'the critical symptoms had appeared' I use the version given by Walz. Muratori followed by Taurisano (*Miscellanea*, p. 185), has 'et cum *non* apparerent in eo signa cretica', which hardly makes sense.

St. Thomas was in fact a Master in Theology for less than twenty years, from 1256 (see Notes to Gui's *Life*, 30 and 33) to his death in 1274.

31. The pope is still Gregory X. The remarks on the *Summa*, 3a *pars* complete those in Book XXII, c. 39 (see above, Note 20). The 'Questions' are the *QQ. disputatae* 'De potentia', and though the text is not clear, I take it that 'on creatures' refers to this same series which in fact includes much on the 'power' of creatures. The *De spiritualibus creaturis* was mentioned separately in XXII, c. 39. Nowadays the *De potentia* is dated earlier, perhaps to Thomas's Roman period and, anyhow, to before 1268 (Eschmann, *Catalogue*, p. 391). The commentary on Aristotle's *De coelo et Mundo*, which Eschmann (p. 402) calls the 'high water mark of St. Thomas's expository skill', belongs probably to 1271–2; that on the *De generatione et corruptione* to 1272–3. In Canonisation Enquiry, LVIII, Tocco says that he saw Aquinas writing the latter work at Naples and that it was his last 'in philosophy'. The commentary on the *Politics* may belong to a slightly earlier phase, perhaps contemporary with the two divisions of the second part of the *Summa theologiae* (1269–71?). See

Eschmann, *Catalogue*, pp. 402–5. Peter of Auvergne was a Master at Paris, 1296–1302; bishop of Clermont in 1302; died in 1304. He completed the commentary on the *Politics* (from III, c. 6) and perhaps also that on the *De coelo*.

32. In the three next chapters are listed most of the *opuscula* of St. Thomas. I refrain from comment for the reason given in Note 87 to the Canonisation Enquiry. Eschmann objects to the category *opuscula* as a meaningless 'catch-all', and breaks the miscellany up into more rational divisions: *Catalogue*, pp. 381, 407–23.

33. Eschmann, *Catalogue*, p. 406. Cf. Note 26 to Gui's *Life*.

34. One might suppose that the *De consolatione philosophiae* is meant; but there is no extant writing of St. Thomas on this work of Boethius, but only on the less famous *De trinitate* and *De hebdomadibus* (the third of the theological tractates, *Quomodo substantiae*, etc.); Eschmann, *Catalogue*, pp. 405–6.

35. Eschmann, *Catalogue*, p. 407.

36. Eschmann, *Catalogue*, p. 401. The first sentence of this chapter is rendered according to Mandonnet's correction of the text in Muratori (*Rev. Thomiste*, VIII, p. 407).

37. Eschmann, *Catalogue*, p. 392.

38. According to Bartholomew of Capua (Canonisation Enquiry, LXXXV, *Fontes*, ed. Laurent, p. 389), St. Thomas's exposition of St. Paul's epistles remains in notes taken by Reginald of Priverno so far as the whole series from I Corinthians 11 to Hebrews inclusively is concerned; only those on Romans and I Corinthians 1–10 being written by the saint. Scholars have corrected this statement in details, but it is agreed that the commentary on Romans is first-hand St. Thomas (see Eschmann, *Catalogue*, p. 399).

39. The student whose notes completed the commentary on John is again Reginald of Priverno, but it is uncertain whether, as Tolomeo asserts, St. Thomas revised this part of the work. The commentary on Isaiah seems to be an early work (1256–9) and survives partly in autograph. On all this, see Eschmann, *Catalogue*, pp. 395–8.

40. For the commentary on the *Sentences*, see Eschmann, *Catalogue*, p. 384; cf. Walz, p. 66. If Tolomeo really saw a second version of the first part, it must have since been lost. Gui, c. 53, repeats Tolomeo on this point. See the Supplementary Note to Gui's *Life*, p. 81 *supra*.

41. My search through the indices of the many-volumed *Histoire littéraire de la France* has failed to identify the *Gesta Gallicanorum*. Schmeidler, in his account of Tolomeo's sources for the *Annales* (*ed. cit.*, pp. xxiss.) mentions the *Gesta Francorum*, and this may be the work referred to.

42. Cf. Gui, c. 19 (Note 51); Tocco, c. 45.

IV

17

III. There was a brother of very noble birth from the neighbourhood of Rome, whom his relatives waylaid while he was on his
way to Paris with the Master of the Order, brother John, who
was taking him thither for the furtherance of his studies.[1] His
relatives counted on the support of the emperor—as he then was
—the lord Frederick, in whose service they then were.[2] They
took the youth to a remote castle and held him there for almost
a year, taking care that none of the brethren should have access
to him, even by letter. Moreover, they did all they could, through
his friends and in other ways, to shake his resolution; but he, by
the power of God that was in him, inflexibly withstood all their
efforts to make him discard the habit or do anything else against
the laws of the Order.[3] Finally they let him go, despairing of
ever inducing him to change his mind; so he, returning to the
brethren, was sent to Paris and became a Master in Theology,
a man of great learning and a pillar of the Order.[4] (Ed. Reichert,
p. 201.)

24

VI. A brother who was a Master at Paris, a famous man whose
life and teaching have been of great service to the Church of
God, had a dream at Paris at the time when the Master of the
Order was being hard put to it, in the court of the lord pope, to
resist the efforts of certain people to destroy the Order.[5] In his
dream this brother saw some of the brethren gazing with astonishment at the sky; and after a while, still gazing, they cried: 'See!
See!' Then he looked and saw, written on the sky in letters of

gold, *Liberavit nos Dominus de inimicis nostris et manu omnium qui oderunt nos*—according to the translation of this psalm in use in the Roman Church. Now this happened just at the time that Innocent's dangerous letter against the brethren was revoked, thank God, by his successor the lord Alexander.[6] (*Ibid.*, p. 215.)

VII. To the same brother his deceased sister once appeared in a dream and told him that she was in Purgatory, but was due to leave it after five years. He then asked her about one of his brothers, and was told that he was already in Paradise. Then he put two more questions: was he going to die soon, and would he be saved? 'You will certainly be saved', came the answer, 'if you persevere; but the manner of your coming will be different from ours.' Five years later that brother appeared to him, of whom he had been told that he was in Paradise, and announced that his sister was now saved; so he asked, 'And I, shall I be saved?' But the other replied: 'Brother, you need not ask that question, for you are in a good state; only keep on steadily to the end. And take this as certain, that none or few of your Order are damned.[7] (*Ibid.*, pp. 215–16.)

VIII. This same brother, when the Chancellor at Paris decreed that he was to receive his licentiate to teach theology, saw in a dream (the night after the decree was published) someone who gave him a book and said: 'Rigans montes de superioribus suis, de fructu operum tuorum saciabitur terra.' So the brother took this text as the theme for his inaugural lecture.[8] (*Ibid.*, p. 216.)

NOTES TO THE *VITAE FRATRUM*

1. Cf. Gui, c. 6 (Note 15). John of Wildeshausen, 'Teutonicus', was Master General O.P. from 1241 to 1252. His successor was Humbert of Romans (1254–63), at whose instance de Frachet compiled the *Vitae Fratrum*.

2. Gui, c. 6 (Note 15). Frederick II died in 1250; de Frachet is writing in the decade following. De Frachet hints, what Tolomeo of Lucca declares, with regard at least to Reginald d'Aquino, that Thomas's brothers later rebelled against Frederick. As we have seen (Note 53 to Gui's *Life*), their sufferings in consequence were reckoned as martyrdom by the biographers of their brother, Frederick being an enemy of the Church: cf. Gui, c. 21; Tocco, c. 37; Calo, c. 20; Tolomeo, xxii, c. 20.

3. Gui, c. 7 (Notes 16–21). Note that de Frachet passes over the attempted seduction; and implies—wrongly (see Note 20 to Gui's *Life*)—that no Dominican was able to visit Thomas in captivity. 'Through his friends' renders 'per amicos', which might of course refer to *their* friends only.

4. Gui, cc. 8, 9 (Notes 23, 24). Note that de Frachet skips the four years (1248–52) at Cologne—a mere preparatory phase; for de Frachet and his contemporaries the theologian-saint's 'workshop', so to say, was the University of Paris. And they were right. 'Saint Thomas hors Paris est inconcevable, spirituellement et institutionellement; Viterbe, Rome, Naples ne sont que des épisodes dans son intellectualité, comme dans sa carrière. Paris est son lieu naturel', Chenu, *Introduction*, p. 22.

5. Cf. Note 29 to Gui's *Life*. The mention of St. Thomas's services to the Church is an allusion, no doubt, to his part in the controversy—so important for his Order—with the anti-Mendicant party in the University led by William of St. Amour. The *Contra impugnantes Dei cultum et religionem* came out in 1256—to de Frachet a very recent event. For the circumstances, see Walz, pp. 62–82.

6. This dream is not mentioned in our other sources. Innocent IV brought out his 'letter' *Etsi animarum*, cancelling the privileges of the Mendicant Orders on 21 November 1254 (*Chartularium Univ. Paris.*, I, pp.267–70, n. 240). He died a few weeks later. Alexander IV's bull *Quasi lignum vitae* of 14 April 1255 restored the *status quo*, to the great comfort of the Dominicans (*Chartularium*, I, pp. 279–85, n. 247). Frachet is writing during Alexander's pontificate, 1254–61.

7. Cf. Gui, c. 20 (Note 52). Tocco, c. 44. De Frachet's account of these visions differs in some points from those of Gui and Tocco. Like them he mentions two 'appearances' (but in *dreams*); but he names no places, while they place the first appearance at Paris, the second at Rome. St. Thomas asks about his brothers' salvation in Tocco and Gui, but not in de Frachet; instead, de Frachet makes the saint's brother—presumably, Reginald—appear to him the second time; implying perhaps a confusion with the incident reported in Gui, c. 21. Finally, the assurance that few Dominicans are damned is only in de Frachet.

8. Gui, c. 12 (Notes 30–3). From the Canonisation Enquiry, xcii—deposition of Peter Capotto, O.P.—an allusion to this passage of the *Vitae Fratrum* throws a sidelight on the use made of this book in the Order towards the end of the thirteenth century. Brother Peter said that he heard of the dream which St. Thomas had before his inaugural lecture as Master in Theology while a student at Paris, where passages from the *Vitae Fratrum* used to be read out to the brethren from time to time. He also tells us that de Frachet's vague 'quidam'—'someone'—was commonly interpreted as 'St. Dominic' at Paris. But if de Frachet had had reason to think that St. Thomas saw St. Dominic on this occasion, he would surely have said so.

(B) *From the 'Cronica Brevis' of Gerard de Frachet*[1]

A.D. 1241. At Paris, brother John was elected Master General; a German from Saxony, born at a town called Wildeshausen in the diocese of Osnabruck, which is in the province of Cologne, John was received into the Order when already advanced in years.[2] Being master of several languages—German, Italian, French, and Latin—and an excellent preacher, his sermons bore much fruit in different parts of the world. For the same reason he had been chosen to accompany many cardinals as penitentiary on embassies from the Pope. He was made bishop of Bosnia while he held the office of provincial of Hungary; but later he succeeded, though with difficulty, in inducing Pope Gregory to allow him to resign the see;[3] and, retaining nothing from the revenues, stepped back into the ranks with his brethren of the Order. But soon they made him prior provincial for Lombardy,[4] and it was from this post that he was raised to the office of Master General. . . . (2nd Redaction, MOPH, III, p. 332.)

This John was well known in the court of the Pope, and also in that of the lord Frederick.[5] And in his time the Order progressed and flourished and gained many valuable privileges. And the lord Hugh was made a cardinal, and many of the brethren in diverse places were made bishops; a fact which greatly displeased John himself and the other brethren who really loved the Order.[6] It was under him, too, that the General Chapters began to be held in various provinces;[7] and he himself visited more provinces than the previous Masters. It was in his time that blessed Peter was martyred.[8] (2nd Redaction, *ibid.*, p. 333.)

. . . From the time of Master Jordan of holy memory down to 1258 the following Friar Preachers received the licentiate as Masters from the Chancellor at Paris, and as such gave lectures on the sacred texts to the brethren and to students in the University:[9]

brother Roland of Cremona,
brother Hugh of Vienne (afterwards a cardinal),
brother John of Saint Giles, an Englishman,
brother Guerric of Flanders,
brother Godfrey of Bléneau, a Burgundian,
brother Albert the German,

brother Laurence of Brittany,
brother Stephen of Auxerre,
brother William of Etampes,
brother John Pointlasne of Paris,
brother Bonhomme, a Breton,
brother Elias of Provence,
brother Florent, a Frenchman,
brother Thomas of Aquino in Apulia,
brother Hugh of Metz,
brother Peter of Tarentaise,
brother Bartholomew of Tours,
brother William of Alton, an Englishman,
brother Baldwin, a Frenchman,
brother Annibaldo, a Roman (afterwards cardinal priest of
the basilica of the Twelve Apostles).

All these, two by two, lectured and conducted disputations at
our house of Saint Jacques in Paris, in the presence of students of
the University and religious and many prelates of the Church;
in a manner pleasing to God and to men, and their teaching and
writing bore much fruit for the Church of God. (1st Redaction,
ibid., pp. 334–5.)

A.D. 1254. At Budapest brother Humbert—from a small town
called Romans in the diocese of Vienne—was elected Master
General.[10] He had been a Master of Arts at Paris; and after
entering the Order became both a lector in theology and prior
at Lyons, and then provincial of the Roman province, and later
provincial of France. He was a man of great experience, but often
severely tried by bodily infirmities.

His election was foreseen in a dream by one of our nuns at
Strasbourg in Germany, where John, the Master General spoken
of above, died and was buried.[11] The vision was like this: the
sister seemed to see John, in his habit but without the *cappa*,
standing at the door of her convent and saying to her: 'I am
going far away, and I shall not return; but the sisters must not
be sad about this, for my place as Master will be taken by the
provincial of France; and he will do much good.' And on that
same day Master John died a good death, and at the Chapter
that followed the prior of France was unanimously elected to
succeed him.

At this Chapter of Budapest took place the baptism of the greatest noble among the Cumans. He was baptised, with his wife and vassals, by brethren attending the Chapter who had for many years been hoping and working for this. His daughter, whose nature showed promise of good things, became the wife of Lord Stephen, eldest son of the then king of Hungary, and now himself king; a man most attached to our Order.[12]

It was owing to the efforts of this new Master, Humbert—with the approval of the lord Pope Alexander IV and the help of that most Christian king, Louis of France—that the difference which had arisen at Paris between the University Masters and ourselves was settled, to the honour of God and of the Order. A letter written in terms unfavourable to the Order by Pope Innocent IV was revoked by the aforesaid Lord Alexander, at the beginning of his pontificate, a few days after the death of Innocent. The reason for this was that Master General Humbert had recourse devoutly to the Blessed Virgin; and she quickly did what to men had seemed almost impossible.[13] (1st Redaction, *ibid.*, pp. 336–8.)

NOTES TO GERARD DE FRACHET'S *CRONICA*

1. Ed. B. M. Reichert; MOPH, III, pp. 321–38.

2. John entered the Order in 1220 or 1221, aged about forty (see MOPH, III, p. 332, note *f*).

3. He was provincial of Hungary after 1231, and bishop of Diakovar in Bosnia, 1233 to 1237, when Gregory IX relieved him of the office.

4. 1238–41.

5. See Note 16 to Gui's *Life*.

6. On Hugh of St. Cher, see W. Gumbley and A. Walz in AOP (1925), p. 189. Hugh filled one of the two Dominican chairs of theology at Paris, 1231–5, and was twice provincial of France. He was the first Dominican cardinal (1244). An extremely strong expression of the feeling in the Order against the accepting of bishoprics by the brethren is the letter of the fifth Master General, Humbert of Romans, to St. Albert the Great, written when the pope appointed Albert to the see of Ratisbon in 1260: a translation is given by Mortier, *Histoire des Maîtres Généraux*, I, pp. 647–8; see also Notes 2 and 3 to Tolomeo.

7. Until 1245 the General Chapters alternated between Bologna and Paris. That of 1245 was at Cologne, and other cities—Montpellier, Trier, London, Metz, Budapest—were chosen in the next few years.

8. St. Peter of Verona; killed by heretics in 1252, canonised by Innocent VI

in 1253; the first Dominican, after St. Dominic, to be raised to the altars. St. Thomas was the next, in 1323.

9. Bd. Jordan of Saxony, the immediate successor to St. Dominic as head of the Order, was Master General from 1222 to 1237. The Dominicans at St. Jacques in Paris at first followed the ordinary theological courses in the University. In 1229 the unusual circumstance of a 'strike' of the University professors gave the Order its opportunity; the bishop, William of Auvergne, asked the friars to give regular theological courses, as part of the University curriculum, at St. Jacques; and at once John of St. Giles, though not yet a Dominican, began to lecture there as a Master with Roland of Cremona as his *baccalaureus*. A year later Roland got his licentiate and began to teach with Hugh of St. Cher as *baccalaureus* under him. In 1231 Roland was sent to open a theological faculty at Toulouse, and Hugh took his chair at St. Jacques; and in the same year the Order was given a second chair at Paris, which was filled by John of St. Giles, now himself a Dominican; and henceforth, as Frachet says, the two courses continued side by side, each under a Dominican Master. St. Albert's period ran probably from 1242 to 1248, after which one of the chairs was reserved to a Master from the French province, the other being open to 'foreigners', among whom was St. Thomas, 1256-9, and again 1269-72. See Mortier, *Histoire des Maîtres Généraux*, I, c. 5, and Mandonnet in *Rev. Thomiste*, VIII, no. 36, November–December 1925; and *ibid.*, IV (1896), pp. 133-70.

10. Humbert, the fifth Master General and a venerated figure in our history, entered the Order at Paris *c.* 1225 (cf. *Vitae Fratrum*, MOPH, III, pp. 170-3). He was elected Master General in 1254 and died in 1263.

11. John died on 5 November 1252.

12. It was at the request of King Bela IV of Hungary that the Chapter of 1254 met at Budapest. This king's daughter, Margaret of Hungary, became a Dominican nun and a saint. The prince mentioned here must be Stephen V (1270-2).

13. See Note 5 to the extracts from the *Vitae Fratrum*, and Note 29 to Gui's *Life*.

V

A letter of the Faculty of Arts in the University of Paris to the General Chapter of the Order of Preachers at Lyons in 1274[1]

The text is in Documenta, *ed. Laurent, pp. 583–6, reproducing A. Birkenmajer's ed. in* Beiträge zur Geschichte der Philosophie des Mittelalters, *XX, fasc. 5, pp. 2–4. It is also in* Chartularium Univ. Paris., *I, n. 447. On the Letter in general, see A. Birkenmajer, op. cit., and* Xenia Thomistica, *III, pp. 57–72.*

To our venerable fathers in Christ, the Master and the Provincials of the Order of Preachers and all the brethren assembled for the General Chapter at Lyons, the Rector and Procurators of the University of Paris, with all the Masters at present teaching in the Faculty of Arts, greeting in Him whose providence graciously and wisely directs all things.[2]

With a clamour of grief and tears we lament the loss that has befallen the whole Church and this University of Paris in particular; lifting our voices to express in common a sorrow befitting such a bereavement. But, alas, nothing less than the voice of a Jeremiah would be adequate now; and indeed our case is sadder than the prophet's: for if he mourned the ruin and destruction of a material Jerusalem, it is the spiritual city, the new Jerusalem, the Church herself whose affliction is the cause of our distress. For news has come to us which floods us with grief and amazement, bewilders our understanding, transfixes our very vitals, and wellnigh breaks our hearts. This report—which we have no choice but to accept as true, coming, as it does, from many sources and with complete assurance—this news which wrings a cry from our lips though we know not what to cry (love, indeed, would choose to stay silent, but so great a sorrow clamours for expression), is that the venerated Master, brother Thomas of Aquino, has been called for ever out of this world.

Who could have expected that divine Providence would permit it—that this morning star which shone on the world, that the light and glory of our time, this 'greater light which rules the day',[3] should already be withdrawn from us? Truly it is as though the sun had withdrawn its splendour or suffered the overshadowing of an untimely eclipse, now that this light of the Church is put out. We must, no doubt, acknowledge that it was by a special privilege that the Creator of Nature willed to concede this light for a time to the world; yet must we also, if we would stand by the authority of ancient philosophers, declare that it seemed that Nature herself had placed this man here amongst us to shed light on her own mysteries.[4]

But enough of such useless laments; we have another purpose in writing. From your General Chapter, reverend Fathers, assembled at Florence we begged that this man be restored to us; begged, alas, in vain.[5] But now we beseech you, out of our gratitude and devout affection towards the memory of so great a cleric, so great a father, so great a master, of your generosity to grant us the bones of him now dead whom we could not recover alive; for it were surely in the highest degree improper and unworthy that any town or place other than Paris, than this the noblest of all university cities, should guard the bones of him whose youth was nourished, fostered, and educated here at Paris, which then received from him in return the inexpressible benefit of his teaching.[6] Does not the Church rightly honour the bones and relics of her saints? Then is this not a desire both reasonable and pious that we should wish to give lasting honour to the body of such a master? Thus he whose fame is kept green amongst us by his writings, may also, by the remembered presence of his tomb in our city, live on for ever in the hearts of our posterity.

That is the first request which eager devotion prompts us to make; and not, we hope, in vain. Our second request concerns some writings of a philosophical nature,[7] begun by him at Paris, left unfinished at his departure, but completed, we have reason to think, in the place to which he was transferred; and these we humbly beg you, of your gracious kindness, to have communicated to us without delay. And permit us also to mention the Commentary of Simplicius on the *De coelo et mundo*, and an Exposition of Plato's *Timaeus*, and a work entitled *De aquarum conductibus et ingeniis erigendis*; for these books in particular he himself promised would be sent to us.[8] Moreover, if there should be any new writings of his own on logic—such as, when he was about to leave us, we took the liberty of asking him to write—we beg you to let us have copies of these also.[9]

In conclusion, it is not for us to remind your sagacity of the evils and perils of this world; being exposed to which, we, your brethren in the Lord, most respectfully recommend ourselves to your prayers, so that now while you are assembled in General Chapter, your charity may grant us a special assistance.

We desire that this Letter be sealed with the seal of our Rector and Procurators. Given at Paris in the year of our Lord 1274, on the Wednesday before the Finding of the Holy Cross.[10]

NOTES ON THE LETTER OF THE FACULTY OF ARTS

1. On the University of Paris in the thirteenth century, and the Faculty of Arts in particular, see Rashdall's *Universities* . . ., ed. Powicke and Emden (1936), I, pp. 269–584, especially 299–333, 398–401, 439–43. Within the scope of these Notes the following points may suffice. (i) Of the four faculties in the University—Theology, Law, Medicine, and Arts—the first was of course the highest in dignity, but the last was by far the most numerous and, within the general academic body, the most powerful. Before the end of the century the rector of the faculty of Arts had become virtually the head or president of the whole University. (ii) The Arts course being introductory to the rest, the 'artists', including both pupils and masters, formed the younger as well as the more numerous element in the academic population. The statutes of 1215 fixed the length of the Arts course at six years, and the minimum age for obtaining the licence to lecture at twenty. Most of the students in Arts were therefore boys in their 'teens, and perhaps most of the masters in the faculty were young men in their twenties. And custom was against remaining many years in this faculty, 'non est senescendum in artibus'. As time went by, the length of the Arts course tended to be shortened (Rashdall, p. 462), but the number of masters in Arts remained considerably greater than that of masters in the higher faculties (cf. *ibid.*, pp. 316, 403, 289). This fact alone explains 'the curious circumstance' (Rashdall, p. 316) that the rector of the M.A.s became head of the whole University. (iii) By the mid-thirteenth century, if not sooner, the faculty of Arts (the old *trivium* and *quadrivium* of the seven 'liberal arts') had become in fact a faculty of Philosophy. The crucial date is 19 March 1255, when the faculty issued a new syllabus imposing the study of all the known works of Aristotle—the whole of his metaphysics, ethics, psychology, and natural science, as well as the earlier established logic: 'the seven arts were henceforth to play the part of auxiliary sciences, no longer of theology, but of the great disciplines of philosophy' (Van Steenberghen). From this setting up of philosophy as a discipline in its own right, and one for which the faculty of Arts was principally responsible, it was but a step to (iv) the emergence in that faculty of more or less rationalistic tendencies—claiming an independence of, and evincing even a certain hostility towards,

the faculty of Theology. There has been much dispute over the exact nature of this 'rationalism', but the reactions of the ecclesiastical authorities in 1270 and, still more, 1277 leave no doubt as to its seriousness. It came out strongly in the late sixties, and its leader was Siger of Brabant (born *c.* 1240). The movement headed by this young M.A.—a genuine philosopher and a brilliant one—was attacked by St. Bonaventure in sermons to the University (1267 and 1268) and criticised on philosophical grounds by Aquinas in his *De unitate intellectus* (1270). Some scholars have called it Latin Averroism, others prefer the name Radical or Heterodox Aristotelianism; in any case it went with what to the theologians seemed an altogether excessive esteem for non-Christian authorities and an implicit contempt for Christian ones (see the text of the 219 propositions condemned by Bp. Tempier in 1277, printed in Mandonnet, *Siger de Brabant,* II, pp. 175–81; the prologue to which expressly denounced men 'studying in Arts at Paris who have overstepped the limits of their faculty'. Cf. Van Steenberghen, *The Philosophical Movement in the 13th century,* pp. 75–115). This crisis was surely a main reason for the recall of St. Thomas from Italy to Paris in 1268–9 (see Note 72 to Gui's *Life*), though in the event some Thomist theses did not escape censure, after his death, in 1277. St. Thomas indeed held a midway position; but while the 'artist' philosophers admired him enough, as a body, to salute his memory with the impressive tribute of the Letter we are annotating, the theologians—in whose faculty Thomas had been twice a professor—offered him no corporate expression of esteem.

2. The General Chapter of the Order met at Lyons in 1274 under the Master General, Bd. John of Vercelli. In the faculty of Arts the titles of *rector* and *procurator* became distinct by the mid-century. The *procuratores* were the elected representatives of the four 'nations'—traditionally called the French (who included all Latin peoples), the Normans, the Picards (who included men from the Low Countries), and the English (including Germans). The rector was a common head elected by the 'nations', and in time, as has been said, the *de facto* head of the University (Rashdall, p. 313). 'At present teaching', etc., renders 'actu regentes in artibus', a 'regens' at Paris being a master 'actually engaged in teaching in the schools' (Rashdall, p. 409).

3. Genesis, 1: 6.

4. There is a studied contrast here between God ('conditor naturae') and Nature ('natura'). The gift of St. Thomas to the world was a special act of God's will, a sort of grace ('speciali privilegio'); so much, say these philosophers, we must as Christians acknowledge. But as philosophers, they continue, as students of *Nature*, must we not admit that Nature had a hand in it?—that Nature upon which the mind of St. Thomas (as philosopher) threw so much light. Both the question and the personification are of course rhetorical; everyone knew that 'nature' had a part in human generation. The appeal to the old philosophers' authority is appropriate; the writers are *ex officio* concerned with them. But what exactly is the authority called in to support? The mere fact that Thomas's generation was (also) 'natural'? Or some *intention* of Nature to have her secrets explored ('ad elucidanda ipsius occulta') by a philosopher whom, for this purpose, she brought into being? The latter seems to be the sense; but I cannot identify the text or texts referred

to. Dante has a phrase about Aristotle, of which this passage reminds one: 'quello glorioso filosofo al quale la natura più aperse li suoi segreti' (*Convivio*, III, v, 7).

5. The General Chapter was held at Florence in June 1272. St. Thomas may have attended it; he had left Paris for the last time shortly after Easter, 24 April, and he was in south Italy by the late summer. See Walz, pp. 138–41.

6. See Note 24 to Gui's *Life*.

7. And so of special interest to 'artists'.

8. It seems that two groups of writings are referred to—first, some philosophical works begun by St. Thomas before he left Paris; secondly, the three works named, which he had promised the Parisian Masters of Arts, before leaving, to procure for them, presumably in Italy, whither he was bound. These latter works were not by St. Thomas. This has been made clearer in the translation than it is in the Latin. My interpretation follows A. Birkenmajer's; see 'Vermischte Untersuchungen' in *Beiträge zur Geschichte der Philosophie des Mittelalters*, xx, fasc. 5, pp. 6ss. The works by St. Thomas alluded to are no doubt the commentary on Aristotle's *De generatione et corruptione*, which was certainly finished at Naples in 1272–3; and that on the *De coelo et mundo*; and perhaps also that on the *Politics*: see Note 31 to Tolomeo.

When this letter was written the commentary of Simplicius (fl. in the first half of the sixth century A.D.) on the *De coelo et mundo* of Aristotle and that of Proclus (the last great Neoplatonist before the closing of the school of Athens in 529) on Plato's *Timaeus* had both been recently done into Latin by the Dominican William of Moerbeke, who was working in Italy and had been in close contact with St. Thomas; who himself used Simplicius for his commentary on the *De coelo et mundo* (1272). There can be little doubt that these two translations are referred to here. The *De aquarum conductibus*, etc., seems to be the *Pneumatica* of Heron of Alexandria (first century B.C.), also translated by William.

9. There are no such works by St. Thomas from this last period of his life.

10. 3 May.

APPENDIX I

NOTE ON ST. THOMAS'S FAMILY

The old Roman town of Aquino, from which St. Thomas's family was named, stands a little north of Monte Cassino, in the Liri valley, about half-way between Rome and Naples. In the thirteenth century this was border country between the States of the Church and the kingdom of Apulia and Sicily, the 'Regno', which, until 1250, was ruled directly by the great Hohenstaufen emperor, Frederick II, the 'stupor mundi' and, in politics, a dreaded enemy of the papacy. The d'Aquino family was Lombard in origin. Rodipert of Aquino in the ninth century was *castaldus* (a sort of bailiff) for the district under the count of Capua. His descendant Adenulf in the tenth century obtained the rank of count (*comes*), but the title seems later to have been lost: St. Thomas's father, Landulf, is only *nobilis dominus* or *miles* (knight) in the documents. Landulf d'Aquino, born perhaps *c.* 1180, was active in the service of Frederick II from about 1210, and in 1220 was named one of the imperial 'justiciars' for the Terra di Lavoro. The chief castle of the family was Roccasecca, where Thomas was born, probably towards the end of 1224 or early in 1225. Landulf's wife was Theodora, of a noble Neapolitan family. She and Landulf may have had as many as twelve children, though one cannot be sure of this. Scandone's researches led him to conclude that there were seven sons—Aimo, James, Adenulf, Philip, Landulf, Reginald, and Thomas—and five daughters—Marotta, Mary, Theodora, Adelasia, and one who died in infancy. Pelster reduced the number of sons to four, holding that James, Adenulf, and Philip (whom a contemporary document represents as brothers) were sons of a second cousin of Landulf, Thomas, count of Acerra. Pelster also subtracted Adelasia, whom he thought was probably the saint's niece, not a sister. In any case Thomas seems to have been the youngest of the sons, and younger, too, than Marotta; he may have been older than Mary and was surely older than Theodora, if this lady was only recently dead in 1318–19 when William of Tocco wrote his *Life* of the saint (see c. 37).

Landulf, the father, seems to have died in or soon after 1244; his wife survived him by ten years or more. Aimo is named as head of the family in a papal document of 1254, which also mentions his fidelity to the Holy See; he was politically therefore on the side opposed to his father's; and as such Charles of Anjou appointed him 'justiciar' for Sicily in 1266. His name does not appear again in this book. We have, however, met with Landulf junior, Reginald, Marotta, and Theodora. Landulf is mentioned in passing by Gui, c. 20; he died before 1260. Reginald is more interesting; see Gui, cc. 20, 21, Tolomeo, xxii, c. 20, and Note 53, p. 71, above. Students of early Italian literature are familiar with the poet Rinaldo d'Aquino whom Dante mentioned with honour in the *De vulgari eloquentia*, i, c. 12. This Rinaldo was certainly related to St. Thomas and *may* have been his brother. He may also have been the 'magister Raynaldus' who is named in a will, dated 1238, as a brother of Philip d'Aquino; the title would imply (if this Raynaldus *was* St. Thomas's brother) that the saint was not the only member of his family to have a university training. Scandone, followed by Mandonnet, De Bartholomaeis, and others, uphold this identification, supposing that 'master Reginald' is the man of 'high standing' in the emperor's court who, according to Tolomeo, had the chief part in the kidnapping of his young Dominican brother in 1244 (see Tolomeo, xxii, c. 20). Pelster will not have this, however, and it remains uncertain so long as we cannot prove that Philip d'Aquino also was St. Thomas's brother. A. De Stefano (*La cultura alla corte di Federico I imperatore*, p. 230) and others identify as St. Thomas's brother a 'Renaldus de Aquino' mentioned in a document of 1240 as one of Frederick II's falconers; and there is nothing improbable in this. To conclude, it is certain that our Reginald served under the emperor and was put to death by him, before the end of 1250, as a rebel; but whether he was either a 'master' (which would here imply, probably, a training in law) or a poet must remain doubtful.

On Marotta, who became abbess of St. Mary's at Capua, see Note 17, p. 63, above. Theodora married Roger, count of San Severino and then of Marsico in the Abruzzi. Her husband and father-in-law (Thomas of San Severino) were implicated in the Capoccio rising against Frederick II (1246); Thomas was executed, Roger fled to the papal States, but returned, after the fall of the Hohenstaufen, in 1266. Theodora is a favourite of the early Dominican biographers of her brother; Tocco (c. 37) and Calo (c. 20) especially record her piety and that of her son, Thomas of Marsico, who was an important source of information on his uncle for Tocco when the latter was gathering materials for his *Life*; see Canonisation Enquiry, lx. For Theodora's relations with St. Thomas, see especially Notes 56 (p. 72), 63 (p. 73), and 96 (p. 79) above. As we have seen, she was given one of the hands from his corpse as a relic. She died *c.* 1310, probably, and was buried in the Dominican church at Salerno.

As for Mary, it is agreed that St. Thomas had a sister of this name and that she married William of San Severino, an elder brother of her sister's husband Roger; but she does not live for us as Theodora does; her interest is incidental. Her marriage, and Theodora's, brought the d'Aquino into relation with the de Morra through Perna de Morra, the mother of William and Roger; a fact of some importance politically to the d'Aquino, since the de Morra were much involved in the revolt against the emperor already mentioned. Moreover, the daughter of William of San Severino and Mary d'Aquino is an important link in the tradition concerning St. Thomas. Her name was Catherine, and she married another de Morra—Francis—who died in 1296. As a girl she had known St. Thomas's mother, Lady Theodora; and as an old lady, still alive in 1318, she was able to repeat to William of Tocco things that Theodora had said to her about her son. One could wish, indeed, that she had told Tocco more than she apparently did; still, through her, he certainly got information on the saint's childhood and early youth from the best possible source. See Canonisation Enquiry, LXII, and Note 47 on it.

Adelasia d'Aquino married Roger dell' Aquila, count of Traetto (now Minturno) and Fondi, after whose death in 1272 St. Thomas was involved in business connected with the wardship of the children; see Note 68 to the Canonisation Enquiry. Pelster, however, supposing that the mother of such young children would probably not have been born much before 1245—twenty years later than St. Thomas, who himself was one of the youngest in his family—considers that Adelasia was too young to have been the saint's sister; he suggests that she was a daughter of Theodora and so St. Thomas's niece.

We may add a word on Frances, wife of Count Annibaldo of Ceccano, who appears at the end of the saint's life as his hostess at Maenza, a few weeks before his death at Fossanova, and was present at his funeral; see Notes 85 (p. 77) and 89 (p. 79), above. Her husband was in bad odour with the Angevin government of Naples; one official document of 1269 even denounced him as a 'traitor and an enemy of the holy Roman Church and of ourselves'. Yet, as a favour to St. Thomas, his 'niece . . . the noble lady Frances' was allowed a passport into the Regno when she wished to take the baths at Pozzuoli in April 1273; which kindness she was able to repay a few months later at her castle of Maenza. She seems to have been daughter to Philip d'Aquino, and so perhaps not the saint's niece but a cousin.

The more relevant data given above may be summarised in the table on the next page: the more important names in the story and tradition are printed in capitals.

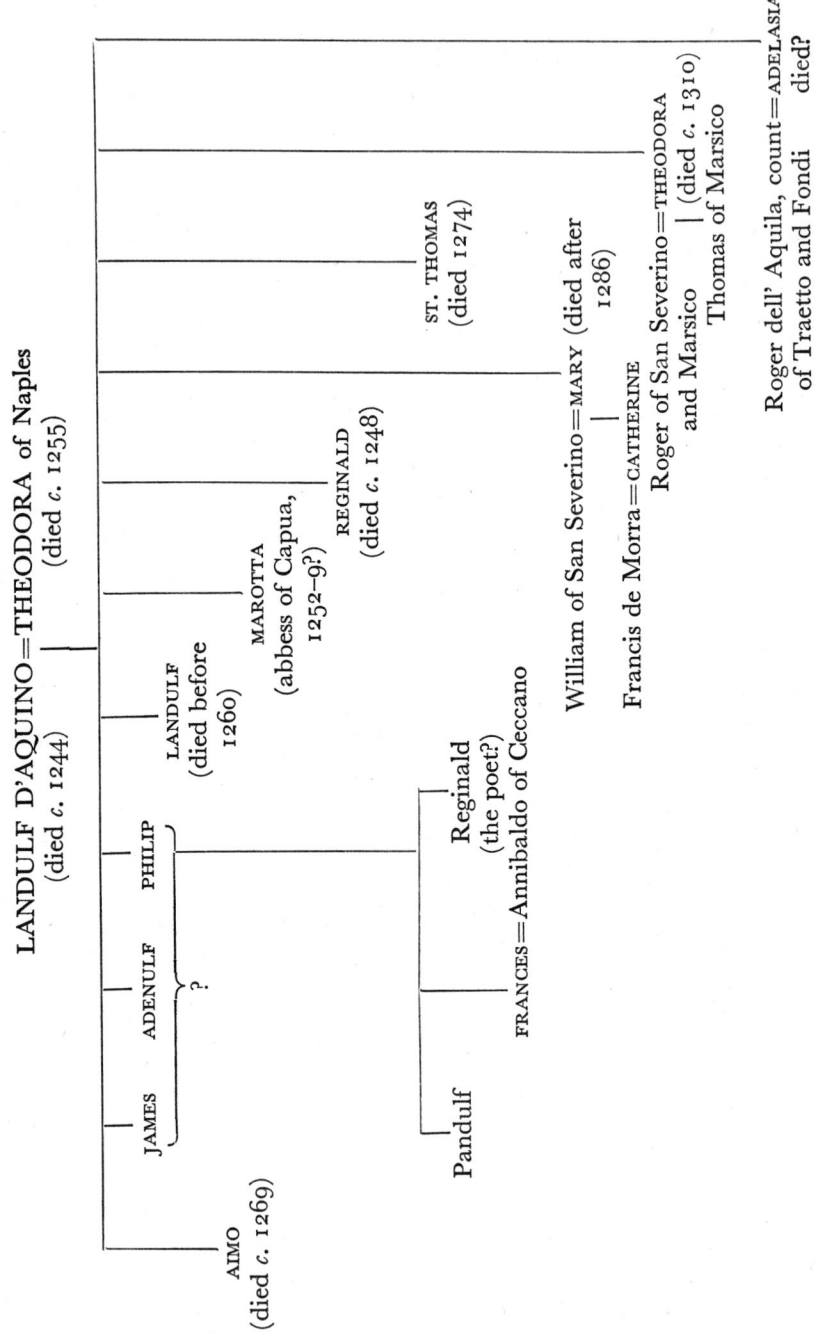

The best account of the d'Aquino family is still Francesco Scandone's in *Miscellanea storico-artistica*, pp. 1–110; it is well documented from contemporary sources. Many of these texts are now available in *Fontes Vitae S. Thomae Aquinatis*, fasc. 6, 'Documenta', ed. M. H. Laurent, O.P. (*Rev. Thomiste*, 1937). Scandone's work should be checked by reference to the articles of F. Pelster, S.J., in *Civiltà Cattolica*, 1923, nos. for 3 March, 2 June, and 17 November. See also Walz, c. 1. On the close relations existing for a time between one branch of the d'Aquino—in particular, Thomas I, count of Acerra, a cousin of St. Thomas's father—and Frederick II, see M. Maccarrone in *Rivista di storia della chiesa in Italia*, x (1956), pp. 165–92.

I have not been able to consult a study by F. Scandone, 'Rocca secca patria di S. Tommaso d'Aquino', in *Archivio storico di Terra di Lavoro*, I (1956), pp. 33–176.

APPENDIX II

AN ITALIAN SONNET ATTRIBUTED TO
ST. THOMAS

It is exceedingly doubtful whether St. Thomas wrote the sonnet printed below, but it is just possible that he did; and so long as the question of authenticity is not finally decided, the poem gains in interest by this 'perhaps' attaching to it. Moreover, its intrinsic quality, in certain respects, inclines one to include it here. Had it not been ascribed to St. Thomas by whoever wrote it out, half-way through the fourteenth century, in a codex preserved at Modena, probably no one would have thought of him as the author; but, this ascription once made, one can find some reasons for thinking it plausible. It is unlikely that Thomas wrote Italian verse after becoming a friar, or at any rate after leaving south Italy, and his aristocratic family, in 1245. But he had been an undergraduate at Naples and had spent, perforce, a year with his family after taking the Dominican habit. Nothing in the content of the sonnet is incompatible with his writing it between, say, 1242 and 1245. It is the work of a thinker, and one who is much more thinker than artist: abstractly conceived, stiff in its syntax, with the logical joints all showing and hardly a touch of imagery, but vigorous, elevated, and intense. It is the sort of poem that might have been writtten by a chaste and intelligent student whose later developments would not be in the field of poetry. And the young Thomas was just such a student. Through his family he was linked—until he chose to break the link—with the courtly world shared by the vernacular poets of the 'Sicilian School'; and the diction of this poem does not seem anachronistic.

But a strong reason against authenticity is supplied by the rhyme-pattern, particularly in the octet. The earliest Italian sonneteers rhymed their octets thus: *abab-abab*; only after the mid-thirteenth century, and indeed not until the Tuscan *stilnovisti* of the 1280s and 1290s, did the scheme that was later called 'petrarchan' prevail: *abba-abba*. If this scheme ever was used before 1250, it must have been rare: Monaci's *Crestomazia* (ed. F. Arese, 1955) gives no examples of it before Guittone d'Arezzo (*c.* 1230–94), while Salinari's *Poesia lirica del duecento*, which includes many more sonnets than Monaci's collection, shows none with this pattern before Cavalcanti (*c.* 1257–1300). This is a serious objection to the ascription of our sonnet to St. Thomas.

It exists in a MS. in the d'Este library at Modena (cod. 9, A.27, fol. 37). Over the text is written 'Fr. Thomas de Aquino'. The date of the MS. is

1347. It was first printed in the eighteenth century. In 1924 F. Scandone reproduced it in *Miscellanea* (pp. 1-2, note 4), adding some over-confident remarks in favour of authenticity; and a little later Mandonnet printed it in the *Revue Thomiste* (VIII, 1925, p. 241). He, too, believed it a genuine work of St. Thomas, and was even prepared to date it to within a year (1244–5), and see in it the young saint's retort to his brother Reginaldo's accusations that he was betraying the honour of the family by becoming a Dominican. Such details are excessively conjectural. Grabmann (*Die Werke*, p. 413) withholds judgment on the authenticity, whilst Eschmann does not even mention the matter in his *Catalogue*. I give the text as in *Miscellanea* (slightly altering the punctuation) and an English translation. The second half of the octet is difficult, and while I am fairly satisfied with my rendering I can only propose it as probably correct.

FR. THOMAS DE AQUINO

Tanto ha virtù ziascun, quanto ha intelletto,
e ha valor quanto in virtù si stende;
e tanto ha 'llhor di ben, quanto l'intende,
e quanto ha d'honor gentil diletto.
E il diletto gentil, quanto ha l'effetto,
adorna il bel piacer, che nel chor scende;
il quale adorna tanto, quanto splende,
per somiglianza del proprio subietto.

Dunque chi vol veder quanto d'honore
altrui è degno e di laude perfecta,
miri in qual desio amante ha il core.
Però ch'esser felice ogni uomo affecta,
massimamente quel, che per l'onore
verace adopra, tal corona aspetta.

TRANSLATION. A man has virtue in proportion to understanding, and is worthy in proportion to his virtue: the good which he aims at[1]—rejoicing, nobly, in all that is of good report—that good he possesses. And this noble joy causes beauty in a consequent desire of the heart—inasmuch as this desire shines with light reflected from it (the noble joy), because of a likeness between their two subjects.[2]

Whoever, then, would judge how worthy of honour and full praise a man is, let him consider what that man's heart desires.[3] While all men strive towards happiness, he most can expect to gain the crown who works for the sake of true honour.

1. Or 'understands'.
2. Latin, *subjectum*; cf. Dante, *Purgatorio*, XVII, 107, and Cavalcanti's canzone *Donna mi prega*, 23. The 'subietto' of a quality or action is that which is such or acts. Here two 'subjects' are compared and seen as similar, the 'heart' and

the proper subject of the 'noble delight', *gentil diletto*, that accompanies the act of the intellect, *intelletto* (line 1): the heart, then, and intellectual appetite, i.e. the will? But the gist of the sestet does not allow us to take 'heart', *core* (line 11) as *mere* sense-appetite. It seems better therefore to understand the two subjects compared, implicitly, in line 8, as (*a*) intellect itself, which has the *diletto gentil*, and (*b*) the affective nature generally, which would include the will proper, designated by *chor, core*. Cf. Dante's *Vita nuova*, XLI, 'Oltre la spera'.

3. Cf. *Summa theologiae*, 1a, 2ae, xviii, 4; xix, 1 and 2: *Purgatorio*, XVII, 103–5.

Index